KOUFAX

KOUFAX

E D W A R D   G R U V E R

Taylor Publishing Company
Dallas, Texas

For Michelle, Patty, and Katie

Designed by David Timmons

Published by Taylor Publishing Company
1550 West Mockingbird Lane
Dallas, Texas 75235
www.taylorpub.com

Library of Congress Cataloging-in-Publication Data
Gruver, Ed, 1960–
  Koufax / by Edward Gruver.
    p. cm.
  Includes index.
  ISBN 0-87833-157-3
    1. Koufax, Sandy, 1935– 2. Baseball players—United States—
Biography. 3. Brooklyn Dodgers (Baseball team)—History. I. Title.
  GV865.K67 G78 2000
  796.357'092—dc21
  [B]   99-056763

10 9 8 7 6 5 4 3 2

Printed in the United States of America

CONTENTS

ACKNOWLEDGMENTS

I wish to thank the following people for their help in this project: Randy Voorhees of Mountain Lion Agency; Mike Emmerich, Fred Francis, and Delia Guzman of Taylor Publishing; and all those gracious enough to share their thoughts and memories in interviews.

Also, thanks to my family for their continuing support.

KOUFAX

INTRODUCTION

The Bronx, New York, 1999.

Joe Torre sat in his office in Yankee Stadium on the night of Friday, September 10, surrounded by media as he answered questions about the performance of Boston's Pedro Martinez. The Red Sox ace had dazzled the defending world champions with a one-hit, 3–1 win in which he struck out 17 and didn't walk a batter.

It was a performance that left the New York Yankees' manager shaking his head in wonder.

"That's the kind of stuff Koufax used to throw," Torre said. "He'd beat your brains out, 1–0."

Koufax.

A certain magic still lingers in the name, stirring memories of the sixties supernova whose half-decade of dominance was so brilliant, yet so fleeting. Decades removed from his final game, Sandy Koufax's statistics still jump from the pages of history like one of his hopping fastballs.

From 1962 to 1966, he went 111–34 with four no-hitters, including a perfect game. He won five straight earned run average titles, including marks of 1.88, 1.74, 2.04, and 1.73. He struck out more than 1,400 hitters in five seasons, including a major league record 382 in 1965. He set another major league mark by fanning 10 or more hitters 21 times in '65, then did it twice more in the World Series.

He won 25 games in 1963, was on pace to win 25 again in '64 before experiencing arm problems, then won 26 in '65 and 27 in '66. Of his 26 victories in '65, 25 were complete games. The one winning game he did not complete was a 1–1 tie through 10 innings.

He won three Cy Young Awards in four seasons at a time when the award was given to one pitcher for both leagues. In 1963, he was the first to win it by unanimous vote, then was a unanimous choice again in both '65 and '66. He was the National League's Most Valuable Player in 1963, and led the light-hitting Los Angeles Dodgers to three pennants and two world championships.

The impression he left on the game, the impression he left on those who saw him pitch, was of something rare and magical.

"The thing I liked about him," said baseball writer Roger Angell, "is that because he was so thin and strong, you could see where all that heat was coming from. You could see the bowed back and the powerful arms and the powerful, thin legs. It was very exciting."

And then it was over.

One month after he had led the league with 27 wins, 317 strikeouts in 323 innings, and an earned run average of 1.73, one month after he had literally carried the Dodgers to a second straight World Series appearance, Koufax announced his retirement from the game in a hastily called press conference. The sporting world was stunned.

"He left at High Noon," one admirer wrote, "a Hamlet in mid-soliloquy."

Boston sportswriter George Sullivan was in Michigan to cover college football's "Game of the Century" between Notre Dame and Michigan State.

"I was at a banquet the night before the game when word spread that Koufax had retired," Sullivan remembered. "Nobody could believe it. It was like Pearl Harbor, one of those times when you remember exactly where you were and what you were doing."

Koufax was retiring from the game because of traumatic arthritis in his left elbow. He had pitched through the ailment for at least two seasons, surviving on painkillers before games and ice baths afterwards, and, in order to keep his muscles loose, lathering his left arm in Capsolin, a skin irritant so hot it watered the eyes of anyone who stood near him and nearly blistered him in the process.

The stress of snapping off flame-belching fastballs and curves that tied professional hitters into Windsor knots had taken its toll. His left arm was bowed, and his suits had to be specially tailored to accommodate the curvature. When Dodgers' team doctor Robert Kerlan told him that he risked permanent injury if he continued to pitch, Koufax retired. He was 30 years old.

"I asked the doctor to keep me going," he said, "and I also asked him to tell me when to stop."

Koufax stopped after having won 53 games in two seasons, consecutive Cy Young Awards, and the admiration of a generation.

"He stood so much farther out from his peer group, it must have been like Babe Ruth hitting in the twenties," said former Dodger pitcher Ed Roebuck. "Bob Gibson was a great pitcher, don't get me wrong. But Sandy dominated so completely that every time he pitched you would think he was a man among boys."

Koufax's early retirement is considered one of the tragedies of sports. Had he pitched in the nineties, he could have undergone surgery to remove the bone spurs on his elbow in the off-season and come back to pitch the next year.

"In those days they wouldn't operate on an arthritic joint," Koufax said. "Today, they'd do arthroscopic surgery, knock off the spurs and send you back out there."

At a press conference in Atlanta honoring baseball's All-Century Team prior to Game Two of the 1999 World Series, Koufax said he didn't regret making the decision to retire. He did however, regret having to make the decision. "I was risking the use of my arm," he said, "the normal use of my arm."

For years, the word was that Koufax had come down from a higher league to pitch in the majors. That was only partly right. He had actually come down from his hillside home above North Hollywood, a bachelor pad whose interior—contemporary living room, Colonial kitchen, and Oriental den—reflected his varied interests.

The location of his 12-room home reflected his private personality.

Situated on a side street in Studio City, a suburb of Los Angeles, it was set back behind a high retaining wall and a thick growth of landscaping.

Solitude is one mark of the man. Modesty is another. On New Year's Day, 1969, the 33-year-old Koufax married Anne Heath Widmark, the comely, dark-haired, 23-year-old daughter of actor Richard Widmark at her father's West Hollywood home. Two years later, in the fall of 1971, the couple moved to a Maine farmhouse, where neighbor MaJo Keleshian said she never once heard Koufax speak of his baseball career in the three years she lived next door to him.

"Maybe that's why we were friends," she mused. "He never saw himself as a public figure."

This explains why, perhaps, he has never understood the public's fascination with him. He wouldn't understand, for instance, why Rob Eshman, who grew up in the sixties and later became managing editor of the *Jewish Journal*, would wander back and forth in front of Koufax's California home just to catch a glimpse of his hero.

Hidden away in Maine, some five years after he had last pitched, Koufax still received bags of fan mail. He read as many letters as he could, but it's small wonder that he has long since instructed the Dodgers not to forward mail to his current home in Vero Beach.

Koufax's distance has heightened the public's interest in him. He deplores talking about himself—"I'd almost rather have a root canal," he said in Atlanta—and if the public sees him as an enigma, a mystery man, friends see him as something else.

"He's a kind friend, a very generous man," Keleshian said. "History might make him out to be more unusual than he is."

Keleshian cringed when she saw the July 1999 *Sports Illustrated* headline on a Koufax story.

"'The Left Arm of God'?" she said, repeating the title. "He's human, just like everybody else."

Human, with frailties. His career is a lesson in the struggle for self-control. Even in his great years, he grimaced in disgust following an ill-timed hit or a walk. At times, he kicked the sheet metal on the bottom of the dugout water cooler in anger over a poor pitch, and once overturned a trainer's table in the locker room in a fit of frustration. After being heckled by Cubs fans in Wrigley Field, Koufax stood on the dugout steps, tipped his cap and bowed in exaggerated fashion. Later, a repentant Koufax blamed his actions on the summer heat. "I think I might have gotten sunstroke or something," he said with some embarrassment.

During the 1963 World Series, the *New York Post* broke a story about his severed relationship with his blood father, Jack Braun, who had divorced his mother when Koufax was three years old. That his father followed his career and attended games in person seemed to carry little weight with Koufax. Even people who knew the family, like then Dodgers' general manager Buzzie Bavasi, weren't aware that Irving Koufax was Sandy's stepfather.

"They were wonderful people, his mom and stepdad," Bavasi said. "I told them they did a great job in rearing this youngster."

Koufax's reluctance to speak about himself extended even to his family. When his autobiography was published in 1966, his mother read it so she could learn more about her famous son. "You never tell me anything," she told him.

Koufax is private, perhaps to an extreme for someone who chose such a public profession. Some friends have refused to speak of him unless they first receive his permission. As one person put it, there is both a respect for Koufax's privacy and a feeling that if you say something he doesn't like, he may stop speaking to you.

That view seems unfounded, since he is said by friends to be highly sensitive to the feelings of others. He discouraged reporters from writing feature stories about him, but he did it politely. "I realize this is your way of earning a living," he would say, "but I wish you wouldn't."

Koufax was embarrassed, he said, to see his name and picture in so many magazines. His sensitivity showed up in other ways as well. As a young pitcher, he put pressure on himself to succeed because he knew he was occupying a roster spot that might have been better served by one of the more established pitchers in the Dodgers' system.

After five years in the majors, his record was an unremarkable 36–40. He led the league in wild pitches, and his manager, Walter Alston, didn't think he could throw a strike under pressure. Koufax contemplated early retirement in 1960, but his determination to prove to the Dodgers, and to himself, that he could pitch in the big leagues persuaded him to try one more season.

He won 18 games in '61, then embarked on a five-year streak of excellence that had observers comparing him to the greatest pitchers in the game's history.

His fastball jumped in the same manner as the great Lefty Grove's had back in the thirties. Unlike most lefties, whose arm angle during delivery varies from the low three-quarters of a Tom Glavine to the sidearm of a Randy Johnson, Koufax threw in a high three-quarters to overhand motion. His delivery was often compared to another great southpaw, Warren Spahn. But as fastballers go, it most resembled the over-the-top arc of Bob Feller, a Hall of Fame right-hander.

Hall of Famer Walter Johnson watched Feller work once and remarked how Feller's overhand motion made it difficult for hitters to see the ball because it blended in with his white uniform. "That's good for him," the Big Train said, "and bad for the hitters."

Koufax enjoyed a similar advantage three decades later. He threw with such velocity that many hitters could hardly see the rotation of the red stitching that tips off whether a pitch is a fastball or curve. They saw only a white blur, a pitch thrown with such velocity it resembled a cueball and emitted a buzzing sound as it approached home plate.

"I don't think I've ever seen batters more overmatched than when he was throwing the combination of that terrific fastball and deadly curveball," Angell said. "They would look back out at him as if, you know, 'What am I doing here?' You would see them go back to the dugout and talk to each other. They were riveted."

As were a generation of fans. It was an unforgettable experience to see him pitch in his prime, sort of like seeing a young Sinatra on stage. Moss Klein, a baseball writer for the *Newark (N.J.) Star-Ledger*, once held his nephew up to the television screen during a Dodgers game just so the youngster could someday say he had seen Koufax pitch. Koufax's style was distinctive—the high leg kick, the bow-taut delivery—but the most distinguishing feature of his delivery was the recoil of his left shoulder after he released the ball. His shoulder would rock back, like the recoil of a rifle, and it was a telling indication of how hard he threw.

Nolan Ryan was a teenager growing up in Houston when he first saw Koufax in person. To Ryan, watching Koufax pitch was like watching a line of poetry come to life. Here was the ultimate pitcher, Ryan thought, dominating with power and control.

Koufax dominated despite being a two-pitch pitcher. He tinkered with a forkball and changeup, but just as he doesn't mince words off the field, he never minced pitches on the mound. He has enormous hands and fingers, and could wrap his hand around a baseball the way most people wrap their hand around a golf ball. His long fingers allowed him to exert extra pressure and extra spin on the ball, and the whipcord motion of his left arm provided greater torque to his delivery.

Because of these distinct physical advantages, Koufax was able to throw a 95-mile-an-hour fastball that flared away from a right-handed hitter and in to a left-hander. His curve dropped like a sinker, and by adjusting his grip on the ball, he could unfurl an 85-mile-per-hour breaking pitch that dipped down and away from left-handers, down and in to right-handers.

"To call his curveball 'outstanding' is not a good enough word for it," recalled Claude Osteen, a teammate of Koufax with the Dodgers on their World Series teams in 1965–1966.

"His curve went straight down," Osteen said, "and his fastball was always going up. He didn't have a great changeup, but he didn't need it. His curveball and fastball were that good."

As elusive as his pitches were for even the best hitters of his generation, Koufax's personality proved just as elusive for those who sought to know him better. In his playing days, Dodger executives complained they could never get in touch with him by phone, so they resorted to telegrams asking him to please contact the club. Legend has it that he hid his phone in the oven to escape its incessant ringing. The fact is, his phone was equipped with a red light that flashed to signal incoming calls. If he wasn't in the room, he didn't know if someone was trying to reach him.

Bavasi said the stories of Koufax being reclusive are overplayed.

"In those days, there was very little contact between the clubs and ballplayers, other than salaries," Bavasi said. "So I don't think Sandy was in our office more than four times in his 12 years with the team."

A person close to the Dodgers said Koufax is only seen on the fringe of the organization these days, "one of those shadow-type things."

Larry Merchant, who knew Koufax from their days together at Lafayette High School in Brooklyn and covered his career with the Dodgers as a sportswriter and later columnist, said Koufax's reluctance to be recognized is a way of maintaining his privacy.

"DiMaggio was like that too," Merchant said, "but DiMaggio nurtured his image as a great player by going to Yankee Stadium (for World Series and Old-Timer's Day games). Koufax shows up at Dodger Stadium unannounced, which is unusual for such a public figure."

Koufax's distance from the club stems in part from the 1998 change in team ownership, when Peter O'Malley and his sister Terry Seidler sold the club to the Fox division of Rupert Murdoch's News Corp. Koufax had been signed to his first Dodger contract by Walter O'Malley and had grown up with Peter and Terry.

"I'm still a Dodger fan," he said in Atlanta, "but it's not the same people."

Ed Linn, who worked with him on his autobiography in 1966, said Koufax is pleasant and laughs easily. Koufax showed a wry sense of humor in Atlanta when he was asked who was the best left-hander ever.

"Warren Spahn's got to be," he said. "Not because he was so good, but because he pitched the whole damn century."

Koufax laughed. For one day at least, he seemed comfortable talking about himself. Asked why he doesn't meet with the media more often, he shrugged. "I think you lose your anonymity," he said.

Koufax is anything but anonymous. He is the only pitcher to be ranked by ESPN among their 50 greatest athletes of the 20th century, and when Spahn was asked who was the best pitcher he ever saw, he wasted little time in answering.

"Koufax," he said. "What do you think I am, crazy?"

Koufax seems humbled by the praise, and if he shows a certain reticence to talk about himself, he manages to turn away inquiring minds in a polite and courteous manner. He is a man, Linn said, who is not only comfortable in his own company, but enjoys his solitude.

"He is reclusive," Linn said. "He's pleasant, and he doesn't want to attack anyone or say anything negative. But he's interesting in a lot of ways. He has tremendous integrity. He could have been the first merchant prince of baseball, but he decided he wasn't going to sell his name. He turned down massive amounts of money."

Though Koufax was cooperative in working on his book, Linn had the feeling that Koufax was forever holding something back, maintaining his private feelings behind what Linn called "a wall of amiability."

It is a wall even old acquaintances have never been able to penetrate.

"Even though I had connections with him, I respected that wall," Merchant said. "Not many people have broken through it."

Koufax has a polished complexity about him. In his Dodger days he was an angelic assassin. Former ballplayers still marvel at how a man so quiet and sensitive off the field was so eager to go for the jugular when pitching. Uncomfortable with the media, he joined NBC as a baseball analyst from 1967 to 1973. He is a homebody who in retirement lived a nomadic existence. His residences have included such diverse places as Maine and Paso Robles, a small, rural town located in the California wine valley, as well as Vermont, North Carolina, Idaho, and San Luis Obispo in California. *L.A. Times* columnist Jim Murray wrote that "Sandy always seemed to be running from something," but Koufax has settled down enough to have kept his Vero Beach phone number intact the past 11 years.

Articulate but guarded, engaging but distant, Koufax is different things to different people. *Boys of Summer* author Roger Kahn said he is courteous but bland; *New York Times* sportswriter Dave Anderson has found him to be bright and engaging.

Perhaps because of these contradictions, Koufax is the one athlete from the sixties that fans want to know better. Ryan wonders if Koufax realizes that modern hurlers consider him a genius at the art of pitching.

Decades after he had thrown his last competitive pitch, coaches and players still quote him, still follow his principles on pitching. Just as Ted Williams is considered the wise old head of hitters, Koufax is thought by many to be the sage of pitching.

On the eve of Game One of the 1998 World Series in New York's Yankee Stadium, San Diego Padres pitching coach Dave Stewart told Larry Whiteside of the *Boston Globe* that one of the keys to his staff winning 98 games and the National League pennant is their new application of an old formula—pitching inside.

"Sandy Koufax always said, 'Make the bat small,' " Stewart said.

"That means you're going to the small end of the bat. If you can keep the ball inside you can keep run production down."

Koufax has worked with a number of pitchers, including Ryan, David Cone, Dwight Gooden, Orel Hershiser, John Franco, and Al Leiter. He admires Atlanta control artists Greg Maddux, Tom Glavine, and John Smoltz because, as he said, "I believe in the outside corner."

Indeed, Koufax harnessed his fastball and curve to the point where he owned the pinpoint control of a dart thrower. Unlike many pitching coaches, he preaches ball movement over changing speeds, which is not surprising since he once dotted the strike zone with pitches that moved not only up and down but in and out.

The extraordinary movement on his pitches allowed him to win despite receiving little run support. Critics called the Dodger offense "Tap Ball." A "Dodger Double" consisted of a walk and stolen base. The L.A. offense was so anemic that Charles Strange, a member of the Dodgers' front office in the sixties, recalled a day in 1962 when Don Drysdale was called away from the team to go to Washington, D.C.

"The team was in New York that night," he said, "and when Drysdale heard that Koufax had thrown a no-hitter, he said, 'Yeah, but who won?'"

"Back in those days, (Maury) Wills would get a bunt single, steal second, take third on a groundout, score on a flyball, and Koufax would win one-nothing."

In his *Historical Baseball Abstract*, Bill James studied Koufax's games from the 1963–1964 seasons. On days in which the Dodgers managed three runs or less, Koufax was 18–4. It was, wrote James, an unbelievable accomplishment.

During the '65 and '66 seasons, Koufax redefined the old baseball adage of pitching with pain. He struck out a combined 699 batters his final two seasons, had a strikeout-to-walk ratio of nearly five-to-one, and posted an ERA of 1.87.

Teammates called him "Koo-Foo," and after he took apart the Mantle and Maris Yankees in the 1963 World Series, *Sports Illustrated* called him "Koo-Foo the Killer." His greatness on the mound thrust him into the national spotlight, a position he was never comfortable with. He never sought fame, and soon sought to elude it. To Koufax, fame meant room service rather than restaurants, and having to go to great lengths to protect his privacy.

"Everyone was looking to get a handle on Sandy Koufax," Merchant said. "But he never gave them much to grab. He was very difficult to probe."

One underlying thread throughout Koufax's life is that he is a realist. When he insisted on a $20,000 rookie contract from the Brooklyn Dodgers back in '55, he did so for several reasons. It was a way of helping his family financially, and he knew if he failed in the majors he would have enough money to return to the University of Cincinnati and continue his architectural studies.

He never complained about pitching for the weak-hitting Dodgers, a club Jim Murray once called the ghastliest-scoring team in history. "They pile up runs at the rate of one every nine innings," Murray wrote. Murray thought Koufax pitching for those Dodgers teams was comparable to Rembrandt painting on the back of cigar boxes, to Caruso singing with a high school chorus.

Koufax, however, saw an advantage in pitching for a team that didn't score many runs. It didn't harm him a bit, he said, to become conditioned to the idea that he didn't have the luxury of throwing a thoughtless or careless pitch.

It was an irony that the very attributes that had allowed him to throw so hard and with such control—the long arms, long hands, and long fingers—proved in the end ill-equipped to handle the physical stress of years of throwing a baseball. Still, Koufax refused to feel sorry for himself. Since he had accepted the advantages of the way he was built, he said, he didn't see how he could complain about the disadvantages.

Like DiMaggio, like Jackie Robinson and Roberto Clemente, Koufax was a significant ethnic figure in major league baseball. He was a star of Jewish heritage, and in the socially conscious sixties, his observances of High Holy Days had a tremendous impact on Jews across the country. When the Dodgers signed outfielder Shawn Green to a free agent contract in November 1999, Rabbi Aaron Kriegel of Los Angeles said Green was "walking in the shoes of Sandy Koufax" as a famous Jewish athlete playing in a city with a large Jewish population.

K
O
U
F
A
X

Michael Wise was a 12-year-old living in Minnesota when Koufax refused to start Game One of the 1965 World Series against the Twins because it fell on Yom Kippur. Later, the executive director of the Jewish Community Federation in Akron, Ohio, Wise said Koufax's stand made him proud to be Jewish.

Teammates called Koufax "Super Jew," and yet while he never pitched on Passover, Rosh Hashanah, or Yom Kippur, research of his career reveals he pitched on Shavuot eight times and Sukkot/Shemini Atzereth twice.

Author Harvey Frommer said Koufax inspired countless members of his faith. Today, Koufax assists veteran ballplayers as a board member of the Baseball Assistance Team, an organization that provides financial help for former major leaguers.

"He saw a need," said BAT executive director James Martin, "and decided to help."

Said former Dodger teammate Carl Erskine, "He's very sensitive to the players that need help. He's made a real contribution to that board."

The contributions he makes are done quietly, without publicity. In July 1999, the *L.A. Times* published a story about Koufax teaching American Legion pitcher Scott Sellz, whom Koufax has known since Sellz was 10, to throw a curveball. He taught Sellz to put his middle finger on the seam and snap down before releasing the ball.

"It moves differently than other people's," Sellz told the *Times* after pitching Valley Chatsworth to the District 20 championship. According to Sellz, the curve broke late and because it looked like a fastball, hitters found it hard to adjust to the pitch.

As with almost everything else he does, Koufax's work with Sellz was done quietly and without publicity.

"He's very private, very withdrawn," said Jack Lang, a veteran baseball writer who covered Koufax for the *Long Island Press* in 1955. Lang recalled that Koufax was on a Caribbean cruise in the summer of 1999 when he learned of the death of former teammate and Dodger captain "Pee Wee" Reese. Immediately, Koufax asked the captain of the cruise liner to make an unscheduled stop at the closest port. The captain obliged, and Koufax flew stateside to attend the funeral of his old friend.

Said Lang, "Sandy's all class."

Koufax ended his self-imposed exile from baseball in March 1979, returning to the Dodgers as a pitching coach. The reason for his return was simple. Having lived on a fixed income for years, he needed the money to keep up with inflation.

But there was more. He had spent eight years doing what he wanted to do, going where he wanted to go. Finally, he realized he'd had enough of that lifestyle. There were only so many holes of golf he could play, he said, and since he couldn't see himself opening a restaurant or owning a hardware store, he knew eventually he would have to do something with his life. Whatever it was he tried, he said, he found it wasn't what he wanted to do. He was searching for a purpose, and his search led him back to baseball.

He was happy to be back.

"It's hard to be away," he said, "from possibly the only thing you ever really did well."

He left the Dodgers in 1990 because his workload had been cut back and he felt he was no longer earning the money the club was paying him. Since then, he has worked with pitchers in various major league camps. Yankees' coach Don Zimmer, who played shortstop behind Koufax on the Dodgers, said Koufax stopped into the Yankees' 1999 spring training camp and talked at length to the club's pitchers.

"He spoke more in 50 minutes," Zimmer said, "than I had heard him speak in the last five years."

When Claude Osteen was a pitching coach with the Texas Rangers, Koufax spent a week with the team in spring training. As Osteen was driving him back to his hotel at week's end, he was surprised to hear Koufax tell him how much he had enjoyed himself. He was surprised, Osteen said, because Koufax rarely spoke about his personal feelings.

"He's guarded," Carl Erskine said, "and I think he wants others to respect his feelings as he would respect theirs. Sandy is a little protective of his private life, and that's his call. I don't think I've ever seen Sandy be rude to a fan or a writer, but if he can avoid a circumstance where it might push him to be a little curt, he avoids that."

Koufax has avoided the spotlight, but when it has been thrust on him, he has responded. Osteen recalled an old-timer's game several years ago in which major league stars from the sixties and seventies headed to Hawaii to play a squad of Japanese stars. Word soon spread that the Japanese team included players who had only recently retired, and that the game was being televised in Tokyo.

"Pride rears its head," said Osteen, "and guys were playing a little harder than they do in usual old-timer all-star games.

"Sandy pitched an inning or two, and he came as close to throwing the way I remembered him as I had seen. Not in terms of velocity but intensity. He snapped off some curves and fastballs that made guys realize, 'Hey, he can still pitch.'"

It was just a glimpse of what had been; yet it served as a reminder of an earlier time, when Koufax and Don Drysdale formed a lefty-righty mound duo unmatched in major league history.

It served as a reminder too, of an October day in 1965. That day, Dodgers manager Walt Alston had to choose between Koufax, a 26-game winner with two days' rest, or Drysdale, a 23-game winner with three days' rest, to start Game Seven of the World Series in Minnesota.

ONE

I n his *New York Times* piece the morning of Thursday, October 14, 1965, sportswriter Joe Durso described Walter Alston's predicament as "a delightfully difficult choice."

Alston didn't think it was so delightful. Talking to reporters on Wednesday, the eve of the seventh game of the World Series in Minnesota, the Dodgers' skipper sighed as he spoke in the visitors' clubhouse of his dilemma.

"The choice is this," he said. "I've got Drysdale with three days' rest and a bruised hand, or Koufax with two days' rest.

"I'll pick one tomorrow. I just want to think about it."

Walter Emmons Alston had taken over as manager of the Dodgers on November 24, 1953, when the franchise was still in Brooklyn, and the team was still known as "Dem Bums." Laconic and controlled, Alston represented a dramatic change from the man he was replacing, Charlie Dressen. Known as "Jolly Cholly," Dressen had led the Dodgers to consecutive National League pennants in 1952–1953, each year falling to their hated city rivals, the New York Yankees, in the Subway Series.

When the New York Giants inked colorful manager Leo Durocher to a three-year contract, Dressen asked Dodger team owner Walter O'Malley for a two-year deal. Dressen argued that his record as a manager was better than Durocher's, but when O'Malley hesitated to extend the contract of his pennant-winning pilot, Dressen's wife fired off a caustic letter to the Dodger front office. "Jolly Cholly" was promptly fired and replaced by the 41-year-old Alston, a man who for the next 23 years became famous for his one-year contracts.

Having spent 13 years in the Dodger organization as a minor league manager, Alston had never enjoyed much major league visibility. In 1936 he had a brief stay in the bigs, striking out in his only at-bat on September 27, 1936, as a member of the St. Louis Cardinals. The day after O'Malley introduced Alston to the New York press, one paper headlined his arrival with the words, "Walt, Who?"

A native of Venice, Ohio, "Smokey" Alston was a big man, standing 6' 2" and weighing 195 pounds. Solid and stable, he was so unassuming that *Los Angeles Times* columnist Jim Murray wrote, "Walt Alston would order corn on the cob in a Paris restaurant."

Inheriting Brooklyn's famous "Boys of Summer" squad of Jackie Robinson, Duke Snider, Gil Hodges, and Pee Wee Reese, Alston delivered a world championship to long-suffering Brooklyn fans in 1955 when the Dodgers finally beat the hated Yankees in the World Series. One year later, Alston skippered Brooklyn to another pennant, and in 1959, managed the Dodgers to a second world title one year after O'Malley had moved the franchise west to Los Angeles.

By the early sixties, the Dodgers had been transformed from a power-packed lineup to one that relied on the speed of Maury Wills and the pitching of Sandy Koufax and Don Drysdale. Their team style represented a dramatic change in the way the game had been played for years by baseball's dominant team, the Yankees. Where New York won with the long-ball power of the "M&M Boys"—Mickey Mantle and Roger Maris—the Dodgers won in a flash-and-dash fashion derided by American League fans as "Hot Wheels." The Dodgers got the best of the Yanks with a four-game sweep in the '63 World Series, but injuries and poor performances doomed the Dodgers to a sixth-place finish in '64. When L.A.'s two-time batting champion, Tommy Davis, broke an ankle in May of 1965 and was lost for the season, the Dodgers' hopes for a pennant appeared dead again.

Instead, L.A. responded with opportunism and raw nerve. Writer

Roger Angell noted that the Dodgers won in '65 not just because of Koufax, Drysdale, and Wills, but because the club's combination of speed, pride, and Alston's managerial intelligence enabled them to overturn the modern structure of baseball—the Yankee style—which was based on the home run.

The Dodgers survived a heated pennant race with the Reds and Giants despite a .245 team batting average that was the lowest ever for a National League champion. L.A.'s popgun offense accounted for just 78 homers, but the Dodgers led their league with 172 stolen bases. They clinched the pennant on the penultimate day of the season, Saturday, October 2, in typical fashion—a 3–1 win over Milwaukee in which Koufax, working on just two days' rest and supported by just two hits, beat the Braves on a four-hitter with 12 strikeouts.

Koufax's herculean effort came on the heels of a 13-strikeout, 5–0 shutout that eliminated Cincinnati on September 30. Koufax was not only winning clutch games, he was winning with little rest. His ability to dominate on two days' rest was prominent in Alston's mind as the manager wrestled with the question of who to start against the Twins in Game Seven. Just two days earlier, Koufax had given the Dodgers a 3–2 Series lead with a 10-strikeout shutout.

Amazingly, Koufax told reporters afterwards, "This was not one of my better games." His cool, unemotional response caused sportswriter Bill Becker to note in the *New York Times* the next day that the life of a perfectionist can be very demanding:

> That was the impression Sandy Koufax, probably the greatest pitcher of modern times, gave today after shutting out Minnesota with four hits and sending Los Angeles ahead in this turnabout 1965 World Series.

"My control was not what it should have been," Koufax explained as perspiration dripped from his dark brows. "I got awfully tired toward the end."

A weary smile followed. "Maybe," he mused, "I was entitled to get a little tired along the 350th inning."

Too tired to get his normal breaking pitches—the curve and fork-ball—over the plate in a season in which he led the majors in innings pitched, Koufax reared back and challenged the Twins' big hitters with his heater. He threw 109 pitches in nine innings, and 70 percent of those were fastballs.

Asked about the possibility of starting Game Seven if necessary, Koufax initially laughed it off. "I'll be ready to pitch the first inning," he said, "but I won't guarantee how long I'll be around."

When the Series shifted back to Minnesota for Game Six and the Twins won to force a seventh game, Koufax's mood shifted as well.

"It doesn't make any difference," he said at the prospect of pitching Game Seven. "After pitching 351 innings this year, a few more won't matter.

"My arm," he said with a smile of resignation, "is, well, tired."

Koufax's 336 innings pitched in 1965 were the most by a left-hander since 1906—an era marked by famous rubber-arms like Cy Young and "Iron Man" Joe McGinnity—and the second most in the modern era behind Robin Roberts' 337 innings in 1954. Koufax won 26 games during the regular season, hurled 27 complete games, and did not miss a start all season. He also broke the major league strikeout record with 382 whiffs, a remarkable set of achievements considering that he was pitching with an arthritic left elbow.

Koufax's physical problems began in 1962, when he developed a circulatory problem in the index finger of his left hand. The mysterious ailment caused the skin on his finger to scale, and forced him to miss two months of the season, ending his hope of winning 20 games for the first time in his career. He finished with a 14–7 record, led the league with a 2.54 earned run average, and struck out 216 batters in just 184 innings. He wasn't told at the time, but his circulatory problem was so severe that doctors privately considered amputating his finger.

Two years later, Koufax rode a white-hot streak in which he won 15 of 16 decisions and was 19–5 entering August. He never won his 20th. Playing in Milwaukee on August 8, he stroked a fifth-inning single off Tony Cloninger and took second on Wills' single. When Cloninger tried to pick Koufax off second, Sandy dove back into the bag safely but endured a hard tag on his pitching elbow.

The elbow stung, but the pain subsided and Koufax stayed in the game. When he awoke the next morning in Milwaukee's Schroeder Hotel, he noticed a lump on his left elbow. Since the elbow wasn't discolored, Koufax knew it wasn't a bruise. The lump was the kind of swelling that results when a joint fills with liquid.

With an elbow that was badly swollen, Koufax pitched through his next two starts, striking out 10 in a 4–1 win in Cincinnati, and 13 in a victory over the Cardinals in Los Angeles that gave him his 19th win of the season. The next morning when he awoke, the swelling in his pitching arm was no longer confined to the joint area, but extended from shoulder to wrist. His elbow was swollen to the size of his knee, and was locked in a hooked position.

Unable to bend or straighten his left arm, Koufax found he had no more than an inch's worth of movement. When he did move the arm, he could hear the sound of liquid swishing around inside the joint, a sound he compared to that of a wet sponge being squeezed.

Showing the elbow to team physician Dr. Robert Kerlan, Koufax was immediately taken for treatment and x-rays. Because Dr. Kerlan had been taking x-rays of Koufax's pitching arm for years, he had images for comparisons. Previous pictures showed an assortment of bone spurs, scar tissue, and adhesions to the cartilage covering the elbow joint that are customary after having thrown thousands of pitches.

This time though, x-rays also revealed traumatic arthritis in Koufax's elbow. The two main forms of arthritis are osteoarthritis, which comes from wear and tear normally associated with old age, and rheumatoid arthritis, an infectious disease. Traumatic arthritis is closely associated with osteoarthritis, since both involve the wearing down of cartilage. The difference is that in traumatic arthritis, the wearing down is brought on by physical exertion rather than old age.

Since every bodily joint has a lining which creates a lubricating fluid, when the lining becomes inflamed, it leaks extra fluid into the joint. In Koufax's case, the lining of his elbow leaked enough fluid to swell not only the joint but the entire arm from shoulder to wrist.

Dr. Kerlan told Koufax the problem could be controlled temporarily, but that it would gradually worsen. Because there were only 10 games left in the season and the Dodgers were 14 games behind in the standings, Koufax and Dr. Kerlan decided to rest the arm over the winter.

Koufax did not pitch again until the spring of '65, but when his arm swelled up following an exhibition outing against the Chicago White

Sox, the Dodgers suggested he pitch just once a week. It was a risky suggestion, since extended rest can sometimes hurt a pitcher's control.

Throughout the season, Koufax's arm swelled the day after he pitched, improved the second day, then swelled again on the third. The arthritis caused him so much discomfort that he found even the act of combing his hair "a very gritty" experience. He took controlled amounts of phenylbutazone, a pill designed to lessen the inflammation in his arm. On days he pitched, he applied Capsolin, a searing skin irritant, on his arm to loosen his muscles before the game, and then submerged his elbow in near-freezing ice baths afterwards.

The media took interest in Koufax's treatments. Mel Durslag of the *Los Angeles Herald-Examiner* called him the pinup boy for the Arthritis and Rheumatism Foundation. Writers described how Capsolin burned the skin almost to the point of making it blister, but at the same time stimulated circulation underneath.

When Koufax first began taking ice baths, his skin would dry and crack and take on the look of frostbite. Dodgers' co-trainer Bill Buhler came up with a way to protect the skin by cutting the inner tube of a tire into an arm-length piece and molding it into a sleeve. Team trainers would fill a small plastic tub with crushed ice until the water temperature dropped to 35 degrees, and Koufax would soak his rubber-sleeved arm in it for 35 to 45 minutes. A photographer from United Press International snapped a picture of a dour-looking Koufax soaking his left arm in a tub of crushed ice in the Dodgers' clubhouse.

Koufax helped his cause by suggesting to Dodger management that he refrain from the normal practice of throwing between starts in order to save his arm for games, and the extra rest allowed him to put together his extraordinary season. Facing the Chicago Cubs on September 9, Koufax achieved that most difficult of mound tasks—a perfect game. Utterly dominating a lineup that included Billy Williams, Ernie Banks, and Ron Santo, Koufax fanned 14, working so briskly the game was completed in one hour and 43 minutes.

Overpowering in his assortment of fastballs and curves, Koufax struck out the last six batters he faced, and seven of the last nine. The Dodgers scored in the fifth in typical style—a walk, bunt, stolen base, and wild throw. Koufax was clinging to the barest of margins when he faced two of the Cubs' hardest hitters, Santo and Banks, in the eighth inning. He struck out both, despite the fact that Cubs hitters were calling every pitch he threw—a fastball if Koufax brought his hands over his head during the windup; a curve if he brought his hands back behind his head.

"I've never seen Sandy throw as hard as he did when he struck me out in the eighth," Santo said. "He threw one fastball right by me and I was waiting for it."

Banks agreed. "He threw it right past us. I thought he might weaken some later on, but he just kept throwing the ball right on through. And he was throwing strikes."

Koufax ended the inning by striking out rookie Byron Browne. In the ninth, he fired a third strike past Chris Krug, then whiffed pinch hitter and boyhood friend Joey Amalfitano on three pitches. With history riding on every pitch, Koufax faced another pinch hitter, Harvey Kuenn, the former American League batting champion. Kuenn also struck out, enabling the 29-year-old Koufax to achieve just the eighth perfect game in major league history.

The Cubs-Dodgers game may have been the best pitched in major league history. Not only did Koufax throw a perfect game, but his opposite, left-hander Bob Hendley, surrendered just one hit and one walk in going the distance in a 1–0 loss.

Ever gracious, Koufax told reporters he sympathized with Hendley's tough loss. "It's a shame," he said, "to lose a game the way he did."

The '65 season represented both pain and glory for Koufax, and his ability to pitch through injuries astounded everyone. "Some sore elbow," scoffed Reds' manager Dick Sisler. "It's sore except between the first and ninth innings."

After whiffing five of the 10 Washington Senators he faced in an exhibition game and getting Doug Camilli to pop up for the final out, Koufax heard Camilli yell over at him, "Sore elbow, my eye!"

"Everyone was aware of his (arthritic) condition," recalled Claude Osteen. "But you couldn't tell how bad it was. There was nothing to lead you to believe how bad it was because of his tremendous pitching performances."

Like everyone else, Pittsburgh Pirates' second baseman Bill

Mazeroski knew about Koufax's arm ailment. Like everyone else, he found it difficult to believe it was that serious.

"I had heard about his arm problems," Mazeroski remembered, "but it was hard to believe because he threw so hard."

Watching Koufax up close for the first time in the '65 Series, Twins' team trainer Dr. William E. Proffitt, Jr. stopped just short of calling the pitcher a medical marvel.

"You would never have thought that Koufax could pitch consistently with that arthritis condition in his elbow," Dr. Proffitt said. "The way he's performed this year is amazing."

Alston was undoubtedly entertaining the same thought as the Dodgers prepared for Game Seven. The day before, he had approached Koufax and Drysdale in the locker room and asked, "Are you both ready?" When they answered in the affirmative, Alston replied, "Well, I don't know yet. I want you both to be ready. I'll let you know tomorrow."

Veteran baseball observers tried to get the scoop on Alston's decision when the Dodgers arrived at Metropolitan Stadium in Minnesota for the game. Pitchers then traditionally shaved on the day of their start, but Koufax and Drysdale both showed up with two days' worth of stubble on their faces.

While the team was still changing from street clothes into their gray road uniforms, Alston met with pitching coach Lefty Phillips.

"It's going to be the left-hander," Alston told Phillips.

When Koufax arrived at his locker before the game, he noticed a baseball on the top shelf. The message was clear. Koufax would start, and Drysdale would be in the bullpen, ready to come on in relief at the first sign of trouble.

Approaching Alston, Koufax said simply, "I'll do my best." He turned to Drysdale. "It's good to know," he said, "that you're out there."

"I'll be there," Drysdale said.

Alston's decision didn't surprise Drysdale. Nor did it anger him, even though it was his turn in the Dodger rotation. Three years earlier, Alston had a similar decision to make when the Dodgers met their rivals, the San Francisco Giants, in a special three-game playoff to determine the National League pennant. Alston opened the series by starting Koufax, who was rusty from inactivity, in the first game. The Giants won 8–0, and Alston, faced with a "must win" game, chose Stan Williams over Drysdale the next day as well.

"What's Alston saving me for, the Grapefruit League?" Drysdale snapped to reporters. Alston reversed his decision, started Drysdale, and the Dodgers won 8–7 to force a third and final game that San Francisco eventually won.

As angry as Drysdale had been at being passed over for the playoff start in '62, he was just as understanding in '65 when Alston named Koufax his Game Seven starter.

Koufax, Drysdale thought, was the best pitcher he had ever seen. When Koufax got the ball, Drysdale always allowed for the possibility that Sandy would throw a no-hitter. That expectation was always there, Drysdale said later, because Koufax was so dominant.

At least one other baseball observer agreed with Alston's decision as well. "If I had a game to win," Mazeroski said, "I'd want Koufax. He'd win it 2–1, 1–0, or 3–2, whatever it takes."

Former Philadelphia sportswriter Larry Merchant believed that by the mid-sixties, Koufax had become so dominant, so overpowering, that the only games that really mattered to him were the big, pressure-filled games of a pennant race or World Series.

Pitching Game Seven against the Twins in Minnesota on two days' rest was the kind of big game Koufax seemed to thrive on. As he prepared to take the field, he had an application of Capsolin rubbed on his throwing arm. He used such a heavy dosage that it made the eyes of those standing close to him tear up. According to veteran Dodger pitchers like Ed Roebuck, Koufax was willing to withstand the extreme heat of the counter-irritant for one reason.

"It burned you so bad," Roebuck remembered, "you couldn't feel the other pain."

Former Dodger catcher Norm Sherry said that most ballplayers cut the counter-irritant by mixing it with petroleum jelly or some other soothing cooling ointment.

"It was hot," Sherry recalled, "and you'd swear it got hotter. It gets in your pores, and it gets so hot you don't feel your arm getting sore or tired."

Before applying the Capsolin to his arm, Koufax underwent a massage from team trainers, who tried to work loose the thick, corded

K
O
U
F
A
X

muscles in his back and shoulders. Capsolin was applied to his left arm straight out of the tube, and as the heating ointment seared his skin, for a moment it helped him forget his aching left elbow.

With that, Sandy Koufax was set to pitch the decisive game in baseball's world championship.

TWO

N BC Sports presents . . . The 1965 World Series. From Metropolitan Stadium in Bloomington, Minnesota, the Los Angeles
Dodgers meeting the Minnesota Twins.

"This is Vin Scully, along with Ray Scott, ready to bring you all the
action of the seventh and deciding game of the 1965 World Series. This
game is being sent your way by the Gillette Safety Razor Company and
Chrysler Corporation . . .

"The big guessing game is over. Sandy Koufax is the Dodger
pitcher . . ."

Scully's opening remarks set the stage for millions of viewers who
had tuned in to the 306 television stations in the United States, Canada,
Puerto Rico, and Mexico broadcasting the World Series. It was a record
number, as was that of the 558 radio stations carrying the game over the
airwaves. The interest in this World Series was so intense, a potentate in
Saudi Arabia requested a kinescope of the NBC broadcast—and got it.

Game day brought bright blue skies to Bloomington on Thursday,
October 14. Metropolitan Stadium sat equal distance between downtown Minneapolis and downtown St. Paul, and the Twin Cities had
been hit by a severe electrical storm the night before. Located on 24th

K
O
U
F
A
X

Avenue South, just off Interstate 494, the Met opened on April 24, 1956, and had undergone major expansion in 1960 to prepare it for the arrival in '61 of the expansion Twins and Minnesota Vikings NFL team.

Writer Roger Angell, in Minnesota for the first two games of the '65 Series, described Met Stadium as "an airy cyclotron standing amid cornfields." The Met was distinctive for the huge scoreboard beyond the center-field wall. Unlike other American League ballparks of the time, the Met offered no idiosyncracies in its outfield dimensions. Lacking a short porch in right field like Yankee Stadium or a Green Monster in left like Fenway Park, the Met measured a symmetrical 365 feet to the power alleys and 430 feet to straightaway center.

Minnesota's hitters had mauled Drysdale, Koufax, and Osteen in winning all three of their home games in the Series, and strafed L.A.'s vaunted staff for 18 runs and 25 hits.

A drenching rain persisted through the early morning hours, but by early afternoon, the sun had melted away the clouds and brought on game-time temperatures of sixty degrees. A cool, northwesterly wind blew in at nine miles per hour. The overnight rain had left the expansive outfield a lush emerald green, and the bright grass shimmered in the sunlight.

Outside the park, fans filing through the ticket gates crunched through fallen leaves as gold and crisp as cornflakes. For the more than 50,000 crowding into the sold-out stadium, game day offered a beautiful, burnished fall afternoon in the Midwest.

Down on the field, the Dodgers and Twins completed their final pregame warmups. The uniforms were classic sixties. The National League champions were dressed in gray old-style road uniforms, featuring large blue numbers on their backs and "Los Angeles" in blue script across their chests. On their heads they wore bright blue Dodgers hats with a white interlocking *LA* on the front panel.

The American League champions wore bright white uniforms with navy blue pinstripes and "Twins" in script across their chests. The backs of their jerseys had large blue numbers, and they wore navy blue hats with *TC*, for Twin Cities, on the front panel.

Introducing the lineups, the public address announcer came to the end of the Dodgers' starters. The sellout crowd fell silent for a moment when the following announcement was made: "Batting ninth and pitching for the Dodgers . . . Number 32, Sandy Koufax."

In the press box, Jim Murray smiled. The *Los Angeles Times* columnist made it a point to watch the opposing team's reaction when they learned Koufax would be on the mound. It was fun, Murray thought, to watch the faces of enemy hitters turn white when they heard Koufax was pitching.

While the lineups were being announced, fans saw a contingent of Dodger pitchers making the long walk to the bullpen. They were led by number 53, Don Drysdale, striding through the short-cropped outfield grass with his cap pulled low over his eyes in trademark fashion.

In the NBC radio booth, Byrum Saam, the voice of the Phillies who was calling the play-by-play for the national broadcast, told listeners that Koufax and Drysdale had taken manager Walter Alston's decision in the fashion of true sportsmen.

Saam: "Either one, I guess, would be a good selection, and as Walt Alston said, 'You writers have a second guess. Maybe they'll best Koufax, and you'll say maybe I should have started Drysdale. But I only have one guess.' "

Talking to NBC-TV before the game, Alston explained his decision to start Koufax over Drysdale:

> I finally decided on Koufax for the simple reason that I think that this club, the Twins, are more susceptible to left-handed pitching than they are right-handed. And the fact that I've got Drysdale in the bullpen if they put their right-hand hitters in there, and I do have to make a switch, I've made them commit themselves again to go to the left-handed side, and I've still got Perranoski ready to go in case they make a second switch.

By starting Koufax, Alston was figuring on a lefty-righty-lefty rotation in which he could first call on Drysdale and then on southpaw relief ace Ron Perranoski if needed. Alston figured the Twins would go with a right-handed hitting lineup to counter Koufax, and that would force Minnesota to make changes if Drysdale entered the game. Once they did, the Twins would be locked into a lefty lineup if Alston brought in Perranoski.

A second reason for Alston's decision was if Koufax came to bat in the third or fourth inning with runners in scoring position, Alston could pinch-hit for Koufax and bring Drysdale in to work the middle innings.

Three more parts to the equation: Metropolitan Stadium was a hitter's park, and Drysdale was more susceptible to the home run than Koufax; a northwesterly wind was blowing out towards left field, meaning Minnesota's hitters would have a better chance of pulling a Drysdale pitch to left; and finally, Koufax's dominating performance pitching on two days' rest at season's end had left an indelible impression on Alston.

Alston, however, was harboring no illusions. Koufax was physically tired. In his Game Five start in Los Angeles, he had consistently fallen behind in the count; he ran up 2–0 counts eight times in nine innings. He had his curve working for seven innings before fatigue forced him to rely solely on his fastball in the final two innings.

Bereft of his curve, he had issued his first and only walk of the game in the eighth, to Bob Allison, but was spared a potential Twins' rally when shortstop Maury Wills made a flashy stop of Don Mincher's tough grounder and turned it into a double play.

In the top of the ninth, Koufax had surrendered consecutive singles and was one hit away from not only losing his shutout, but being pulled from the game. Relying on his fastball, he got Joe Nossek to rap a solid liner that Wills turned into another double play—a Twin-killing in more ways than one.

Asked afterwards by Scully how he felt, Koufax issued a weary smile. He was not a man given to exaggeration, and his response to Scully came in careful, measured tones.

"I feel," Koufax said, "a hundred years old."

Before leaving the locker room to start Game Seven, Alston pulled Koufax aside. "If you feel like you haven't got it anymore, let me know right away," he said. "We've got Don ready. We'll get him in there quick."

Asked how long it would take him to get loosened up in the bullpen, Drysdale responded quickly. "Fifteen pitches," he said. It was a startlingly low number, since it usually takes starting pitchers as many as 40 pitches to warm up. Drysdale's answer was a clear indication to

Alston that while Koufax was being given the start, Drysdale's arm was the fresher of the two.

Between them, Koufax and Drysdale had won 49 games in 1965, plus two more in the World Series. Fans packed ballparks whenever Koufax or Drysdale pitched, and the Dodgers were drawing an incredible 2.5 million fans a year in the early sixties.

Drysdale and Koufax gave the Dodgers a matched set of power pitchers unequalled in major league history. Drysdale, a side-arming right-hander who intimidated hitters with a quick temper and even quicker fastball, won the Cy Young Award as baseball's best pitcher in 1962. Koufax, an over-the-top left-hander who rarely hit batters but wasn't afraid to pitch inside, captured the Cy Young in '63, '65, and '66.

Drysdale pitched for the Dodgers from 1956 to 1969, won 209 games, and struck out 2,486 batters. Koufax was with the team from '55 to '66, won 165 games, and fanned 2,396. Drysdale posted a career earned run average of 2.95; Koufax 2.76. Drysdale threw 49 career shutouts and set a major league record with 58⅔ consecutive innings of shutout ball. Koufax had 40 career shutouts and set a major league record by throwing a no-hitter in four consecutive seasons. Both have been enshrined in Cooperstown.

"They were something," recalled Charles Strange, who saw Koufax and Drysdale firsthand as a member of the team's front office. "They had different personalities but they got along very well.

"Sandy didn't care for all the celebrity; he tried to stay in the background. But Don ate it up, he thrived on it."

When Koufax took the mound in the bottom of the first inning of Game Seven, his jersey number—32—reflected his lifetime record in the World Series: Three wins and two defeats.

While everyone in the Dodger organization and many in the sports world debated whether Koufax or Drysdale should start Game Seven, Koufax seemed sure who was going to get the call.

"No one knew who was going to pitch, everyone was arm weary," remembered Strange. "The decision was up in the air. But Sandy was definitely our go-to guy.

"Lou Johnson was a rookie outfielder with us that year, and he tells the story of sitting nervously in the hotel lobby the morning of the seventh game. Sandy walks in, sees Lou, and says, 'Don't worry, Lou. They're going to give the Jew boy the ball, so don't worry about a thing.'"

Claude Osteen, the Dodgers' number three starter, recalled thinking that although Alston waited until game day to make his decision, the players already knew who would get the call.

"No contest," Osteen said. "When you talk about great pitchers, Sandy stands right at the top. I liken him to Greg Maddux of the Braves. Maddux isn't as flashy as Sandy was, because Sandy had a lot of strikeouts, but in comparing Maddux to his contemporaries, he's a lot like Sandy."

Said then Dodgers' general manager Buzzie Bavasi, "I loved Donald, and I was always a Drysdale guy. But when you've got the best, you go with the best. And Sandy was the best."

Out on the mound, Koufax took comfort in the thought that Game Seven was much like a spring training game. The Dodgers were set, if needed, to go with three pitchers for three innings each.

But as he went through his warmup pitches, Koufax said later, he wasn't thinking about pitching just three innings. He was going to try to do the job for nine.

Jim Kaat, the Twins' lefty, also planned to go nine innings. He had defeated Koufax in Game Two in Minnesota, then dropped Game Five to him in L.A. To Kaat and the Twins, there was little mystery as to whether Koufax or Drysdale would start Game Seven.

"We didn't have any doubt," remembered Kaat, who went on to pitch until the age of 44 and won 283 games. "If they had started Drysdale, and no disrespect to him because he was a great pitcher, psychologically that would have been a big lift for us.

"First of all, we were a stronger team against a right-hand pitcher because we had Jimmie Hall and Don Mincher and some pretty good left-hand hitters. We had gotten to (Drysdale) in Game One so I think certainly we would have been a more confident team had Drysdale started. But I don't think there was any doubt in our minds that Koufax was going to start."

Twins' hitters Tony Oliva and Harmon Killebrew agreed.

"Both pitchers were great," Oliva said. "But it would have been better for us if Drysdale had started."

Killebrew said the Twins believed Koufax would get the start, based on what they knew of him.

"Of course we had known about Sandy for a long, long time and faced him in spring training," Killebrew recalled. "He was one of the dominant pitchers of that era. I can't say that I can compare him with anybody (in the American League). There may have been some guys who had a similar type fastball but didn't have the control Sandy had. That was the thing that set him apart, was that great, great control that he had."

As the pitcher opposite Koufax, Kaat's goal was to pitch as tight a ballgame as he possibly could. Like Koufax, Kaat was starting on two days' rest, and like the Dodgers' ace, he was a workhorse. A solidly built southpaw, Kaat started more than 40 games in a season twice in the sixties and three times in his career. He led the league twice in games started, once in innings pitched, and once in complete games. He worked more than 200 innings in a season 14 times in his career.

Arguably the finest fielding pitcher in baseball history, Kaat won a record 16 straight Gold Gloves, an annual award given to the most skillful fielder. Squaring up following each delivery, Kaat was in essence a fifth infielder, and his presence on the mound added an extra dimension to the Twins' defense.

In 1965, Kaat ranked second on the Twins in wins with an 18–11 record, and he was one year away from posting a league-best 25 victories. He started 42 games in '65, threw 264 innings, and yielded 267 hits and 63 walks while striking out 154. His earned run average was a respectable 2.83.

Koufax countered with numbers that dazzle latter-day historians. He led the majors with a 26–8 record and a .765 winning percentage. He started 41 games, pitched in 43, and led the National League with a staggering 27 complete games. Koufax registered eight shutouts, and struck out 382 batters in 336 innings pitched, a league-high average of eight per game. He walked just 71, surrendered only 216 hits, and finished with a league-best 2.04 ERA. Opponents' batting average against him was a paltry .179.

With the 26-year-old Kaat considered by some historians the American League's best left-handed pitcher in the sixties, and the 29-year-old Koufax the best lefty in baseball, Game Seven offered a classic matchup between the top two southpaws of the mid-sixties.

Yet as good as Kaat was, he felt he had to pitch an almost perfect game to beat Koufax.

"Looking at Koufax, it was such a helpless feeling," Kaat said. "It was almost demoralizing going into a game like that because you feel pretty helpless. I had made a comment to Johnny Sain, I said, 'If I give up a run, the game is over.' And (Koufax) had a tougher lineup to face than I did. The Dodgers were not known as a home run hitting lineup, and they were a little more vulnerable to left-hand pitching.

"We had an awfully strong lineup. I think we hit something like 150 home runs as a team, which tied a record, so just to see him dominate our lineup (in Game Five) was pretty impressive. I just felt he belonged in a higher league, seeing him for the first time like that."

To a man, the Twins were surprised that Game Seven had even become necessary. They had routed Drysdale in Game One with a six-run third inning, eventually winning 8–2. Koufax, who had skipped the opener because of his observance of Yom Kippur, was driven off the mound in the seventh inning of Game Two, a 5–1 Twins' victory. Twins' fans inside the Met celebrated Minnesota's 2–0 Series lead with chants of "It's all over now!"

One Minnesota writer made his way through the stands after the game and belittled the L.A. wives, making it a point to tell them what the Twins were going to do to the Dodgers the rest of the Series.

Baseball writer Roger Angell wasn't so sure. Visiting the Dodger clubhouse after Game Two, Angell found Koufax, who had actually surrendered just one earned run in the loss, offering what he later described as a precise, unapologetic, and totally unruffled analysis of the game. After hearing Koufax speak, Angell left the clubhouse with the curious conviction that the Twins, after consecutive victories, were now only slightly behind in the Series.

The Twins had other ideas. "After we won the first two games," Killebrew recalled, "we thought we might be able to sweep the Series in Los Angeles."

The Dodgers thought otherwise. The ridicule of their wives by the

Minnesota writer fired the club up. Years later, Koufax recalled the effect it had on helping turn the Series around.

"It sort of lifted up the team," he told John Devaney and Burt Goldblatt in their book, *The World Series*. "There's a good chance you are going to be down after losing the first two and I think the writer may have helped."

Dodger pitching snapped back in Los Angeles. Osteen won Game Three 4–0, and Drysdale evened the Series at two games apiece with a 7–2 triumph in Game Four. Koufax gave L.A. the Series lead the next afternoon, surrendering just four hits and striking out 10 on a sun-drenched afternoon in Chavez Ravine.

Having swept their final three home games in Los Angeles, the Dodgers flew back to Minnesota hoping to wrap up their second Series title in three years. But Twins ace Jim "Mudcat" Grant, making his second start in three days and third of the Series, went the distance and downed the Dodgers, 5–1.

The Series was tied at three apiece, each team winning at home in the first six games. Twins fans hoped the trend would continue in Game Seven, but the celebratory mood of the first two games had vanished. Success and disaster would be riding on every pitch, and the enormous expectations of a long summer of baseball would now be decided in the space of a single afternoon.

The grim nature of Game Seven caused Twins fans in the Met to watch in almost complete, eerie silence.

Kaat held the Dodgers scoreless in the top of the first, stranding Jim "Junior" Gilliam at second base when Oliva made a skidding catch of Lou Johnson's sinking two-out liner to right.

Interestingly, the Twins had taken pregame batting practice against a left-hander named Sandy—Sandy Valdespino. Now, however, they were prepared to face the other Sandy in the bottom of the first. Twins hitters searched Koufax's mechanics as he warmed up, looking for any clue to his physical condition. Unlike most power pitchers, like Bob Gibson or Roger Clemens who tend to explode off the mound, Koufax seemed to implode. His left leg and arm coiled so much that in mid-delivery, he appeared to be compressing energy. His arm angle was unusually high for a left-handed power pitcher, particularly when compared to sidewinders like Randy Johnson, and it whipped through his delivery with tremendous thrust. His dynamic delivery continued with a smooth follow-through and a dramatic downward sweep over his front leg.

"He had a straight over-the-top delivery," remembered Osteen. "He was very smooth, very fluid."

Former Dodger teammate Ed Roebuck said Koufax's over-the-top delivery allowed him to throw something most left-handers do not, a four-seam fastball that because it came over the top had what is known as "true rotation."

"Most left-handers," Roebuck said, "throw from their left shoulder to their right knee and they've got a moving fastball. Warren Spahn threw right over the top, but you don't see too many true four-seam left-handers. Vida Blue was one too."

Many southpaws throw a two-seam fastball that sinks as it arrives at home plate. By throwing a four-seam fastball, Koufax made the ball jump as it exploded in the strike zone at speeds estimated between 95 and 99 miles an hour. In throwing a four-seam fastball, Koufax threw what is known as a "light" ball that was easy for his catchers to handle. Southpaws who throw a two-seam fastball sacrifice speed for sinking action and thus throw a "heavy" ball more difficult for catchers to handle.

To throw his four-seam fastball, Koufax gripped the ball so that his long fingers crossed all four seams. A two-seam fastball is gripped with the fingers between the two seams. The difference in the grip, Roebuck said, is critical in determining the air resistance that affects the ball's movement and speed. Koufax's extremely long fingers allowed him to grip the ball properly for the four-seam fastball.

"He really has long fingers," Roebuck said, "and it's a plus for the fastball, it's a plus for the curve, it's just a real physical plus."

Among the Twins watching Koufax closely that day at the Met was Kaat, who thought Koufax's delivery reminded him of another Hall of Fame lefty, Warren Spahn.

"Pitchers fall into two categories," said Kaat, who became a broadcaster for the New York Yankees. "They either cock that back leg and get up over—Spahn used to call it toe-to-toe—and that's kind of what Sandy did. He would bend that back leg and he was kind of up over the top, much more of a vertical motion than a lot of the pitchers you'll see, like a Cone or a Maddux, or a Clemens. They make much more of a horizontal turn where they turn their back pocket to the hitter, they pivot almost horizontally. Koufax was just the opposite. The way I would refer to it, he would cock that back leg and come up over the top. His pitching motion was much more vertical than horizontal. Spahn is another left-hander who comes to mind that did that. I don't know of any other pitcher today that really delivers the ball like that. Most of them pretty much make more of a horizontal turn.

"The guys that make the turns, if you look at Tom Seaver, Nolan Ryan, guys like that, they have a big trunk, big butt, big legs. Sandy was the opposite. He was wiry with a huge upper body, and it's probably why it was a little tougher on his elbow. He was much more of an upper body pitcher. He pushed off the rubber, but in a different way than the others did."

A unique aspect of Koufax's pitching style was the odd little recoil of his left shoulder as he followed through on his delivery. It simulated the recoil of a powerful rifle, and it indicated the power behind Koufax's pitches.

"If you talk to a doctor," Kaat said, "they will tell you about a group of muscles called the 'antagonistic muscles.' What determines how hard you can throw a ball is how strong the muscles in the front part of the shoulder, which are the antagonistic muscles, how strong they are because they're the ones that cushion the blow. If you didn't have those, your arm would just come right out of the socket. Ron Guidry was an example of a guy that was fairly skinny and wiry but threw exceptionally hard. But he had big upper back muscles like Sandy did. If you ever saw Sandy from the back with his shirt off in his playing days, his shoulders and upper back muscles were huge. And then when you let that ball go, the muscles in the front of the shoulder have to be strong enough to absorb that speed. And that's when you get that recoil."

Koufax was the premier power pitcher in the game in '65, but because he threw a 95-mile-per-hour fastball, had thrown over 350 innings during the season, was suffering from an arthritic left elbow, and was now coming back on two days' rest, his task in Game Seven was daunting even for him.

"I'm sure one of the reasons he had to retire after the next year," Kaat said, "is all the innings he had pitched and coming back the way he did on short rest with that arthritic elbow, that's what forced him into retirement.

"So for him to come back on two days' rest . . ."

Kaat got a reminder of Koufax's condition before the game. Photographers had gotten the two starting pitchers together for publicity photos. As the two shook hands and made small talk for the cameras, Kaat smelled the Capsolin, the heating ointment Koufax used to loosen up his heavy back and shoulder muscles before each start.

"I remember standing next to Sandy before the games in the World Series when they took pictures of us," Kaat said. "He had this Capsolin on, and it made your eyes water. It was an ointment that you put on that heated up your arm and killed the pain. There was Capsolin and we had some stuff called 'Atomic Bomb,' and it was so hot that you cut it with a cold cream or Vaseline, something to lessen the strength. He just put tubes of that stuff on his arm to basically make the pain go away.

"That was kind of the law of survival for pitchers then. Fortunately for pitchers today, the laws have changed."

Lathered in Capsolin and sweat, Koufax finished his warmup pitches and prepared to face the Twins in the bottom of the first inning. Kaat had retired the Dodgers without a run in the first, and now it was Koufax's turn.

Facing leadoff hitter Zoilo Versalles, Koufax started with a fastball that sailed high out of the strike zone. With seven hits and a .292 batting average in the Series, with league-high numbers for doubles (45) and triples (12) and a team-high 27 stolen bases, Versalles represented an immediate challenge to Koufax.

On NBC Radio, Saam briefly outlined Koufax's situation as he started his second game in three days:

> Here's a man that's close to 350 innings (pitched) and actually in the last three years has had two ailments and he has overcome those. When he is right, I dare say, there is not a better pitcher in baseball. And he can be sure that the whole bullpen is ready, and Drysdale is in that bullpen. But he realizes that coming back on just a couple of days' of rest is unusual.

Adjusting his navy blue batting helmet, the bespectacled Versalles fouled the next delivery back into the crowd, then turned his glittery glare to Koufax and took ball two. He fouled off two more Koufax pitches, then struck out swinging on a fastball.

Saam: "And Koufax is off and running . . ."

One of the reasons Koufax seemed so deceptive to hitters was his smooth delivery. "It looked like he was throwing nice and easy," Roebuck said with a laugh, "and then the ball was by you in the blink of an eye."

Koufax's long fingers allowed him to exert extraordinary pressure on the seams of the ball. That combined with his tremendous wrist action and torque in his delivery provided a backspin rotation that allowed his 95-mile-an-hour fastball to flare upwards just as the batter was following through on his swing.

Norm Sherry, who was a catcher for Koufax, said Koufax's long stride and over-the-top delivery carried him so far out in front of the mound that he was actually closer to the hitters than most pitchers, who take a shorter stride.

"You reach out there and throw the ball like he did, my God," Sherry said. "You're catching him and you see the ball coming and the guy swings and it looks like the ball jumps over the bat. That was his velocity and his pulling on the seams that made the ball spin like that. When he threw the ball, it was white, a little white tablet coming at you. When you throw a four-seam fastball and you throw it correctly, you're not going to see any spin, you're just going to see the white, you're not going to see the red seams."

Along with not being able to see the spin on Koufax's fastball, hitters also had to deal with the late hop of the ball as it jumped into the strike zone.

"It did have a rise to it," Sherry said. "They would swing at where they thought they saw the ball, and because the ball had moved, it appeared to jump. It did have a lift to it."

Carl Erskine, a former pitcher and teammate of Koufax on the "Boys of Summer," said the Dodgers' theory on left-handed pitching was to come over the top the way Koufax did.

"Sandy and I had some things in common," Erskine said. "We both threw over the top and our curveballs broke almost straight down. A four-seam fastball, thrown with good velocity, has a life to it, has movement to it. It's not just perfectly straight. But you have to have good velocity to make that happen. Sandy had speed that I didn't. He had these big hands, and a huge wrist flex, and that gave the ball tremendous rotation. That had to be a big part of the movement on the ball. The rotation on a four-seam fastball is what made the ball have life. And when you throw a ball cross-seams over the top, you put a lot of back rotation on the ball. It looks like a cueball. You don't see any seams because it's rotating rapidly. And you could hear his ball, because of that real tight rotation.

"I think it had a lot to do with the length of his fingers, and his wrist, and all that power in his legs. He was a muscular, defined guy, what baseball men said a pitcher's build should be—long, lean muscles. He had a lot of bulk in his shoulders and chest and powerful legs, and that helped him get tremendous movement on his fastball, where players would swing right through it."

Koufax got Joe Nossek, who followed Versalles to the plate, to swing through a first-pitch fastball, then got him to swing late at his second offering, which Nossek fouled back to the screen behind home plate. A breaking ball was low and outside, and Koufax ran the count to 2–2 with a pitch high and out of the strike zone.

Some baseball men thought the best strategy for hitting Koufax's curve, which was estimated at a startling 85 miles an hour, was to wait on the pitch. The idea was that if the ball was below the letters, take it, because you weren't going to hit it anyway. It was easy to see the curve coming, because pitchers who have a great curveball, like Koufax and Clem Labine, need to get a bigger grip on the ball and will dig their hands a little further into their gloves as they begin their windup. Experienced hitters can also spot the curve by the wrist action of the pitcher. Since most pitchers bend the wrist to throw the curve, hitters will watch to see if the wrist is bent as it comes out of the glove during the windup.

Sherry said that because Koufax had long fingers and big hands, he could turn the ball in such a way as to make the pitch turn over and drop straight down. That, Sherry said, was the way the Dodgers always taught their rookies to throw the curve.

"He threw it out and straight down," said Sherry. "It didn't have any break to the opposite side like most left-handers did. It would break straight down. It would start at your shoulders and end at your toes. And it had the same rotation—white. A lot of guys throw breaking balls and you can see the rotation, you can see the red seams.

"Guys knew when he was throwing the curve because they could see him turn that hand and grip that ball. Everybody knew when he was throwing the curve, but they still couldn't hit it."

From his third-base coaching box, Billy Martin flashed signs to Nossek. Koufax rocked and delivered, and Nossek tapped a bouncer to shortstop, where Wills threw to first for the second out.

Two outs, and Tony Oliva stepped to the plate. Like Koufax, Oliva was something of a medical marvel in 1965. Finishing the season with a .321 batting average, the 24-year-old Cuban became the first player to claim consecutive American League batting championships since Ted Williams in 1957–1958, and did it despite a painful injury. The Twins' star injured his middle finger in May while sliding into second base, and the injury caused his hitting to tail off, so that Oliva's average fell below .250 in June.

Experts counted him out of the race for the batting title, and doctors advised him to have the hand operated on, but the player who had won American League Rookie of the Year honors in 1964 pushed on. The Twins were locked in a pennant race, and Oliva refused not only to have his hand operated on but also to take time off to rest the injured digit.

"If I take one or two days' rest, it does not help," he told the Minnesota media in halting English. "You must take four or five days. But if I take four or five days, I will lose my timing and I will not hit. So it is better not to rest. It is better to play every day."

Oliva's pain became so unbearable that he was practically swinging the bat with one hand, but he gradually broke out of his slump. On July 21 he slammed five hits against Boston. On August 8, he rapped Washington pitchers for three singles and a double. As the pennant race heated up, so did Oliva. He lifted his batting average to .290 in September, then faced the second-place Chicago White Sox in a crucial two-game series.

In the opener Oliva, batting lefty, singled through the middle on his first at-bat, then followed with a single to right and a double to left to lead the Twins to a 3–2 win.

The Twins won the second game as well, and Minnesota manager Sam Mele singled out his injured star after the series sweep.

"That kid," he said of Oliva, "could hit wearing boxing gloves."

The year before, Oliva had hit .323 with 32 home runs and 94 RBI, and had become the first rookie in the history of the American League to win the batting title. After winning his second straight batting title, Oliva was already being compared to legendary hitters Ted Williams and Ty Cobb.

"Whoever can hit for high average, whoever can run, whoever can throw, he is the new Ty Cobb," Versalles told a visitor. "Oliva is Ty Cobb."

Oliva was one of a number of solid major league players to come out of Cuba over the years. Minnie Minoso, Mike Cuellar, Luis Tiant, Jose Cardenal, Bert Campaneris, Tony Perez, Juan Guzman, and Orlando Hernandez were all products of Cuba. But the player Oliva drew the most comparisons with was Martin Dihigo, who played in the Caribbean and Negro leagues and is regarded by many as the finest baseball player ever.

A victim of the color barrier that existed prior to 1947, Dihigo never played major league ball. But the man known in Havana to this day as "El Immortal" excelled at the plate, on the mound, and in the dugout as a manager, and is enshrined in the Hall of Fame in three different countries.

Though the trend in the majors during the sixties was to pull the ball for power, Oliva concentrated on hitting to all fields. American League pitchers were soon struggling to solve his hitting style. If they pitched him inside, he was strong enough to pull the ball to right field. If they pitched him outside, he was disciplined enough to stroke the ball to left. He could handle high heat and golf-low sinkers, yet his power forced infielders to play back and his speed helped him outrun bunts and slow rollers. His league-high 185 hits were testament to his considerable skill at the plate, and he had impressed broadcaster By Saam through the first six games of the '65 Series: "He is one of the fine-looking young hitters in baseball, and he is still quite a young man. He looks like he's going to be a star for quite a few years to come . . ."

Oliva did indeed look like a star. His bright white uniform with the navy blue pinstripes shone in the hazy sunshine, and his appearance at the plate—he used a wide-legged stance with his back foot planted at the edge of the batter's box—stirred the big crowd.

NBC cameras closing in on Koufax showed he was respectful, not awed—and Oliva returned the attitude.

"I faced a lot of good pitchers before I faced Sandy Koufax," Oliva recalled, "but he was the best left-handed pitcher I ever saw."

Later a minor-league hitting instructor for the Twins, Oliva said the Twins, unlike National League hitters who were used to seeing Koufax, were unaware that he tipped his pitches. That made it more difficult to pick up the ball as it raced towards home plate.

"His ball was different," Oliva remembered. "It did something different. Everybody knew he threw hard, but he threw every pitch from the same motion, and that made it very hard to pick up his pitches.

"His curveball went straight down, and his fastball was in the high nineties and moving up. Every delivery was the same, and every pitch was off one motion."

As much as Oliva respected Koufax's abilities, he felt a certain comfort hitting against him. Koufax threw hard, but Oliva knew that he rarely relied on brushback pitches and that his control was excellent. Koufax was the National League's preeminent power pitcher, but he differed from "Sudden" Sam McDowell, the hard-throwing 23-year-old lefty who led the American League that season with 325 strikeouts, an average of 10.4 per game.

"I preferred to face Koufax more than McDowell," Oliva said, "because Sandy's control was perfect. McDowell was wild. He might throw the ball behind you or over your head."

Touching the bill of his blue cap with his left hand, tugging on the matching blue of his classic three-quarter-length sleeve, Koufax started the American League's two-time batting champion off with a big curve for a strike. Oliva, who had five hits and a homer in the Series, fouled off the next delivery to fall behind 0–2.

Backing out of the chalk-lined batter's box, Oliva headed to the on-deck circle, where he rubbed his bat down with pine tar and rosin. Before stepping back in, he fidgeted with his stance, adjusted his batting helmet, and took time before returning his focus to the mound.

The delay seemed to disturb Koufax, who had been working with quick rhythm. He flamed the next pitch high and inside for a ball, then issued another high and tight pitch that backed Oliva away from the plate and drew a chorus of boos from the crowd. Another high offering brought the count to 3–2. Oliva, showing excellent bat control, stayed alive by fouling the next pitch back. With the count still full, Koufax stared at the American League's best hitter and delivered another high, inside pitch that sent Oliva to first base with a walk. It was just the third walk Koufax had surrendered in his three Series starts.

Working from the stretch for the first time in the game, Koufax now faced Harmon Killebrew. The Twins' slugger led the team in homers with 25 despite missing part of the summer due to injury.

"That was an interesting year for me," recalled Killebrew, later a member of the Twins' front office. "On August 2 of that year I had dislocated my elbow in a play at first base. It looked like after all those years of struggling, we were going to win the pennant and I wasn't going to get a chance to play in the World Series. Fortunately for me at least, I played the last ten games (of the regular season) at third and then played in the Series."

Nicknamed "The Killer," the Idaho native stood 5' 11", weighed 215, and had forearms like the village blacksmith. Killebrew's strength was legendary around the American League. Teammate Bobby Allison described him as "strong, strong, strong." Yankees' slugger Mickey Mantle said Killebrew was so powerful, "he muscles a pitch out of the ballpark."

Killebrew led the American League in homers in '62, '63, and '64, and the book on him was to pitch low and away since he was a pull hitter. Yankee hurler Steve Hamilton told writer Alexander Peters, however, that the scouting reports weren't always right. Hamilton recalled delivering the ball right where he wanted it, low and outside, and then watching as Killebrew connected. At worst, Hamilton thought it was an opposite-field hit to right. But as Hamilton watched from the mound, the ball kept traveling and cleared the right-field fence for a home run.

"That's what I call overpowering the ball," Hamilton said.

Killebrew had already overpowered a Drysdale pitch for a homer earlier in the series, and he dug in against Koufax with a chance to do some early damage to the Dodger ace.

"The main thing with Sandy was that he had such an outstanding fastball and great control," Killebrew said. "He had that curveball that looked like his fastball coming up there and then went straight down. The thing that I tried to do, and I'm sure the rest of our hitters were thinking the same thing, was that you couldn't swing at that high fastball. You might as well forget it if you were swinging at that one. He was going to get you. So I tried to lay off the high fastball against Sandy, tried to make him bring the ball down a little bit."

The other part of Killebrew's hitting strategy against Koufax was to lay off the big breaking curve and look for a fastball that wasn't sailing.

Matching power against power, Koufax's first delivery to the Twins' slugger was outside. Switching gears, Koufax came back with a breaking ball that sailed low.

Because his fingers were so long, Koufax could wrap them almost entirely around the ball. "He could put spin on the ball," Roebuck said. "If you could just imagine how much more friction he could put on the ball with his long fingers."

Roebuck, who has seen all the great major league pitchers of the last half-century, said Koufax had the best curve of anyone. The reason, he said, was the speed of the pitch.

"Let's say you have a 93-mile-an-hour fastball," Roebuck said. "The curveball would be about 77 or 78. Sandy was probably between 97 and 100 on his fastball and his curveball was way up there too, probably up around 85 or 86, and that's unheard of. That is hard to pick up with that kind of spin.

"Another remarkable thing about Sandy was that he did not knock you out with his changeup. It was just two pitches, baby, and you'd try to hit 'em."

Like the rest of the Twins, Killebrew had been dazzled by Koufax's curveball and location in Game Five. He told reporters after the game in Los Angeles that Koufax's curveball was the best he had ever seen from a southpaw. The first inning of Game Seven saw Koufax again relying heavily on his curve, but he was beginning to realize he didn't have his good breaking stuff that day. His curve, which cracked like a long whipcord on good days, was sailing rather than breaking. It was a sure sign that his arm was fatigued.

Down 2–0 in the count, Koufax was outside with his next curve. Killebrew stared down the third-base line at Martin for the sign, then stepped back into the box and took a high and tight fastball for ball four. Having lost Oliva on a 3–2 count, Koufax walked Killebrew on four straight pitches.

Saam: "And we've got some action going in the bullpen . . . Don Drysdale already warming up, right under the scoreboard in right field. A lot of people were wondering if Sandy should get into a little trouble here, how soon would they make the move?"

Metropolitan Stadium had not been kind to Koufax in 1965. Game Seven marked his third mound appearance at the Met that season. He was wild during an All-Star Game appearance in midsummer, then driven from the mound after six innings in a 5–1 loss in Game Two of the Series.

Koufax, Drysdale, and Osteen had all struggled at Met Stadium during the series. Drysdale started and was gone after less than three innings of Game One in an 8–2 loss. Koufax dropped Game Two, and Osteen, who stopped the Dodger slide with a Game Three victory when the Series shifted to Chavez Ravine, dropped Game Six.

"When you pitch as long as we pitched, you get to identify certain mounds with certain ballparks," Osteen said. "Some ballparks do have high mounds. We had groundskeepers in Los Angeles who fixed the mound the way we liked it."

Dodger catcher John Roseboro thought Met Stadium's mound was a big concern for L.A.'s staff. Groundskeepers in Chavez Ravine tailored the mound to the pitcher's needs, making it a sharp-breaking hill that helped keep the ball down. The mound at the Met was flat, which the Dodgers thought was helping to keep their pitches up in the strike zone.

Catching Koufax in his great years was never a problem. Sherry, who used to get shaken off by Koufax in their early years together, said that calling a game for Koufax became easy once he harnessed the control on his pitches.

"You'd get a hitter up there," Sherry said, "and really, you knew darn well Sandy could throw his fastball right by him. All you do as a catcher is suggest to the pitcher that this is what we should throw. And if you have their confidence, everything will go along pretty good."

Still, Koufax was his own man, and there were times he'd get two strikes on a hitter and when his catcher would put the sign down for a fastball, Koufax would shake him off and throw the curveball.

The difference between the Koufax of '59 and the Koufax of '65 was that in his early years he never had enough confidence that he could consistently throw his curve for a strike. He would shake off his catcher and throw the fastball. By the mid-sixties, however, his curve was considered the best the game had ever seen, and he would shake off the sign for a fastball and throw the curve. The result was that hitters gearing up for the fastball would stand stock-still at the plate as the curve dropped unimpeded over the plate for a called third strike.

On such occasions, Sherry recalled hitters mumbling after strikeouts that Koufax "belongs in a higher league."

Seeing Koufax struggling with his control during Game Seven's first inning, the Met Stadium crowd stirred. Koufax rolled his shoulders, his gray uniform damp with sweat and Capsolin. The voice of the Twins, Ray Scott, was broadcasting the first 4½ innings for NBC-TV before turning the game over to Scully, the voice of the Dodgers. After Killebrew walked on four pitches, Scott remarked on the rarity of Koufax issuing a free pass: "In regular season play, Koufax was the number one worker. Three hundred thirty-six innings, and to give you an idea of his remarkable control, and ratio of walks versus strikeouts, seventy-one walks versus three hundred eighty-two strikeouts . . ."

Earl Battey, a .297 hitter during the regular season, stepped to the plate. The stocky catcher had tripled the day before, and was looking to deliver another clutch hit. Bearing down, Koufax started the right-hander out with a strike, then quickly got ahead 0–2. Rubbing the ball down between pitches, he followed with a curve that missed outside, then tied him up with a big curve that fell untouched in the strike zone.

Dodgers' reliever Ron Perranoski said once that the break on Koufax's curve was so big at times, the ball looked as if it was coming out of the third deck. Koufax didn't know it, but as he headed off the mound after a shaky first inning, he had just thrown his best curveball of the entire afternoon.

THREE

S tanding on the mound in Metropolitan Stadium at the start of the second inning, Sandy Koufax represented different things to different people.

To a young Jewish boy named Lee Bycel, Koufax was a great baseball player, a great Jewish baseball player who refused to pitch the opening game of the 1965 World Series on October 6 because it was Yom Kippur.

In the Jewish religion, Yom Kippur is a solemn occasion. It is the day of Atonement, the day Jews believe God inscribes and seals the Book of Life as to what will happen in the coming year, the holiest day of the Jewish year. Koufax's decision to remain faithful to his religion even though it could cost his team a World Series win inspired a generation of youths to embrace their religious identity.

"He was the real Jewish icon," said Harvey Frommer, the author of numerous books, including *Growing Up Jewish in America*. Frommer said Koufax's decision not to pitch on Yom Kippur in 1965 had a marked impact on people of his faith.

"It was savored not only by Jews in Brooklyn," Frommer said, "but by Jews around the world."

Koufax was born Sanford Braun on December 30, 1935, in Brooklyn, New York. His parents, Jack and Evelyn, divorced when he was three; at the age of nine he took the name of his stepfather, attorney Irving Koufax, when his mother remarried. He grew up playing sports in the streets, school yards, and Jewish community clubs, excelling in the face of early stereotypes that physical achievement was looked down upon by some Jewish parents—though not by Koufax's parents. There had been professional Jewish baseball players as early as 1871, in the persons of Lipman Pike and his brother Jacob. But to many turn-of-the-century Jewish parents, a baseball player was regarded as, in the words of Eddie Cantor, "the king of all loafers."

In his autobiography, Cantor recalled his grandmother denigrating him as "You baseball player you . . ." That, said Cantor, was "the worst name she could call me."

In *Growing Up Jewish in America*, Harvey and Myrna Katz Frommer quoted Murray Polner's experience as a nine-year-old in Brooklyn dragging his father Alex to a Dodgers game in Ebbets Field. Later that night, Alex was sitting outside his home when someone asked how his day had been.

The father sighed. "Oysgemattert farloirener tog," he said, meaning an exhausting, wasted day.

Some fathers grew resentful at their son's desire to be Americanized, seeing it as a departure from their Old World culture. To compensate, they would take them to see soccer teams from Europe. But to American children whose patriotism was to America and the Brooklyn Dodgers, European soccer seemed slow and irrelevant.

By the forties and fifties, the Jewish attitude towards baseball was changing. Walter Harrison, in an article titled "Six-Pointed Diamond: Baseball and American Jews," wrote that while baseball did not supplant Judaism as the religion of American Jews, it was one of the areas of American life that many Jews mixed with Judaism to create a new, secular faith.

"Baseball," said renowned lawyer Alan Dershowitz, "was our way of showing that we were as American as anyone else."

Many immigrant families did indeed find baseball to be an "Americanizing" process. The Dodgers, a team with varied ethnic backgrounds, appealed to a large number of immigrant children. While blacks may have looked to Jackie Robinson, Roy Campanella, and Don

Newcombe and seen a way out of confinement, Jewish families identified with the Dodgers. They saw in them a team whose cry of "Wait 'til next year!" played into the Jews' messianic hope of looking to the future. The Dodgers always came up short in the World Series against the victorious goyim—the New York Yankees. The Dodgers were cast in a Judaic context, and many Jews followed them with religious fervor.

In many Jewish households, the two radio voices heard all the time in the forties were those of President Franklin Roosevelt and Dodgers' announcer Red Barber, whom many Jews thought was Jewish. The honey-smooth deliveries of FDR and Barber taught many the power of the spoken word. One Jewish youngster, Neil Postman, heard Barber use the word *extemporaneous* and liked it so much that he used it in his bar mitzvah speech. In an era when most major league games were played during the day and broadcast live on radio, Jewish families ate dinner in complete silence in order to listen to the ballgame on the radio.

Though Jews continued to relax their stance towards baseball by the midpoint of the 20th century, their emphasis remained on education. Julius and Elaine Barr, longtime Brooklyn residents, recalled that in the years of their youth in the forties, children were expected to do their homework first before going outside to play after school. In some Jewish households, everything but learning was considered a waste of time. Socializing was idle talk. Baseball, however, was a different story. Feeling a tremendous pull to assimilate into America, to Americanize, Jewish fathers and sons followed the game and studied the players and their statistics. Baseball was no longer *narrishkeit*. Baseball was America.

In their book the Frommers relate a story concerning the 1960 World Series between the Yankees and Pittsburgh Pirates. Solomon B. Freehoff, one of the most renowned Reform scholars, was rabbi of Rodef Shalom, a prominent reform congregation in Pittsburgh. A huge fan of the Pirates, Rabbi Freehoff invited Assistant Rabbi Fred Schwartz to join him at a Series game in Forbes Field after the service for the High Holy Days. Rabbi Schwartz went, but because he was embarrassed to be seen at the stadium in the striped pants and morning coat he had worn to the service, he covered his outfit with a trench coat and watched the game in the sweltering sun.

There were still not a lot of Jewish players in the majors, and most

Jews still tried to steer their children towards intellectual pursuits. They wanted their children to become doctors and lawyers, in order to live better than they did. That was the philosophy of many Jewish families living in Brooklyn at the time Koufax was growing up, and in his household, his parents made it clear to him he would someday go to college.

Koufax's notoriety as a Jewish ballplayer preceded his public stance against pitching on Yom Kippur in Game One of the '65 World Series. After achieving stardom with the Dodgers in the early sixties, he was sometimes referred to in national magazines as the "World's Most Eligible Jewish Bachelor."

Koufax was one of several American Jews who have occupied a special niche in baseball history. In their book *Diamonds in the Rough*, authors Joel Zoss and John Bowman state that the story of Jews in organized baseball is one that has largely been told by Jewish writers. There is a Jewish Sports Information Service that provides material on Jewish sports figures. Baseball players, for instance, are listed under the headings of *Jewish mother, Jewish father, converted in, converted out, possible convert, unconfirmed,* and *disputed.* In 1986, Shapolsky Books published *The Jewish Baseball Hall-of-Fame.*

Magazine articles dealing with Jewish ballplayers have appeared through the years as well. In 1926, an article appeared under the headline "Why Not More Jewish Ballplayers?" In 1954, a magazine article dealing with racism was titled "Anti-Semitism in Baseball."

Anti-Semitism was a problem encountered in baseball's earlier years, even among Hall of Famers like Detroit Tigers first baseman Hank Greenberg. Born in Greenwich Village and raised in the Bronx, Greenberg broke into the minors playing in small southern towns. Fans at those games were said to be as curious to see a Jew as they were to see the outcome of the game itself.

As a Jewish slugger, Greenberg was following in the footsteps of Moses Solomon. A member of the 1923 New York Giants, Solomon hit 49 home runs for Hutchinson of the Southwestern Class C League. Solomon was called "the Jewish Babe Ruth" and "the Rabbi of Swat."

Like Koufax, Greenberg honored Jewish holy days. When he joined the Tigers in 1933, Greenberg faced the problem of missing a critical game with the Boston Red Sox in order to observe Rosh

Hashanah. He resolved his dilemma by going to services the evening of the holiday, which started at sundown, then playing the game the next day. Greenberg hit two home runs to beat Boston, prompting the *Detroit Free Press* the next day to declare both homers "strictly Kosher." A Jewish newspaper in Cleveland told readers, "Only one fellow blew the shofar yesterday . . . He was Hank Greenberg. He blew the shofar twice and the ears of the Boston Red Sox are still ringing."

Congratulated by a rabbi after the game, Greenberg remarked, "I guess I didn't do anything wrong." The big slugger then announced his intentions to go home to pray and thank God for those home runs.

Edgar Guest later penned a poem about Greenberg's Yom Kippur observance:

> Come Yom Kippur—holy fast day world-wide over to the Jew;
> And Hank Greenberg to his teaching and the old tradition true
> Spent the day among his people and he didn't come to play.
> Said Murphy to Mulrooney, "We shall lose the game today!
> We shall miss him in the infield and shall miss him at the bat,
> But he's true to his religion—and I honor him for that!

The following season, Greenberg earned unanimous Most Valuable Player honors as he led the Tigers to the American League pennant. Despite his outstanding season, which saw him drive in 170 runs, Greenberg still had to deal with anti-Semitism. One Detroit writer patronized him as the "Pants Presser," and fans and opposing players alike aimed racial taunts at him.

Greenberg acknowledged there was added pressure. By his own recollection, he was called a "Jew bastard," "kike," and "sheeny." The taunts frustrated Greenberg so much, the 6' 3½", 210-pound slugger had to exert enormous self-control to refrain from charging into the stands or the opposing dugout.

"If you struck out," Greenberg said once, "you weren't just a bum, but a Jewish bum."

By the late thirties, Jewish athletes like Greenberg and world heavyweight boxing champion Max Baer had become heroes to a generation of Jewish fans alarmed at the anti-Semitism in Germany. Realizing he was representing a couple of million Jews among a hundred million gentiles, Greenberg knew he was always in the spotlight. He felt a responsibility to perform, to make good despite the fact that on the few bad days he did have, he said, "every son of a bitch was calling me names."

Greenberg didn't have many bad days. In 1938 he blasted 58 homers, just two shy of the major-league mark set by the New York Yankees' Babe Ruth in 1927. As time went on and the Holocaust in Germany became known, Greenberg came to feel that as a Jew, whenever he hit a home run, he was hitting one against Hitler.

In 1940, Greenberg was one of the first major leaguers to join the military. There was a sense among many that he was setting an example, as both a Jew and an American athlete.

Aviva Kempner, who produced a documentary about Greenberg, said the Tigers' star defied the stereotype of Jewish men, many of whom are seen as what she called "nebbishes, Woody Allen types."

Al Rosen, a star for the Cleveland Indians who drove in 100 or more runs in each of his first five full seasons in the majors, made it a point to prove that Jews are tough. Rosen told writer Roger Kahn that he had been thrown at a lot in his career, and had taken more than one 90-mile-an-hour fastball on the left elbow. But, Rosen added with grim pride, no one had ever seen him try to rub the pain away.

Koufax, lean and muscular and overpowering, defied the stereotypes as well. He pitched grittily through searing pain, and his tough-mindedness made him the best clutch pitcher in the game from 1963 to 1966.

Like Greenberg and Rosen, Koufax had experienced discrimination on the ballfield as well. He was called "Super Jew" by other players, and Kahn wrote once of an incident dealing with Koufax's days on the Brooklyn sandlots. Pitching for a Jewish-Irish team near Coney Island, Koufax was said to have been taunted by a team of Italian Americans. Name-calling followed, and Koufax quieted the catcalls by firing inside fastballs.

Koufax was also stung during the '65 Series by what he considered the anti-Semitic comments of Minneapolis sports columnist Don Riley. Writing in the *St. Paul Pioneer Press* on the morning of Game Two,

Riley titled his column "An Open Letter to Sandy Koufax" and warned Koufax of what the Twins' sluggers had in store for him that afternoon:

> . . . Sandy, can you back guys away from the plate who see T-bones on the dish? Can you overpower people who carry sticks in their hands and belong to a cause? Can you win with two runs? I don't believe so.

Koufax actually found the column amusing until he reached the end, when Riley closed his column with a reference to Koufax's Jewish heritage.

"The Twins," Riley wrote, "love matzoh balls."

Coming off a day-long fast and pitching out of rotation, Koufax was beaten by the Twins in Game Two. But he clipped Riley's column and saved it, using it as fuel for his fire. In his next start, he responded with an overpowering victory in Game Five.

Just as Greenberg had set examples as a Jewish American, Koufax set an example by refusing to pitch or even go to the ballpark when Yom Kippur coincided with the opening game of the '65 World Series in Minnesota. Though he has never talked extensively about his decision, newspapers reported that he spent the day of the opener attending services at a synagogue in St. Paul.

The attention paid to his decision seemed to make Koufax uncomfortable. When Kahn was working on a story for the *Saturday Evening Post* about Jews in sports, he contacted Rosen and Koufax. Catching up with Koufax in the Dodgers' locker room, Kahn found him polite and cordial, but with misgivings about the topic. Koufax told Kahn he thought too much was made of his being a Jewish pitcher, and not enough as just a pitcher. Koufax's reluctance to be portrayed as anything special, a reluctance that sportswriter Larry Merchant observed firsthand, extended not only to his athleticism but also to his Judaism.

As a Jewish boy and ardent baseball fan during the '65 season, Lee Bycel felt a need for Jewish heroes. Koufax's decision, he said, filled him with pride, and he realized then that no person should ever be embarrassed about their religion or ancestral culture. Ethnic and religious identity, Bycel thought, should engender fulfillment and hope. He felt it was a courageous act for Koufax to abstain from playing in an era when some Jews were afraid, for fear of losing wages or being mocked for asserting a religious difference, to take off from work in order to observe the Jewish High Holy Days. Koufax's decision not to pitch was an important reminder to Bycel that America harbors people of different faiths and religious practices.

Bycel learned from Koufax the power of personal acts, and he would in time become a rabbi and eventually the dean of the Hebrew Union College-Jewish Institute of Religion and president of the Los Angeles County Commission on Human Relations.

Bycel looked back at October 1965 and remembered a personal challenge he too had to overcome. He wanted to listen to Game One on his transistor radio, but felt that if Koufax had the courage not to play, Bycel could find in himself the discipline not to turn on the radio. The rabbi still thanks Koufax for his inspiration and the example he set.

In 1997, Steven Schnur wrote a children's book called *The Koufax Dilemma*. The book centers around a young boy named Danny, who is the best pitcher on his baseball team and must make the decision whether to pitch the season opener, which falls on Passover. Like Koufax, Danny has to choose between loyalty to his team and loyalty to his family and faith. Danny finds an example in Koufax, who faced similar decisions throughout his career.

Like many Jews, Koufax worked on Saturday, the Jewish Sabbath; and while he did not observe every religious holiday, he did feel a desire to observe Yom Kippur as a day of worship. Passover, an eight-day spring holiday, often overlaps with the opening week of the major league baseball season in April. Observant Jews do not work on the first and last two days of the holiday. While Koufax never pitched on the Passover Seder that occurs the first evening of the holiday, he did pitch on this holiday four times in his career.

He also pitched eight times on Shavuot, a two-day holiday in late May and early June that is the least observed of major Jewish holidays. Koufax never pitched on Rosh Hashanah, a two-day holiday in September that is the start of the high holiday season. He did pitch two World Series games on Sukkot/Shemini Atzereth, a combined nine-day holiday that occurs in October.

Yom Kippur, a one-day holiday that occurs in late September or early October, is the holiest day of the Jewish year. Observant Jews fast for 25 hours, taking no food or water, and are in religious services for 10 hours. The fact that Koufax was beaten by the Twins in Game Two may have had something to do with his being weakened by a lengthy fast in the two days prior to his start.

After Drysdale had been driven from the mound in the Game One loss, Lefty Gomez, a Hall of Fame pitcher with the Yankees in the thirties, walked into Walt Alston's office. "I'll bet you wish Drysdale was Jewish too," Gomez smirked.

While Koufax never pitched on Yom Kippur, he did come close twice. On October 1, 1960, Koufax threw two innings of relief in a night game. Because Yom Kippur had officially ended at 6:45 P.M. that night, Koufax technically did not pitch on the holiday. Very likely, however, he was in the clubhouse and suited up before sundown that day.

On September 20, 1961, Koufax worked a 13-inning night game in which he threw a staggering 250 pitches. Again, Yom Kippur had ended by 7 P.M., before the start of the game. Yet what makes Koufax's performance so incredible is that he was able to work as many innings and throw as many pitches as he did coming off a 25-hour fast.

Koufax's willingness to publicly declare that he was a Jew brought enormous pride to the Jewish community. "We have a good person to look up to," Rabbi Mendy Sasonkin told Arnie Rosenberg of the *Akron Beacon Journal* in a 1995 article concerning the observance of Yom Kippur despite the Cleveland Indians' drive to the pennant. "He did what a good Jew does on Yom Kippur."

Dr. Sidney Steinberger, an Ohio resident and former president of Beth El Congregation, had four tickets to an Indians' playoff game on Yom Kippur but chose to trade them for another game.

"If Sandy Koufax, who had the opportunity to pitch on Yom Kippur, said, 'I'm not going to,' it is easy for me," he said.

Jim Carney, the religion writer for the *Beacon*, wrote that Koufax's decision not to pitch in the 1965 Series opener that fell on Yom Kippur was "a moment of clarity and pride" for Jews across the United States. Rabbi Donald Goor of Temple Judea in Los Angeles said what's important is not that a successful athlete was born with Jewish blood but whether they live by Jewish principles and tradition, as Koufax did when he took his famous stand in '65.

Brad Farber, a 16-year-old student at Cherry Creek High School in Colorado, sat out a state tennis tournament in 1997 because of his observance of Yom Kippur. "I've heard Koufax's story since I was a little kid," he told the *Denver Post*. "If you can't respect your religion, what can you believe in? You do what's right in your heart, and you can never turn your back on that."

Koufax never did, and he wanted to make sure people knew it. Doing an interview with Larry King on the eve of Rosh Hashanah, he told King, "Don't forget to say we taped this the day before."

Koufax gained lasting admiration among Jewish people, including a couple of young boys who went on to become major leaguers. Jose Bautista was born to an Israeli mother and Dominican father. A hard-throwing lefty, Bautista's childhood idol was Koufax. "He was one of the best pitchers in the world," Bautista said, "and he was Jewish and a left-hander, so I really admired him."

Jesse Levis, who grew up in the Jewish suburb of Elkins Park in Pennsylvania, also drew inspiration from Koufax. "I know Koufax's story and I admire him," Levis said. "If you look at him as a player, Koufax was a Hall of Fame pitcher and deserved all the attention he got. Not many guys can throw a curveball like he did."

Along with Bautista and Levis, a University of Southern California student named Tom Seaver was inspired by the examples set by Koufax. To Seaver, however, the example set by Koufax came from his pitching artistry. Seaver used to watch Koufax closely as the Dodger ace went through his warmup pitches. Seaver noticed that Koufax would tug on the left side of his jersey, in effect pulling his shirt some two inches outside his belt. Since Koufax felt the baseball was an extension of his body when he pitched, he was loosening his jersey so it would not restrict the extension of his pitching arm.

Seaver, a right-hander who in 1965 was still three years away from being named National League Rookie of the Year and four years away from a Cy Young season, learned from Koufax's tip and began pulling his uniform jersey two inches outside his belt when he pitched. It was a practice he maintained throughout his own Hall of Fame career.

Seaver learned later that Koufax, bothered as he was by an injured index finger, was powerful enough to throw the curveball off his middle finger alone. The point illustrates the physical strength of the 210-pound Koufax, since most major league pitchers require the use of both the middle and index fingers.

Koufax's curveball in the sixties was legendary. He threw it with such velocity that it was said to emit an audible hum; hitters shook their heads years later, recalling the "melody of the sphere" thrown by Koufax. Pittsburgh Pirates' Hall of Fame slugger Ralph Kiner said that on days when Koufax had both his letter-high fastball and down-dropping curve working in unison, the Dodger pitcher was almost guaranteed a three-hitter.

Wally Moon, a teammate of Koufax on the Dodgers, agreed. "He can win with his fastball and he can win with his curve," Moon said. "And when he has both, forget it."

Los Angeles Times columnist Jim Murray wrote once that Koufax's curve disappeared like a long putt going into a hole. Murray said the definitive story on Koufax came from the first man Murray ever heard swear on the radio, San Franciso Giants' third baseman Jim Davenport. Davenport hit Koufax better than most, and one night after beating Koufax with a base hit, Davenport appeared on the postgame show. The result was classic radio.

"Jim, with Koufax, do you look for the fastball?"

"Oh, shit, yeah," Davenport told a startled listening audience. "The curveball you can't hit anyway!"

Koufax's curve was thrown with a sudden wrist snap to the outside. A lefty's curve breaks right and down; a right-hander's curve breaks left and down. For years, physicists have argued whether a pitched ball can actually curve. In 1877, the editors of the *Spalding Guide* remarked that the perfection of "curved pitching" was the most important trend of the decade.

"Any professor," the *Guide* claimed, "can in his study prove from the books that the thing is impossible, and many ballplayers can show him in the field that it is not only possible but common."

In 1941, *Life* ran strobe-light photos that the magazine said proved a baseball doesn't curve. Interestingly, *Look* magazine argued that photos proved it does curve. Physicists have determined that the ball does indeed curve, albeit in a continuous arc.

Yet because the arc of curve is continuous as it travels towards home plate, the ball only appears to hitters to break sharply as it arrives at home; it's an optical illusion of sorts. Unlike a fastball, which picks up a backspin rotation from the middle finger, the curve acquires top-spin from the index finger. Aided by a topspin rotation, the raised seams of the ball create a thin layer of air underneath that reduces air pressure and causes what is referred to as an "outdrop." The more rapid the rotation, the more the ball seems to break and drop. The curve is thrown with maximum spin. It starts high, and begins its break about 15 feet from home plate. Thrown by a southpaw, the pitch drops down and in to a right-handed hitter; down and away to a lefty.

Through the years, the unique arcs of the curve have created a number of colorful nicknames—"bender," "jug," "Uncle Charlie," "yakker," and "yellowhammer."

The last two are long-standing terms relating to birds. The yakker was named for a yawker, a type of woodpecker whose undulating pattern of flight resembles the path some curveballs take. The yellowhammer is another type of woodpecker that drops suddenly in flight. Whatever nickname it goes by, the curveball has spelled trouble for hitters for more than a hundred years.

The discovery and mastery of the curve is credited to William Arthur "Candy" Cummings, a 5' 9", 120-pound pitcher who in 1867 unleashed the first known curve while throwing underhand for the Excelsior Club of Brooklyn against Harvard. Cummings is said to have discovered the curveball in 1863, when as a 15-year-old he was throwing clamshells along with some friends. He was experimenting with his throwing motion to determine the best way to make the shells sail.

Believing he could make a baseball sail too if he altered his delivery, Cummings spent the next four years experimenting with different ways of throwing a ball. His attempts were a standing joke among his friends, but Cummings got the last laugh when he unveiled the curve against Harvard. Pitching underhand according to the rules and giving the ball a sidespin with a finger snap upon delivery, Cummings' curve dipped and moved so much, it dazzled not only Harvard hitters but its author as well. "It almost seemed," he said of his curve, "to have life."

Rules changes helped popularize the pitch. A wrist-break was allowed in the pitcher's delivery in 1872, the year Cummings turned professional, and over the next six seasons he won 145 games in the

National League and National Association. When overhand pitching was legalized in 1884, pitchers found the curve could be thrown faster and with a sharper downward break. Another rules change in 1893 gave pitchers an additional five feet to gain movement on the curve.

The first great practitioner of the pitch in the 20th century was Mordecai Brown, nicknamed "Three Fingers" because of a damaged hand. Brown's physical handicap worked to his advantage when throwing the curve, just as Koufax's finger ailment ultimately helped him. Because he released the ball with a final finger-snap of his middle digit rather than the index finger as is common, Koufax's curve picked up a three-dimensional look. While other southpaws threw a curveball that broke down and in to right-handed hitters and down and away to lefties, Koufax's unique delivery caused his curve to break almost straight down. Thus Murray's observation that the Koufax curve seemed to disappear into a hole, and Dodger executive Chip Strange's exclamation that the pitch dropped "like it was falling off a table."

Pirates' second baseman Bill Mazeroski, who faced Koufax numerous times in the fifties and sixties, said Koufax's curveball was the best he had ever seen.

"It was hard to hit," Maz said, "because it went straight down. You could look for his curveball and still not hit it."

Koufax owned the best curve of the decade, perhaps the best of modern times, and ranks with Bob Feller and Nolan Ryan as a famous fastballer who mastered one of baseball's most difficult pitches. The curveball has proven so difficult to control that even as accomplished a pitcher as Seaver said that after 17 years in the major leagues, he was still not satisfied with his curve.

Koufax said that before he mastered the curve, his career was like a camera in which the film always came out blank. He struggled for years before learning to control the pitch, and Seaver points to Koufax as a model of someone who ultimately harnessed his great abilities, and with hard-earned insight, became a Hall of Fame pitcher.

In Game Five, Koufax's curve had been his best pitch for the first seven innings. But when he tired in the final two frames, he lost control of his curve. Rearing back, he challenged the Twins' hitters with his letter-high fastball. Two solid defensive plays by shortstop Maury Wills, the second a game-ending double play, allowed Koufax to walk off the mound with a four-hit shutout to put the Dodgers ahead in the Series, three games to two.

Working on two days' rest and with more than 350 innings pitched already logged on his arthritic left elbow, Koufax had struggled to control his curve in the bottom of the first inning of Game Seven. Minnesota sluggers Harmon Killebrew and Tony Oliva were bobbing and swaying at the waist to avoid Koufax's wild first-inning deliveries, but after walking both men, Koufax had settled down enough to end the inning by freezing catcher Earl Battey with a big, breaking curve for a called third strike.

The streak of wildness saw Koufax throw 26 pitches in the first inning as opposed to just eight from his opposite, Twins' southpaw Jim Kaat. Kaat cruised through the second as well, retiring L.A. on 11 pitches and ending the inning by fanning Dick Tracewski on a checked-swing strikeout.

Koufax's pitch count and his trouble with the curveball would not have been great cause for concern in most games. But as radio announcer Byrum Saam noted as the Twins came to bat in the bottom of the second, every move is magnified in the World Series, especially in a Game Seven setting.

"This is it," Saam said. "There's no tomorrow."

In the bottom of the second, Koufax got leadoff hitter Bob Allison, whose 23 home runs was second on the team to Killebrew, to foul off three straight pitches, then struck him out swinging with a sharp breaking curve. Working to left-handed slugger Don Mincher, Koufax picked up a first-pitch called strike, then forced Mincher to foul off the next two pitches, including a curve that brought a reaction from Saam:

"Sandy's best curve is an overhand pitch. It has what old-timers describe as 'the drop.' And it really breaks off."

Koufax followed with two pitches out of the strike zone, and with the count at 2–2, rode a fastball in on Mincher, jamming the slugger who had bashed 22 homers in the regular season. The 215-pound Mincher tried to fight off the pitch, but it tied him up inside and all he could do was check his swing. Home plate umpire Ed Hurley pumped his fist in the air to signify the strikeout, and though it was a borderline call, Mincher didn't argue. Koufax now had three straight strikeouts and four in less than two innings.

Facing Frank Quilici, Koufax retired the side when he got Quilici to pop out to Wills in shallow left field. He had thrown 11 pitches in the inning, less than half his first-inning total, but his pitch count of 37 after just two innings was still high, still a cause for concern in the Dodger dugout.

FOUR

A rm-sore, Sandy Koufax could not control his curveball in the first two innings of Game Seven against Minnesota. His streak of wildness at the start of the game indicated that. As the sun broke through the overcast sky over Metropolitan Stadium and warmed temperatures to 65 degrees, the Dodger ace stood sweating in his gray road uniform at the bottom of the third inning of a scoreless game.

Larry Sherry, a right-handed reliever with the Dodgers from 1958 to 1963, said Koufax could sometimes be wild in the early innings because it took his heavy muscles a while to loosen up. Since this concerned him, Koufax would rub Capsolin on his shoulders, back, and left arm before he pitched to stimulate circulation in his muscles. Because it heated skin so quickly, players sometimes snuck Capsolin into the jockstrap of a teammate as a locker-room prank. It was so hot most athletes could barely stand it, but because he had thick skin, Koufax would lather it on his muscles to help him get loose. Sherry recalled walking past Koufax during games and noticing the overpowering smell of ointment from Koufax's long-sleeve, blue cotton undershirt.

Bereft of his curve, Koufax faced the prospect of challenging the Twins' sluggers with his fastball alone. He had always had a strong arm. Growing up in Brooklyn, he soon found he could retreat a little farther than the other neighborhood kids during snowball fights and still have the range to pepper them without getting hit in return. On the sand-lots, he could make long throws from the outfield, which he didn't find particularly useful since he didn't enjoy playing the outfield. His strong arm stood him in good stead in basketball games at Lafayette High. Taking the ball out of bounds after an opponent's score, Koufax had the arm strength to rifle it the length of the court to a forward streaking for the basket. The maneuver drove opposing coaches crazy, but Koufax sometimes drove his own coach crazy when he threw the ball so hard it would fly over the forward's head and bang off the backboard or the gymnasium wall.

Koufax was born in the Borough Park section of Brooklyn into an environment consisting of single- and double-story wooden houses, streets, school yards, playgrounds, parks, and community centers that constituted Flatbush. The Brooklyn of his youth in the thirties and for-ties offered a mingling of small, middle-class neighborhoods. Each neighborhood was distinctive in style, and a walk of five blocks in any direction usually meant you were not only in another part of town, you were in another town altogether.

"Our neighborhood was sort of on the borderline between where the Jewish neighborhood and Italian neighborhoods came together," remembered Richard Kauffman, a friend of Koufax and the younger brother of Larry Merchant.

"Lafayette was an area that was very Italian. It was lined with stores and shops that had Italian names. Not just the owners but the stores themselves. It was very heavily Italian, and there were a lot of Italian kids. So the school was a heavy mixture of kids with Jewish and Italian names. There were a few blacks, but very few. Most of the Ital-ians were Catholics, but there were a few kids who were neither Catholic or Jewish and they were referred to as Protestants."

The Jewish influx into Brooklyn began at the start of the 20th cen-tury. Seeking to escape the tenements of Manhattan's Lower East Side, Jews emigrated into Brooklyn by traveling across the bridge into Williamsburg. The passageway was later known as "Jew's Bridge" and Williamsburg was called "New Jerusalem."

By the mid-1920s, the emigration of Jews changed the face of

Brooklyn. The plate-glass windows of kosher butchers bore hand-painted silver-and-black signs that read "boh-sor ko-sher" (kosher meat). Jewish delicatessens, stores offering Old World delicacies, enticed shoppers with window displays of grilled knishes. Visitors to Jewish delis were greeted by rows of smoked meats, trays of garnishes, and bottled beer and soda.

More than a third of the immigrants moving into Brooklyn in the years following the First World War were European Jews of Russian and Polish descent. Many settled in Brownsville apartments, others sought homes in Bedford-Stuyvesant, Borough Park, Brighton Beach, Crown Heights, and Flatbush.

Virtually every home in Koufax's neighborhood had a three- or four-step porch, called "stoops" in Brooklyn, and it was against these steps that the young Koufax played "stoopball." It was a game played by throwing a pink Spalding rubber ball against the steps of the stoop, and it continued until someone's mother came out and chased the kids away.

In Brooklyn, "Spalding" was pronounced "Spal-deen" and to kids like Koufax, it was important to hit the last syllable as hard as possible. Doing so gave the game a special flavor and the players a special status; hitting the last syllable hard made the kids feel like hard guys playing hard ball.

As they grew older, Koufax and friends graduated from stoopball to stickball and punchball. The former was sometimes played in the street, sometimes in the playground. Street games were bordered by cars parked along the curb, and home plate was a manhole cover with a hexagon pattern and the BPB monogram—Borough President of Brooklyn. Stickball was also played in the school yard of PS 103 with a broomstick and a tennis ball or Spalding. Painted on a wall at the far end of the school building was a rectangular strike zone, and hitters aimed for the far end of the open court. Games ended prematurely only when someone launched the ball into the protective screening in front of the school windows, hitting it hard enough to break the glass, or if the ball was hit onto a neighboring roof.

Punchball was played in the streets, where parked cars, fire hydrants, and sewer covers served as bases. In punchball, the pitch was served on a one-hop bounce, and the batter attempted to hit it with his balled-up fist. A sponge ball was preferable, since the hard rubber Spalding usually left a bright pink mark on a player's wrist or palm if he didn't hit the ball cleanly with his fist.

Among the older neighborhood kids who played an occasional game of ball with Koufax was future comedian Buddy Hackett. Four years older than Koufax, "Butch" Hackett, as he was called in those days, had a sister who was Koufax's babysitter at times. Talk show host Larry King also grew up in the area, though Kauffman remembered him as Larry Zeiber. Singer Vic Damone, then Vito Franola, also hailed from the neighborhood.

To the other kids, Koufax was a hemisha boy, a mensch. He liked to have fun, but he never did crazy things. When his friends sneaked down from the cheap seats into the box seats at Ebbets Field, Koufax stayed put. Koufax was as close to being an orthodox Jew as any of the kids in the neighborhood. While most of them observed the dietary laws, Koufax refused even to drive a car on Saturdays.

Koufax's childhood was divided into three stages—the divorce of his parents, Jack and Evelyn Braun, when he was three years old; his mother's marriage when he was nine to New York attorney Irving Koufax; and his high school years in the Bay Ridge section of Brooklyn. Koufax lost contact with his blood father at the age of nine, when Jack Braun remarried and stopped making alimony payments. A short time later, Evelyn and Irvin married, and Sandy took his stepfather's name.

"When I speak of my father," Koufax said in his autobiography, "I speak of Irving Koufax, for he has been to me everything a father could be."

A solidly built man with slicked-back hair, Irving delighted his young son with his ambidextrous sleight of hand. Not only could he write with each hand, he could put a pencil in each hand and write backwards with the left and forward with the right—at the same time.

"Darnedest thing I ever saw," Koufax said years later. During his early interviews with New York sportswriters, Koufax actually preferred talking about his stepfather to talking about himself.

His mother, an attractive woman with dark hair and features, was an accountant. Neither Irving nor Evelyn was a big baseball fan until their son joined the Dodgers.

"My wife and I became enthusiasts as soon as Sandy made

the Dodgers," Irving Koufax said years later. "We went to every game possible."

Dodgers' general manager Buzzie Bavasi remembered Koufax's parents as people of great integrity.

"He came from great stock," Bavasi said. "His mother was a wonderful woman, a marvelous woman, and when you come from that kind of stock, you know you've got to be a good person. He had the right genes."

Because his parents had to work, Koufax frequently stayed with his grandparents. He often spent Saturdays with his grandfather, Max Lichtenstein, going to the theatre, the movies, or a concert.

When his mother remarried, the family moved to Rockville Centre, a town whose country atmosphere led New Yorkers to consider it "out on the Island" although it was just 19 miles from Manhattan. Koufax's uncle, Sam Lichtenstein, did architectural work in Rockville Centre, and he purchased a two-story home in the area. The Koufax family moved into the first-floor residence, the Lichtensteins into the second.

Koufax and his family moved from Rockville Centre to Bensonhurst in Brooklyn the day of his ninth-grade graduation. Their new residence was a three-story, red-brick garden apartment in a housing development bordering the Belt Parkway. Brooklyn in the forties was an animated and colorful city. In his book *When Brooklyn Was the World*, Elliott Willensky wrote of a city whose streets were a natural amphitheater. The Brooklyn air was filled with the chatter of neighbors visiting on front stoops; the clattering of stores on wheels selling baked goods and fruit; and the voices of mothers calling their sons for dinner—"Ants" for Anthony, "Yussy" for Joseph. It was a city filled with its own language—"dem," "dese," and "dose"; "idear" for *idea;* "erl" for *oil* and "oil" for *Earl.*

Brooklyn was dinner at a Chinese restaurant, where 99 percent of the guests were not Chinese; it was the Bossert Hotel and the Paramount Theatre; and it was Ebbets Field, the BMT subway, and Nathan's hot dogs.

Koufax enjoyed his Brooklyn upbringing, and in the fall of 1949 enrolled at Lafayette High. He also made the Jewish Community House on Bay Parkway his second home. The "J" or "JCH" as it was called, offered a neoclassical facade that to some seemed ostentatious. Inside, it resembled the YMCA in that it featured a basketball court, handball court, swimming pool, weight room, and steam bath. With his outsized hands and feet, and with his body control and coordination, Koufax excelled at basketball. He joined a neighborhood team, the Tomahawks, and played in Brooklyn's Ice Cream League, where he was named Outstanding Player of the Junior Division.

At Lafayette High, the school newspaper welcomed him to the team by spelling his name as "Coufax." By his senior year, however, he had been named team captain, and he scored 24 points against rival Lincoln High in one memorable game. He finished the season with 165 points in 10 games, second highest in his division.

Richard Kauffman lived on Dahill Road and 64th Streets in Brooklyn and was one year ahead of Koufax at Lafayette High. But the two had common friends and soon formed a friendship.

"I knew him probably almost as well as anybody else, because he was always reserved, even as a kid," said Kauffman. "He came over to my house a couple of times; I don't think I was ever over to his.

"I do recall our first meeting. It was a touch football game and we were playing in the street with a group of guys. He was in that group, and we were just throwing the ball around. He was quiet, he wasn't always leading the group to go do something. But he was not a solemn person. My image of him is that he always laughed a lot, and whenever the guys got together there was a lot of laughing. He had a good sense of humor and he was always laughing with everybody else and playing games, playing sports at the JCH.

"I dug up my old high school yearbook recently, and I had almost forgotten that he had signed my book. Now he was a year behind me, and it was a little bit unusual to get guys signing your book from the other classes. I thought that was interesting; it shows he wasn't hiding out in corners or anything."

Kauffman recalled Koufax as a terrific, all-around athlete who could run, catch, throw, and hit. He was not a first-string pitcher. Koufax was a good-hitting first baseman who was used in relief of starter Fred Wilpon, who went on to become the president and CEO of the New York Mets. Years later, Wilpon was said to be taken aback when he learned that Koufax, his former backup, had signed a major league contract with the Brooklyn Dodgers.

Koufax didn't make the Lafayette High baseball team until his senior year, and only played the game to keep occupied. "I played baseball mostly because I had nothing to do," he said once. "My friends played so I played."

"All he ever was was an athlete," biographer Ed Linn said. "People have attempted to make him into something he wasn't, everything but a violin player. He was an athlete. He spent his life in Brooklyn on the playgrounds."

A solid but unspectacular baseball player, Koufax excelled in basketball. Lafayette High was not the dominant city team at the time, but had a loyal following among the students and games were well attended. Kauffman remembers Koufax as one of the team's best players.

"He was a fabulous basketball player," Kauffman said. "It was amazing what he could do. He could jump so high it was astonishing."

Harvey Frommer, the author of numerous books on both Jewish life and baseball, recalled playing basketball against Koufax at the JCH.

"We both grew up around the same time," remembered Frommer. "He was a much better basketball player than baseball player. I had thought I was a very good basketball player, and when I played against him it was like going up against someone from a different league."

One of the highlights of Koufax's basketball experience occurred when the Police Athletic League of Bath Beach arranged for the New York Knicks to play a benefit game against Lafayette High. Koufax was a Knicks fan, and he followed the on-court exploits of Harry Gallatin and "Sweetwater" Clifton. Gallatin was supposed to put on a dunking exhibition at Lafayette High, but when he missed on two of his first three attempts, basketball coach and later NBA color analyst Al McGuire grabbed the 6' 2" Koufax by the elbow.

"I've got a kid right here," McGuire announced, "who can show you how to do it."

Dribbling from the foul line, Koufax soared and dunked the ball easily.

"I'll bet he can't do it again," Gallatin laughed.

Koufax did, and played well in the benefit game against the

Knicks. After it was over, Gallatin approached him, and wrote his name on a piece of paper.

"I'm going to be looking for you in future years," Gallatin said. "You're going to be in the NBA."

Kauffman said everyone who saw that event still remembers it. "The Knicks came to our high school and there was Sandy jumping with the best of them," he said. "One of those players remarked afterwards about how high the kid could jump. I mean, he was going up above the hoop, and it's not like he was 6-foot-6."

Among the spectators at the gym that day was Merchant, an assistant football coach at Lafayette. Merchant was impressed by what he saw of Koufax's basketball skills.

"I noticed he did very well as a rebounder," Merchant said. "He had a presence on the court. He was a good player."

Merchant also recalled seeing Koufax in the hallways of Lafayette High, and that he carried himself in a manner that would become his trademark in his superstar years with the Dodgers.

"In high school, he just wanted to be one of the guys," Merchant said. "He was not a strutting person. But he was very competitive and he wanted to win. He liked competition and he liked to perform in front of people."

Years later, when Merchant covered Koufax as a sportswriter and columnist in Philadelphia, he found him to be the same low-key person. "He didn't want to blow his own horn," Merchant said. "Even though he was a superstar, he didn't want to be considered a star among his teammates. He was very sensitive to that."

Basketball and baseball overlapped for Koufax. Springtime found him playing baseball after school, followed by basketball in the playground. On the Tomahawks baseball team, he played catcher and first base, and helped the team go 10–0 and finish first in the Junior Division. In the best-of-three playoffs, Tomahawks ace Mike Fields started Game One on Friday, and would have pitched Game Two on Saturday had the team lost. But with a game in hand, the team needed a pitcher, someone who could throw the ball hard. All eyes turned towards Koufax.

He walked five batters in the first inning and forced in two runs. His control improved as the game went on, but the Tomahawks lost 4–1. Fields returned the next day and pitched the team to the title.

At the age of 15, Koufax had pitched his first baseball game. Until that time, he had been used largely as a decoy; coaches would warm him up in the bullpen to scare the other team. Inevitably, a Koufax fastball flew over the head of his catcher and rolled out onto the field, forcing the umpire to stop the game momentarily. It would be another two years before he began pitching regularly. He pitched two more games for the Tomahawks, losing 6–2 before finally winning his first-ever game, a 4–2 decision in which he knocked in the winning runs.

At Lafayette, Koufax hadn't even thought about pitching until Milt Laurie, who attended the games because he had two sons on the team, took notice of Koufax's arm strength as he rifled the ball around the infield.

Koufax, however, wasn't interested. "Not only am I not a pitcher," he said, "I'm not even a baseball player. I'm a basketball player."

His pattern of pitching in his early days was to both walk and strike out hitters by the handful. Laurie, a former minor league pitcher, managed a team called the Parkviews in the Coney Island League. Convincing Koufax to join, he worked with him on controlling his fastball. In an early game with the Parkviews, Koufax hurled his first no-hitter. Though he had little control over his curve, he was strong enough to overpower hitters with his fastball.

"He was amazingly strong," Kauffman said. "He didn't look overpowering; he was very wiry and he had long arms and long legs. But he was very, very strong."

Kauffman said he got a taste of Koufax's strength firsthand when he wrestled him one time and gained both a draw and a fierce headache from the tenseness of the match.

In time, Koufax became Parkview's "money" pitcher in a literal sense. Teams put up $50 to $100 before each game, and more often than not Koufax pitched the money games. Because of the dollars involved, he became accustomed to pitching under pressure.

Scouts from the Boston Red Sox and Philadelphia Phillies turned up at Parkview games, but Koufax accepted an athletic scholarship to the University of Cincinnati, where he would study to be an architect and, he thought, play more basketball than baseball.

"He came to us on his own," recalled Ed Jucker, the Bearcats' freshman basketball coach and head baseball coach. "He saw us play in

Madison Square Garden, and I don't know if it was the way we played or the way we cut our hair or what, but he apparently liked what he saw.

"He just showed up, and I was happy to have him. He did tell me he had seen us play at Madison Square Garden, he did tell me that. So we gave him a scholarship to play basketball and baseball.

"He was a youngster that I enjoyed being the coach for, and the players loved him. We got together as a team and we played as a team."

As a 6' 2" forward on the freshman team, Koufax averaged 9.7 points per game and helped the Bearcats post a 12–2 record.

"I saw enough in him that he could have played varsity basketball, and we had great teams there," recalled Jucker, who went on to coach the Bearcats' varsity to consecutive national championships in 1961–1962.

"He had long arms and he could jump, and he had big hands and long fingers. He wasn't one of those gunners. He worked great around the boards and he could put the ball back in (for a rebound basket). He was quick enough to play defense. He didn't have great speed, but he did a good job. He was intense, an intense player, and he had motivation to do well. You have those ingredients, that motivation, that ability that he had, and the kind of person he was, why, he couldn't lose."

Koufax's interest in the baseball team increased when he learned that freshmen were allowed to play on the varsity in non-conference games. Hearing that Cincinnati would be playing in New Orleans over Easter vacation, Koufax approached Jucker.

"Coach, I'm a baseball player. I'm a pitcher."

"Yeah, everybody's a pitcher these days," Jucker responded. "But what kind of a pitcher, that's the thing."

"I can pitch pretty good."

Jucker held a tryout for pitchers and catchers in the university gym, which was poorly lit. Squatting behind home plate, the catcher stared out at the dark silhouette of a southpaw going into his windup. Out of the shadows came a whistling fastball that buzzed the ear of the catcher. The shaken catcher stood up, handed his mitt to Jucker and said, "Get somebody else. I don't want any part of this guy."

Jucker laughed at the memory. "The gym was dark," he said, "and there was no catcher who wanted to handle his speed ball. He had a terrific curve too. It went straight down, and with speed. You know, when you have a youngster come along and you see something like this, it's like a revelation to see someone throw the ball that fast."

Jucker's story is similar to one involving a game Koufax pitched for Parkview against their Coney Island League rivals, Gravesend Youth Center. Pitching in a fog so dense that pitchers and hitters could barely see one another, one batter facing Koufax failed to see his fastball from the time it left Koufax's hand to the time it exploded into the catcher's mitt behind him. When the umpire shouted "Strike!" the hitter walked out of the batter's box and refused to return.

Since no one on the Bearcats wanted to catch Koufax because of his speed and wildness, he spent his time throwing at wooden planks near the ball field. Despite his wildness, Jucker was surprised Koufax had not gained more attention from major league scouts.

"He played sandlot baseball in Brooklyn, and to me, I just wondered, 'How could they overlook this guy?'" Jucker said. "I couldn't believe it."

Jucker said Koufax fit in well with the university's surroundings. He joined a Jewish fraternity, and his personality earned him numerous friends.

"Everybody liked him," Jucker recalled. "He was a quiet individual, not boisterous, and kept within himself. He kind of knew what his goals were."

Koufax's immediate goal was to improve his control. Jucker said Koufax presented a coaching dilemma. "He would walk three and strike out three," Jucker said. "He was fast and had a great curveball, but he was wild. But he just got better and better, and at the end of the season, he said, 'I'm coming back next year.'

"So he came back, and said, 'I've got a $20,000 Brooklyn Dodgers contract in my back pocket. I haven't signed it yet, but I'm thinking of doing it.'

"I said, 'Wait a minute, let's take a look at the Cincinnati Reds. They're right here.' I had a meeting, a luncheon, with Birdie Tebbets, a Reds' coach, and he said, 'We'll give you $4,000.' At that time, if you gave a rookie a penny more than $4,000, you had to keep him. You couldn't send him out (to the minors).

"He wasn't interested in the $4,000. He said he had $20,000, so he took that. The rest is history."

Koufax's fastball had attracted the attention of major league scouts, and his ability to throw it past major league hitters kept him in the big leagues through his formative years. Surprisingly, his fastball was a pitch most hitters preferred to see since they knew he wasn't a headhunter.

Braves' slugger Hank Aaron thought Koufax didn't test a hitter's courage the way Bob Gibson or Don Drysdale did. The Hammer believed Koufax was too nice a guy to throw at anybody; he simply challenged hitters with his speed and confidence. Aaron spoke from experience. During one at-bat against Koufax when both were in their prime in the mid-sixties, Aaron fouled off numerous Koufax pitches. Finally, as Koufax walked halfway to home plate to take yet another new baseball from the home plate umpire, he told Aaron he was tired of seeing his pitches fouled off. The next pitch, Koufax declared, was going to be a fastball, and Aaron was either going to strike out or hit a home run. Koufax fired his fastball, and Aaron popped out.

Koufax's challenging of the Hammer had been done quietly and without fanfare—one of the things hitters respected most about Koufax. Because he never showed hitters up, they accepted what they called "comfortable outs." In other words, even when hitters struck out against Koufax, they didn't feel as if their manhood had been tested. They had merely faced the best, and been beaten. Aaron recalled a day when Koufax worked against the Braves with a blister on his pitching hand. Despite knowing they would see nothing but fastballs, Milwaukee hitters were still beaten by Koufax, 2–1 in 13 innings.

Koufax lacked the hard edge attributed to Gibson and Drysdale. But Joe Torre, later the manager of the New York Yankees and a teammate of Gibson's in the sixties, said Koufax intimidated hitters with his fastball in the way Roger Clemens did.

Koufax was aware of the edge his fastball gave him in pitcher-batter confrontations, and he used it to his advantage. "The art of pitching," he said, "is to instill fear in a man by making him flinch."

Tom Seaver remarked that Koufax's statement wasn't intended to be malicious. It meant that a pitcher cannot be afraid to throw his fastball on the inside part of the plate.

"Show me a guy who can't pitch inside," Koufax said, "and I'll show you a loser."

Willie Mays recalled a crucial Giants-Dodgers game in the final days of the hotly contested '65 pennant race when Koufax came inside with what Mays called "a courtesy pitch." From his position in center field, Mays watched San Francisco starter Juan Marichal deck Maury Wills and Ron Fairly with pitches high and inside. Since he was the Giants' leadoff hitter in the second inning, Mays figured Koufax would throw at him in retaliation for what Marichal did. Koufax did, but he issued a sailer, a pitch that flew a foot over the Giant slugger's head. The pitch was different from what a headhunter would have thrown, and even Mays termed it "nothing dangerous." But Koufax's message was clear: "Don't throw at my teammates."

Courtesy pitches are an accepted part of the game, and Koufax had such excellent control that he could fire fastballs at the inside corner of the plate and never touch the hitter. In 1966, he set a major league record by pitching 323 innings and not hitting a batter. Mays said Koufax used the inside fastball, "a jammer," Mays called it, to set up his great curve. The tight fastball forced the hitter to lean back, and Koufax followed by breaking a curve so sharply over the plate that it froze even great hitters like Mays.

National League batters differed on how to beat Koufax. Aaron believed that Koufax knew exactly what he was going to do with each pitch, and that allowed the Hammer to think along with the Dodger ace. Hitters of the late sixties followed a vastly different approach against Cleveland Indians' ace Sam McDowell, who succeeded Koufax for a time as the game's most dominating southpaw. Ron Smith wrote in *True* magazine in 1969 that McDowell throws fastballs, and if that doesn't work, Smith wrote, "he throws a faster one." McDowell himself warned hitters against trying to think along with him. "Most of the time," he said, "I don't know where the pitch is going."

Mays felt his confrontations with Koufax were more elementary than Aaron's. Mays believed that you had to beat Koufax pure and simple, or not at all, and that meant making contact with his great fastball.

Koufax enjoyed the confrontations with great hitters. Baseball, he said once, is a form of warfare. He never believed in fraternizing with opposing players, because the guys in the other uniforms represented the enemy. He never wanted to get to know an opponent well enough to feel anything towards them except, as he put it, "sheer hostility."

Koufax carried an air of animosity towards hitters, but he hid it behind a cool demeanor, unlike his contemporaries, Gibson and Drysdale. Torre said that Gibson wasn't unfriendly when he pitched. "I'd say it was more like hateful," Torre remarked.

Gibson on the mound posed a fearsome sight for hitters. Tall and athletic, he had striking, dark features and strong self-confidence. On the mound, he pulled his bright red Cardinals' cap low on his forehead, almost obscuring his dark complexion, and the bright red sleeves of his undershirt extended to his wrists, even in the hottest of summer games. He had an exploding fastball and wicked slider, and delivered his pitches out of a windup so powerful it ended with him falling away towards first base as the pitch rocketed towards home plate and the hitter.

Gibson rose to stardom in the sixties, and some saw in his defiance on the mound a kind of black militancy. Gibson saw in himself a realistic attitude towards himself and the world he lived in. It was nice to get attention and favors, he said, but he could never forget the fact that if he were an ordinary black person he'd be in the doghouse, like millions of others.

From 1963 to 1968, Koufax and Gibson dominated the National League, and their teams rode their pitching talents to multiple pennants. Koufax's Dodgers won league championships in 1963, '65, and '66; Gibson's Cardinals captured the National League flag in '64, '67, and '68. They dueled both on the field and in the record book. On October 2, 1963, Koufax set a World Series record by striking out 15 Yankees; five years to the day later, Gibson broke Koufax's mark by fanning 17 Detroit Tigers.

Like Koufax, Gibson excelled in big games. In the 1964 World Series, he ended the Yankee dynasty by beating New York twice within three days, in Games Five and Seven, the latter coming on two days' rest, and set a Series strikeout record with 31 strikeouts in 27 innings. Gibson's Cardinals took a backseat to Koufax's Dodgers in 1965 and '66, but following Koufax's retirement in 1966, Gibson led the Cardinals to consecutive Series appearances in '67 and '68. He went 3–0 against Boston in the '67 Series, and earned another Game Seven victory when he three-hit the Red Sox at Fenway Park. The following season, Gibson dominated the National League with a blistering 1.12 earned run average that was the lowest in the major leagues since the introduction of the lively ball back in 1920.

Gibson utterly dominated the National League in 1968, posting league-high totals with 13 shutouts and 268 strikeouts. He also won 15 straight games and pitched 28 complete games, a startling number, en route to winning both the Most Valuable Player and Cy Young awards. He peaked in the Fall Classic, striking out 17 Tigers in a 4–0 shutout win in Game One. He won Game Four 10–1, his seventh straight complete-game Series victory dating back to '64. Ironically, Gibson's final Fall Classic appearance, a Game Seven loss in '68, was strikingly similar to Koufax's Series finale, a Game Two loss to Baltimore in '66. Just as Koufax was hurt by errors from center fielder Willie Davis, Gibson's chances of victory were hurt when his center fielder, Curt Flood, slipped on a fly ball to center that led to the deciding runs.

In style and demeanor, however, Gibson resembled Drysdale more than Koufax. Gibson and Drysdale used power principles that allowed them to catapult the pitch towards home plate. Maximizing hip and torso rotation, they dropped their arms to a three-quarter angle that pulled them through an unorthodox delivery, a fallaway follow-through towards first base.

Drysdale terrorized hitters with his flailing delivery and fiery demeanor. Physically imposing, Drysdale followed the rules of the game as taught to him by ex-Dodger Sal Maglie. Nicknamed "The Barber" because he "shaved" batters with pitches high and tight, Maglie said that he never wanted to get to know his opponents too well. "I might like them," the Barber reasoned, "and then I might not want to throw at them."

Former Giants' hitter Alvin Dark said once that "Maglie got by on meanness."

Drysdale got by on meanness as well. "If they knocked one of our guys down," he said once, "I'd knock down two of theirs. If they knocked two of our guys down, I'd get four. You have to protect your hitters."

Drysdale protected them so well that Cardinals' slugger Orlando Cepeda said that the trick against Drysdale was to "hit him before he hits you."

New York Yankees' Hall of Fame slugger Mickey Mantle batted

against Drysdale in the 1963 World Series and in several spring training games. Regardless of whether it was a Series game in October or an exhibition game in March, Mantle hated to hit against Drysdale.

"After he hit you," Mantle said once, "he'd come around, look at the bruise on your arm, and say, 'Do you want me to sign it?' "

In a sense, Gibson and Drysdale perpetuated the game's ancient rivalry between pitcher and hitter. Cleveland Indians' pitcher Early Wynn, who worked in the major leagues from 1939 to 1963, considered the mound his office, "a place where I conduct my business." Wynn's business was pitching inside; he once dusted his own son in a game. "That son of a bitch is so mean," said Mantle, "he'd knock you down in the dugout."

Countered Wynn, "I've got a right to knock down anybody holding a bat."

St. Louis Cardinals' pitcher Dizzy Dean once stared at a hitter digging in at the plate, and yelled, "You all done? You comfortable? Well, send for the groundskeeper and get a shovel, because that's where they're gonna bury you."

Philadelphia Phillies manager Jimmie Wilson said in 1935 that a batter couldn't get a hit off of either Dizzy or his brother Paul without getting beaned the next time up.

Koufax, however, wasn't cut from that mold. "With the kind of stuff he had," Hall of Fame lefty Warren Spahn recalled, "he didn't have to throw at people."

Among history's great fastballers, Koufax may have most closely resembled Washington Senators' Hall of Famer Walter Johnson, who pitched in the majors from 1907 to 1927. Johnson's fastball was called "The Big Train" because it moved so fast, and Birdie McCree, an executive for the New York Highlanders, said in 1908 that there was only one way to time Johnson's heater. "When you see the arm start forward," McCree said, "swing."

Batting against the Big Train in 1915, Cleveland Indians' infielder Ray Chapman began heading for the dugout after two strikes. Informed by the umpire he had one strike left, Chapman remarked, "Keep it. I don't want it."

Boston Red Sox pitcher Joe Wood was Johnson's main competitor in throwing the heater during that era, but even the man nicknamed "Smokey" for the velocity of his fastball acknowledged Johnson's speed. "He could throw the ball by you so fast," Wood said, "you never knew whether you'd swung under it or over it."

Koufax, like Walter Johnson, awed his contemporaries with the speed of his fastball. Hall of Famer Richie Ashburn said after facing Koufax in 1962 that "either he throws the fastest ball I've ever seen, or I'm going blind." Dodgers' pitcher Don Sutton said hitters considered foul balls against Koufax to be moral victories.

The Twins didn't get many moral victories against Koufax in the third inning of Game Seven. Working against his opposite, Jim Kaat, a man whom the Dodgers respected as a hitter as well as a pitcher, Koufax got ahead quickly in the count 1–2. He followed by striking Kaat out on the next pitch.

A .247 hitter during the regular season, Kaat batted just .167 over three games against Koufax. "I can't even recall if I got a foul ball or not," Kaat said with a laugh. "I hit off him a couple of times in Game Two and maybe once each in Games Five and Seven. I doubt that I even put the ball in play. It was just a blur."

Fanning Kaat on four pitches, Koufax registered his fifth strikeout of the game. He had also struck out three of the last four hitters to face him.

"That's an old habit for him," said NBC Radio announcer Byrum Saam, who went on to remind his listeners that just two days earlier, Koufax had whiffed 10 Twins in his last outing, and that during the '65 season, he had struck out at least 10 hitters in a game 22 times.

Returning to the top of the Twins' batting order, Koufax got Zoilo Versalles to foul off two pitches, then hung a breaking ball that the Minnesota leadoff man chopped into short center field for the Twins' first hit of the game.

Versalles led the team in steals in '65 with 27, and as he took a lead against Koufax, the Met crowd began chanting "Go! Go! Go!" Working to Joe Nossek, Koufax blew a high fastball past Nossek on the first pitch, followed with a ball, then delivered another high fastball, this one way outside, as Versalles broke for second base on a steal attempt. Trying to protect the runner, Nossek swung across the plate at the outside pitch, and in the process tipped the glove of catcher John Roseboro. Umpire Ed Hurley ruled catcher's interference, called Nossek out, and returned Versalles to first.

With two outs, Koufax faced the dangerous Tony Oliva for the second time in the game. The Twins' Number Three hitter and American League batting champion, Tony O. had worked Koufax for a walk in the first inning.

Despite having quick wrists and excellent bat control, Oliva struggled with Koufax's pitches—the flaring fastball, the down-breaking curve, all thrown off the same picturesque motion and with pinpoint control.

"I made a living hitting baseballs," Oliva said, looking back. "And in those days if I swing at five pitches, I'm going to hit at least one. But I didn't touch some of his pitches. He threw fastballs 96, 97, maybe 100 miles an hour, and the ball was moving."

Oliva quickly fell behind Koufax 0–2 when he fouled off a pitch and swung through the second. Working against Oliva, Koufax kept an eye on Versalles. Four times he threw to first in an attempt to shorten Versalles's lead, bringing a game-stopping protest from Twins' third-base coach Billy Martin, who hollered at Hurley that Koufax was guilty of a balk.

Hurley disagreed, and Koufax ended the running argument and the inning when he struck Oliva out swinging. It was his sixth strikeout of the game, and though he had extinguished the Twins' threat, he walked off the mound at the end of the third framed by the sight of Drysdale warming up in the Dodger bullpen in left field, ready to come on in relief should Koufax's sore arm give way.

FIVE

At the end of the third inning, Sandy Koufax approached his catcher, John Roseboro, in the Dodger dugout.

"John, bad curveball."

Looking at Koufax, Roseboro replied, "Well, there's one thing about it. It's got to get better. There's just no other way for it to go."

Koufax's wildness and inability to control his curveball in the opening innings was reminiscent of his early development as a pitcher. Despite being on a basketball scholarship at the University of Cincinnati, it was as a freshman baseball pitcher that he began attracting the attention of pro scouts. After pitching a four-hitter against Wayne and striking out 16, Koufax followed with a three-hitter and a school-record 18 strikeouts against Louisville.

Bill Zinser, a bird-dog scout for the Brooklyn Dodgers, scouted Koufax. Zinser filled out a report on May 15, 1954, that rated the Cincinnati freshman an A-plus for his arm and A-minus for his accuracy. In the Dodgers' system, an A equaled the major league average. Zinser's report classified Koufax as owning a major league arm but minor league control. The Dodger scout described Sandy as tall and muscular, well coordinated, and with quick reflexes and outstanding aggressiveness. On the question, "Definite Prospect?" Zinser noted "Yes."

Indeed, years later, Dodger executive Al Campanis told writer Roger Kahn that there had been only two occasions in his life when the hair on the back of his neck literally stood on end. One, Campanis said, was when he saw Michelangelo's paintings in the Sistine Chapel. The other was the first time he saw Sandy Koufax throw a fastball. It appeared headed for the dirt, Campanis recalled, then it rose for a knee-high strike.

Koufax's record his freshman season stood at 3–1, with 51 strikeouts and 30 walks in 31 innings. A start against Xavier College proved customary—six walks and seven strikeouts in seven innings.

The New York Giants' baseball team invited Koufax to a tryout at the Polo Grounds, and the wildness that had scared off the scout reappeared. Giants' catcher Bobby Hoffman told Koufax, "Just loosen up at first," and Koufax responded by firing a fastball that flew over Hoffman's head and landed three rows back in the grandstand behind home plate. He never heard from the Giants again.

Returning to Brooklyn for summer vacation, Koufax rejoined the Parkview club in the Coney Island League. He did well enough to attract the attention of more major league scouts, including the New York Yankees. The Yanks sent two scouts to the Koufax household, and offered Sandy a standard $4,000 contract to join their Class D minor league team. He balked when the Yankees refused to increase their salary offer and replaced their first two scouts with a Jewish scout. The latter was a patronizing move that offended Koufax.

That same summer, the Pittsburgh Pirates learned about Koufax from Ted Gale, a projectionist at the Fox Theatre in Flatbush who telephoned Ed McCarrick, the Pirates' supervisor of scouting for the New York and New England area. Calling McCarrick on a Saturday night, Gale told him to to come to Abraham Lincoln High School field the next day to watch a kid named "Koo-fax" pitch a playoff game.

Gale managed sandlot teams in Brooklyn, and he had seen Koufax pitch the week before. When McCarrick told him he already had plans to scout someone else, Gale responded, "Cancel it. This kid has a great arm."

McCarrick arrived at Lincoln High the next day, and sat in the bleachers as Koufax struck out 15 hitters in seven innings. After the game, McCarrick phoned Pirates' president Branch Rickey, Sr. He told Rickey of Koufax's blazing fastball and power curve. Rickey agreed to send his son, Branch Jr. and Clyde Sukeforth, the Pirates' bullpen coach, to watch Koufax in his next playoff outing the following Sunday.

McCarrick also arranged for Branch Jr. and Sukeforth to scout Koufax in a private workout the morning of the game. Sunday dawned cold and foggy, and with the workout scheduled for 8:30 A.M., Koufax struggled to get his arm loose in the damp, heavy air. As wisps of fog settled in on Dyker Field, Koufax took the mound and began throwing for the Pirates' brass. Days earlier, he had injured his ankle in a swimming pool accident, and the combination of the cold air and sore ankle prevented Koufax from finding his pitching rhythm, and he threw with a cramped, strained motion.

Later that day, he took the mound for Parkview against the rival Falcons, champions of the Shore Parkway League. With McCarrick, Branch Jr., and Sukeforth in attendance, Koufax had one more opportunity to impress the Pirates' scouts. As he was going through his warmups, however, Koufax felt a blister breaking out on the middle finger of his throwing hand. He tried to pitch through it, but in the second inning the blister broke, and blood spotted the ball with each pitch he threw. Surrendering four runs in three innings, he was taken out of the game.

Despite Koufax's poor showing, McCarrick talked the elder Rickey into one final workout. Explaining that there had been "complications" with Koufax's injuries, McCarrick said, "Before you make up your mind, I want you to see him when he's right."

Rickey agreed to give Koufax a workout at Forbes Field, home of the Pirates. Sitting in a box seat just behind third base, the Pirates' president watched, chin in hand, as Koufax fired fastball after fastball, each pitch exploding into catcher Sam Narron's mitt with a crackling sound that seemed to reverberate around the old ballpark. At one point, Rickey got down behind Narron at home plate to see how much movement Koufax's pitches had. Koufax's big hands and long, powerful fingers allowed him to throw the fastball with so much spin and velocity that when the ball got to within seven or eight feet of home plate, it literally jumped. Dodger reliever Larry Sherry, whose brother Norm was a catcher with the Dodgers, thought Koufax's fastball picked up so much movement those final seven or eight feet, that it looked like somebody had thrown it a second time.

Narron recalled Koufax being wild in his workout at Forbes Field, but he could see that the kid had a major league fastball. Others saw it too, and at the end of the workout, Rickey turned to McCarrick and said, "Ed, we want this boy." McCarrick quietly worked out a verbal agreement with Koufax in which the Pirates would sign him to a $10,000 major league contract. Rickey had revolutionized scouting when, as general manager of the St. Louis Cardinals in the years following World War I, he built the first modern farm system. The Cardinals signed amateurs in droves, separated the pretenders from the contenders, and trained them in the Redbirds' system of baseball. Rickey's biggest impact on the game was when he signed Jackie Robinson from the Negro Leagues, thus integrating the majors for the first time and opening the sport up to black and Latin talent.

Red Smith once described Rickey as a curious man full of contradictions. To Smith, Rickey was "a God-fearing, checker-playing, horse-trading, cigar-smoking, double-talking, nonalcoholic, sharp-shooting blend of eloquence and sincerity and profundity and guile." Nicknamed "The Mahatma," Rickey was, an observer said, "a man of many faucets, all turned on."

Smith said that while Rickey's agile mind raced on, his facile tongue pattered after. The result, said Smith, was verbal obscurities, speeches as twisted as a hoopsnake.

Smith once heard Rickey give a speech in which he told his listeners, "When there comes a stoppage of vertical mobility among the society strata . . ."

Rickey's twisted verbiage prompted a man in the audience to exclaim, "Guys get drunk and don't say things like that!"

John Drebinger of the *New York Times* once asked Rickey a question in a press conference, and The Mahatma responded with a 20-minute discourse.

"Does that answer your question, John?"

Said Drebinger, "I have forgotten the question."

It was important to Rickey never to be beaten in a business deal.

He was a master persuader, and owned a fearsome reputation for handling ballplayers coming into his office for a raise. Gary Schumacher of the New York baseball Giants once described the ground rules for dealing with Rickey: "Don't drink the night before, keep your mouth shut and your hands in your pockets."

Rickey struggled to adapt to the postwar practice of big bonuses, and it cost him Koufax. The Phillies' signing of pitcher Curt Simmons for a $65,000 bonus in 1947 presaged big bonus deals, and Rickey fell in line in 1950 when, as general manager of the Pirates, he signed a southpaw named Paul Pettit for a $100,000 bonus. Pettit won one major league game for Pittsburgh, and Rickey was maligned in the press for the deal.

Ever-increasing bonuses drained the Pirates' organization in the early fifties, and for Rickey to sign Koufax for even the comparably modest sum of $10,000, he acknowledged he would have to get the money "somehow." Before his father could sign, however, Branch Jr. talked him out of it. The memory of Koufax's poor showing in his morning workout at Dyker Field and against the Falcons that same afternoon convinced him that Koufax wasn't ready for the major leagues.

"Don't do it," said Branch Jr., who was mindful of the negative press his father had received for earlier bonus deals gone bad. "He's not ready. I've seen a sandlot team clobber him. All he'll do is take up space and give the papers extra ammunition to throw at you. And then when you need extra money again for some kid who will really be able to help us, you won't be able to get it."

Branch Jr. wasn't impressed with Koufax's showing against the Falcons, but Jimmy Murphy, a reporter for the *Brooklyn Eagle*, was. Murphy had seen Koufax pitch on previous occasions, and was impressed that he would try to pitch despite a painful and bloody blister on his middle finger. Murphy had also been kept informed of Koufax's strikeout totals at the University of Cincinnati by Parkview manager Milt Laurie.

Just as negotiations with the Pirates hit a snag, Murphy ran into Campanis, who was scouting for the Dodgers during a game at Ebbets Field. Campanis called Koufax, whose last name he initially thought was "Kovacs," and arranged to meet him. A tryout was setup at Ebbets

Field. Amid a steady drizzle, Koufax stood on the mound as Campanis, Dodgers' manager Walt Alston, and club vice president Fresco Thompson watched, along with a few fans scattered in the seats.

"Alright," Campanis shouted, "let's see a few fastballs."

For the next 15 minutes, Koufax hurled high heat through the drizzle and into the mitt of second-string catcher Rube Walker. Koufax knew he was throwing well, and felt the grayness from the overcast skies made his pitches seem even faster.

The sight of Koufax's fastballs elicited "ooohs" and "aaahs" from those in attendance, and Campanis followed by calling for some curves. Eager to see how long Koufax could throw before he tired, the Dodgers let the workout run for almost a full hour. When it was over, Campanis approached Walker.

"What do you think?"

"Whatever he wants, give it to him," Walker said. "I wouldn't let him out of the clubhouse."

Campanis filed a scouting report that graded Koufax an A-plus for his fastball and curve, and A-minus on change of pace and control. On a scale of 80, Campanis rated him a 77 for velocity, and a 72 for how sharply his pitches broke. Under the area left for "Remarks," Campanis wrote: "Good poise and actions . . . Lad appears to possess confidence in himself. He has the tools. Whether or not to make him a bonus player is the question."

Upon reading the Campanis report and conferring with Dodger scout Art Dede, team president Walter O'Malley gave Brooklyn general manager Buzzie Bavasi permission to sign Koufax.

"Everyone was high on him," Bavasi remembered. "I hadn't seen him play of course, but his father came in asked for $14,000. So I called Arthur in and said, 'Arthur, Mr. Koufax wants $14,000.'"

"He said, 'If I had it, I'd give it to him.'"

"That was enough for me."

A handshake deal was concluded in July between Bavasi and Irving Koufax. "Five minutes after he left my office," Bavasi said, "a scout for the Pittsburgh Pirates passed him in the hall and said, 'You're just the man I want to see. Mr. Rickey told me to give you more $5,000 more than the Dodgers offered you.'"

"His father said, 'No, I made a deal.' A month later, John Quinn of the Milwaukee club offered him $32,000, and he turned him down."

On December 14, 1954, the Dodgers officially signed Sandy Koufax to a two-year contract at $6,000 for the 1955 season, plus a $14,000 signing bonus. The signing came on the same day the Dodgers sold pitcher Preacher Roe and third baseman Billy Cox to Baltimore, and ran in New York newspapers the next day as a brief under the Roe-Cox story.

Dave Anderson, a Pulitzer prize winning columnist for the *New York Times*, was working for the *Brooklyn Eagle* in 1955 and covered Koufax's signing. "He was a nice kid," Anderson recalled, "but he was just the 25th player on the roster."

Arriving in the Dodgers offices that day, Koufax donned a Brooklyn baseball cap and shirt and smiled for photographers as he posed with Campanis and Thompson. Behind them was a blackboard listing all the Dodgers' minor leaguers.

As photographers snapped away, Koufax thought of the names on the board behind him, players he knew had more baseball experience than he did. How, he thought, could the Dodgers give me all that money? How could a team fighting for a pennant every season clear a roster spot just for someone who hadn't pitched in even 20 games his entire life?

I've fooled them, he thought. All the experts who are supposed to know so much. I've fooled them.

By 1965, when he had matured into baseball's best pitcher, Koufax was no longer fooling anyone, either with his talent or his pitch selection. While most pitchers tried to hide their next pitch by shielding their grip on the ball from the hitters, Koufax tipped his pitches in a number of ways before each delivery. Writer Daniel Okrent noted that Koufax held his elbows out for a curve and his elbows in for a fastball. Ed Bouchee of the Cubs remembered sitting on the bench while the team called every pitch Koufax threw. If Koufax was going to throw a fastball, he would bring his hands way up over his head in his windup. If he brought his hands back behind his head, the next pitch was certain to be a curveball. Film study revealed yet another tip-off. Whenever Koufax bent forward at the waist before his delivery, he invariably followed with a changeup.

Despite tipping his pitches, Koufax continued to overpower baseball's best hitters. Willie Mays said that he knew every pitch Koufax was going to throw, and he still struck out against him. Koufax would let hitters see what pitch he was going to throw, Mays said, and they still couldn't hit him.

The reason Koufax was so successful, Mays thought, was simple. Koufax had a fastball hitters had trouble seeing, and his curve jumped a foot. Ernie Banks of the Cubs said Koufax overpowered hitters with his fastball by throwing it right past them. Ken Boyer, a slugging third baseman for the Cardinals, agreed. No ball, Boyer said, should get to the plate that quickly.

Pirates' great Bill Mazeroski laughed when asked what a hitter's strategy was against Koufax in his prime.

"Just try to hit it," Maz said. "You could look for his fastball and not hit it, and you could look for his curve and not hit it. His fastball went almost straight up. It was very unusual for that to happen. He had to be throwing 96 or above for that to happen."

Surprisingly, Koufax's best fastball was measured at just 93 miles per hour, but those who saw him pitch scoff at that figure. Dodger teammate Ed Roebuck said the method used to time pitchers in the sixties was believed to be one mile off for every ten feet. Since the pitcher's mound is 60 feet, six inches away from home plate, a Koufax fastball clocked at 93 miles an hour was actually traveling between 99 and 100 miles an hour.

It's a figure Koufax's former catcher, Norm Sherry, agreed with. "He could throw the living crap out of the ball," Sherry said. "He threw overhand, and he got way out in front because he really had a long stride. By the time his hand released, he was on top of the ball. He had real long fingers and real strong hands; his fingers could probably hold a baseball like someone would hold a golf ball. His hands were big and his fingers were long, so when he gripped that ball it probably felt small in his hands.

"Now, when you can get the ball to feel small in your hands, you can pull hard on the seams at your release point to make the ball spin and get that velocity. He could do that. He probably ripped those seams. And you could hear the ball coming—'Sssffftt.'

"What we try to say in pitching is 'Make one side longer than the other.' He did, because his stride took him out so far that when he went to throw, the backside had to come way over to the front side. So if you look at his body, one side is longer than the other. This gives you torque and strength to throw the ball hard, besides having the strength in his hands and fingers to rip those seams off. He had a unique delivery, because not everyone can do that."

Gripping the ball across the seams with his long fingers and relying on his broad shoulder and back muscles, Koufax threw a four-seam fastball with such force and backspin that it was able to overcome nature's gravitational pull downward. The rise on his fastball was steady, but to hitters it appeared sudden because the human eye is unable to focus quickly enough on objects moving that fast. Hitters still speak with awe of the last-second "hop" of Koufax's fastball as it rocketed through the strike zone. Some hitters have estimated the ball jumping as much as six to eight inches as it crossed home plate. Pete Rose, whose career spanned three decades, called Koufax the hardest thrower he ever faced.

Yet as overpowering as Koufax's fastball was at times, the challenge of consistently throwing it past Minnesota's heavy hitters going into the fourth inning of Game Seven was daunting. Leadoff man Zoilo Versalles led the American League by rapping 45 doubles and 12 triples and was named league MVP; Tony Oliva was the American League batting champion, and the Twins' offense featured six hitters with 16 or more home runs and a team batting average of .254 that was the highest in the league. Harmon Killebrew led the majors in home runs during the sixties, and ranks second behind only Babe Ruth among American League home run hitters.

The Twins literally attacked the ball, and their aggressiveness at the plate stemmed in part from fiery third-base coach Billy Martin. The former second baseman of the New York Yankees' dynasty that dominated baseball in the early fifties, Martin had been a fierce competitor on the field, and he carried with him a combative air, on the field and off.

"I don't throw the first punch," he once said, "I throw the second four." Martin inherited his fighting nature from his mother, Joan, who told her kids, 'Don't take nothin' from nobody. If you can't hit 'em, bite 'em.'"

Chicago sportswriter John Schulian said Martin was "a mouse studying to be a rat," and former Cleveland Indians' general manager Frank Lane referred to Billy as "the little bastard." Said Lane, "He's the kind of guy you'd like to kill if he's playing for the other team, but you'd like ten of him on your side."

The Twins were glad to have Billy the Kid on their side in '65. He joined the team at the start of the season, and told the players in spring training he was going to make them more aggressive base runners. Martin said he would get the Twins' players thrown out at home deliberately just so they would be more daring. Though some in the organization disliked Martin's methods, Minnesota manager Sam Mele appreciated his ability to teach and allowed him to coach third the way Martin felt was right. By season's end, the Twins listed seven regulars who drove in 60 or more runs, and Martin said later that Minnesota won the pennant that season because they had learned to play aggressive baseball.

Martin coached third aggressively during Game Seven, and his loud dispute with home plate umpire Ed Hurley concerning Koufax's move to first base in the bottom of the third inning exemplified Billy the Kid's combative style and fired up the Minnesota dugout.

The Twins came out swinging in the bottom of the fourth inning. The Dodgers had scored in the top half of the inning when Lou Johnson hooked a leadoff homer off the left-field foul pole. Ron Fairly followed by driving Jim Kaat's next pitch the opposite way into the right-field corner, and took second when the ball skipped away from Oliva. With the Twins' infield drawn in to cut down the lead runner and prevent another runner, Wes Parker ruined the strategy by punching a hopping grounder over the head of drawn-in first baseman Don Mincher, scoring Fairly for a 2–0 L.A. lead.

The Dodger uprising forced Kaat from the game, and reliever Al Worthington came on to retire the side.

"I was trying so hard that game to not give up the first run," Kaat recalled. "Johnson hit a pretty good pitch. The ball was actually out away from him and he hooked it down the line and hit it off the foul pole. That was such a crushing blow, even though it was only the fourth inning, because being down one run to Koufax was like being down five to any other pitcher. Looking at Koufax, it was almost a helpless feeling. You knew that unless he was wild, you weren't going to hit the ball very hard."

With their southpaw ace out of the game, Minnesota's big hitters looked to even matters against Koufax in the bottom of the fourth. Killebrew led off, and took ball one outside. Throughout his career, the Killer averaged a home run every 14.22 at-bats, a ratio ranking him third all-time behind Babe Ruth and Ralph Kiner.

A power hitter whose power ran in awesome streaks, Killebrew outslugged Detroit's Norm Cash for the 1962 home run title 48–39 by going deep 11 times in his last 11 games of the regular season. The following season, the Killer missed 20 games with a twisted knee, then blasted seven homers in his last six games to overtake Boston's Dick Stuart in the home run race, 45–42. When the Senators named him their everyday third baseman in 1959, Killebrew responded to the starting assignment with five two-homer games in a two-week streak from May 1 through May 17. He tied Cleveland's Rocky Colavito for the American League lead with 42 homers, and from 1962 through '64, led the league with respective home run totals of 48, 45, and 49.

Killebrew missed 48 games of the '65 season with a dislocated elbow, but he still managed a team-high 25 homers and a .501 slugging percentage. The Killer owned a short, violent swing, and he fouled Koufax's next delivery back into the press row. Killebrew said that it took him five years to catch up with major league pitching, and he struggled to catch up with Koufax's next delivery, a fastball that he almost went to his knees trying to hit.

Killebrew knew that Koufax was relying heavily on his heater, almost to the point of ignoring his breaking stuff.

"He threw mostly fastballs in that game," Killebrew remembered, "which was pretty unique and unusual because he had a great, great curveball. You still knew that he had that great curveball and there was a possibility he might throw it."

Down in the count 1–2, Killebrew took a breaking ball low to even the count at 2–2. Twins fans accustomed to seeing the Killer's high, majestic homers hoped he could time one of Koufax's fastballs and drive it deep. But Killebrew swung late on a low hummer and tapped a grounder back to the mound. Fielding the ball cleanly, Koufax flipped to Wes Parker at first base for the out.

Earl Battey followed, and after taking a fastball outside for a ball, fell behind in the count when he swung at and missed another fastball away and then fouled a belt-high heater back to the screen behind home plate.

Battey struggled against Koufax throughout the Series, striking out six times and managing just one hit, a pulled single to left. Down in the count 1–2 and facing his second strikeout against Koufax in the game and seventh in three games, Battey caught hold of another belt-high fastball and drove it to right-center field, where Willie Davis gloved it for the second out of the inning.

Having retired Killebrew and Battey on a handful of pitches, Koufax now faced Bob Allison. A strikeout victim at the start of the Twins' half of the second inning, Allison struggled to find his stroke. Having produced 23 homers and 78 RBI during the season, he had reached Dodger pitching for just two hits—a homer and a double—and two RBI, and was hitting .125.

Koufax continued Allison's frustrations, inducing him to swing at a first-pitch breaking ball; the Twins' outfielder pulled it down the third-base line. Junior Gilliam gloved the hard-hit grounder behind third base and quickly fired to Parker to retire the side.

In the Minnesota dugout, Twins' players were awed by Koufax's machine-like efficiency in the fourth. Killebrew looked up at the scoreboard and saw the Dodgers with two runs in their half of the fourth. Those runs were huge, he said, because with Koufax, sometimes all he needed was one run.

"Hitters never want to give you any kind of indication that you don't have a chance," Kaat said. "But you could almost see the mood in the dugout as he mowed down one after the other, you almost felt sorry for the hitters that had to go up there."

Koufax had retired the side on just 10 pitches to preserve L.A.'s 2–0 lead. In the packed press box, one writer looked at the scoreboard beyond the center-field wall, saw the two runs in the Dodgers' half of the fourth, and said, "That's enough."

Paul Zimmerman of the *L.A. Times* wasn't so sure. It isn't often, Zimmerman would write later, that a man can win the deciding game of the World Series with a fastball alone. Nor was it often that a man could go all the way on one pitch, as Koufax was trying to do.

Walking off the mound, Koufax felt the same way. His arthritic elbow was sore, and he had little control of his curveball or changeup. Heading back to the dugout, the best pitcher in baseball didn't know how long he was going to last in this Game Seven.

SIX

Minnesota Twins' manager Sam Mele watched Sandy Koufax work through the first four innings of Game Seven, and recalled an earlier meeting with the best pitcher in baseball.

In 1955, Mele was a 32-year-old member of the Cincinnati Reds, an outfielder in his next-to-last season as an active player. Sitting in the Reds' dugout prior to a game with the Brooklyn Dodgers, Mele watched Koufax, just 19 years of age, warm up for his second game as a starter in the majors.

"He's fast," Mele thought. Still, the Reds were a fastball-hitting team. Their lineup featured sluggers Ted Kluszewski, Gus Bell, Wally Post, and Smoky Burgess and accounted for 181 home runs and a combined .425 slugging average. Next to the Dodgers, the Reds boasted the best offensive team in the senior circuit.

Working with pinpoint control that allowed him to spot his blazing fastball and big-breaking curve, the kid southpaw baffled the Reds with a two-hit, 14-strikeout masterpiece. It was the first start in 50 days for Koufax, whose initial major league start had come against Pittsburgh. He worked 4⅔ innings in his debut, allowing three hits, striking out four, and walking eight.

Despite the long layoff between starts, Koufax was so command-
ing against the Reds that the only outfield hit he allowed was a two-out
double in the ninth to left—a ball hit, incidentally, by Mele.

Accolades rang down on the young lefty, but when he followed by
getting bombed four days later in one inning of relief work against Milwaukee, it marked a pattern of highs and lows that frustrated Koufax's
early years with the Dodgers and threatened his future in the game. He
had signed with Brooklyn in '55, and because he was a bonus player, the
Dodgers had to keep him on their roster for a year or risk losing him to
another team in the annual player draft.

The year before, the Dodgers lost a talented 20-year-old outfielder
to the Pittsburgh Pirates when they tried to hide him on the roster of
their Montreal farm team. The Dodgers had signed him to a $10,000
bonus, but because Brooklyn in the mid-fifties was talent-rich in
outfielders—with Duke Snider, Carl Furillo, and Sandy Amoros—they
sent the young prospect down to the minors for more seasoning. They
tried to hide the right-handed hitter by not batting him against left-
handed pitchers, a move they hoped would prevent him from fattening
his batting average. The Dodgers even benched the kid once after he
had lined three triples in a game.

The Pirates, however, discovered the Dodgers' hidden gem, and
picked him in the player draft. His name was Roberto Clemente.

Rather than risk losing another bonus baby, the Dodgers kept
Koufax with the big club. To make room for him on the roster, they de-
moted another young lefty, Tom Lasorda, to the minors. Lasorda was
livid. "That kid can't win up here," he said of Koufax.

Lasorda jokingly takes credit for Koufax's rise to stardom. "If it
hadn't been for me (being sent down)," he said, "there'd have been no
Koufax."

The '55 Dodgers were a devastating team. They opened the season
with 10 straight wins and victories in 22 of their first 24 games. By July
4, the traditional midpoint of the major league season, Brooklyn led
the National League by 12½ games.

The Dodgers' dominance that season both helped and hurt Koufax.
Because they were so far ahead in the pennant race, the Dodgers
could afford to spot-pitch the young Koufax. Still, Koufax's mound

experience was extremely limited—he had pitched in fewer than 20 games before signing with Brooklyn—and the time he could have spent honing his craft in the minors was lost to him.

"He had great stuff, and you could see he had great potential," recalled Ed Roebuck, a teammate of Koufax's on the '55 Dodgers. "But he couldn't throw strikes because he didn't have experience at the big league level. Because of the bonus rule he couldn't be sent down. So it was a very bad situation for him because he should have been in the minor leagues developing rather than sitting around on that level.

"But he took it very well, and he ended up working himself into the big league rotation. Which is a very tough thing to do, really."

Nor was there any resentment among the club's veterans about this kid pitcher taking a spot on the roster and languishing on the bench. "I think most of the people accepted him," Roebuck said. "He was friendly with Furillo. He and Furillo used to go out and eat together on the road. He had no problems making friends, because there were some young kids on the team too. Myself, Roger Craig, we were sort of in his age group."

As was Don Drysdale, who joined the club a year later. They differed in many ways—Drysdale was from Van Nuys, California; Koufax from Brooklyn, New York. Drysdale was outgoing; Koufax was reserved. Though the public perceived Koufax as a quiet, introverted guy, Drysdale saw a different side to him.

In his book, *Once a Bum, Always a Dodger*, written with Bob Verdi, Drysdale remarked how Koufax never relaxed around the media or a lot of people. But get him away from the crowd or off for a beer, Drysdale said, and Koufax was a funny guy who told great jokes in his distinctive Jewish accent. Drysdale and Koufax spent the winter of '57 in the Army Reserves in Fort Dix, New Jersey. Being from the West Coast, Drysdale had little experience with snow and ice, and Koufax actually had to teach him how to negotiate walking on snow and ice without falling. Drysdale spent a lot of time with Koufax that winter, accepting invitations to his family's house for dinners. When the club moved to Los Angeles, Drysdale returned the favor by inviting Koufax, who was still a bachelor, to his family's home for the holidays.

Appearing in 12 games with the Dodgers in '55, Koufax posted a 2–2 record with a respectable 3.00 earned run average. He started five games and completed two, both shutouts. He struck out 30 in 42 innings, but also surrendered 28 walks and 33 hits—not a useful ratio. He was a thrower who hadn't yet learned how to pitch, and he had difficulty gaining command of his humming fastball and sweeping curve.

"At that time, he was just wild," remembered Dave Anderson, who covered the Dodgers. "He could throw the ball through the brick, but he couldn't find the brick. He just had no control."

To help their pitchers find their control, the Dodgers had a device known as the "pitching strings." It was a setup handed down by Branch Rickey. The strings were slipknots adjusted to the approximate width of home plate—17 inches—and the idea was for pitchers to work on throwing to spots by widening or narrowing the strings on the inside or outside part of the plate, and up and down in the strike zone.

"The strings were a very consistent pitching aid in spring training," recalled Carl Erskine, a member of the Dodgers' staff from 1948 to 1960. "They were a Dodger innovation and they still use them. If a pitcher's having control trouble, then that was one of the places to spend some time. I work with Little Leaguers today, and if a dad says, 'My son needs a little control,' I'll say, 'Well here, put these (strings) in your back yard and work with them.' It's a real good visual outline of the plate."

Rickey devised another pitching aid consisting of a large, black tarpaulin with holes cut in it an inch or two above an outline of home plate and an inch or two below it. The device allowed pitchers to work on their control for as long as they wanted, without need of a catcher. Pitchers like Koufax and Drysdale threw at the tarp, then collected the balls at the back of the tarp and resumed throwing.

Despite working for hours on improving his control, Koufax still struggled to gain command of his pitches. Jack Lang, who covered the Dodgers for the *Long Island Press*, recalled Koufax's early problems with control.

"When he first came up," Lang said, "he was as wild as can be. And everyone knew he was wild. But he had a great fastball."

Lang remembered covering the Dodgers in spring training in 1956. The first pitch Sandy threw in warmups that day, Lang said, sailed over the backstop and clattered on the roof of the press box, startling an old writer who had been snoozing in his seat.

"As far as his throwing, he was kind of an unpolished kid," Carl Erskine recalled. "What I observed of Sandy was that he was a great talent. He had a good, live fastball and a hard curveball, but he was totally inexperienced. And Sandy was a very sensitive young man. He had to stay on the roster because of the bonus rule. They paid him $20,000 and that excluded him from going to the minors.

"He came out of the sandlots without very much experience and with a lot of raw talent. He was very sensitive about that, and knowing Sandy in the years after that, it bothered him a lot that he was staying on the roster. The Dodgers had close to 800 players under contract in those days because of their farm system, and he was aware that some kid was down there trying to make it and he had never spent one day in the minors. And I think that was a psychological load for Sandy. Secondly, he felt very unsure of himself because he didn't know the refinements of pitching, like holding men on base and all of those things."

In a clubhouse filled with famous personalities, the subdued, 19-year-old Koufax went almost unnoticed by writers covering the team.

"He smiled and said hello, but there was no reason to talk to him," Anderson said. "He never pitched. He was just there. He may as well have been a batboy in a way. He was just on the team; they didn't use him."

Dodger manager Walt Alston used Koufax at times to pitch batting practice. The club's veterans, however, soon grew wary of his wild deliveries. "Taking batting practice against him," one Dodger said, "is like playing Russian roulette with five bullets. You don't give yourself much of a chance."

Snider said Koufax's pitches were all over the batting cage. To the Duke of Flatbush, the Jewish kid from Brooklyn was just another wild, hard-throwing left-hander, albeit one who already had lots of local fans because of his ethnic background.

When the Philadelphia Phillies traveled to Ebbets Field for a series against the Dodgers, Robin Roberts, the Phils' ace right-hander and future Hall of Famer, took the field early to watch the hitters take batting practice. On the mound, Roberts saw a southpaw who could obviously throw very hard, but was also very erratic. Some of his deliveries missed not only home plate, but the batting cage surrounding it.

Standing next to Furillo, Roberts asked, "Carl, who's that?"

"Some Jew kid," said Furillo, "who'll never learn to pitch as long as he has a hole in his ass."

Learning to pitch was something Koufax knew he had to do. He learned the mechanics of his craft from Joe Becker, a tough ex-catcher who became the Dodgers' pitching coach the same day Koufax joined the club in the spring of '55. Becker worked on eliminating Koufax's exaggerated windup before the pitch, and explained to the young lefty that he was leaning back too far, which made it more difficult to keep the ball low.

The act of pitching, Koufax learned, is a mechanical exercise involving the same movements over and over. If the mechanics are correct, pictures taken at every step of a pitcher's delivery should look the same, right down to the wrinkles in his uniform. If the delivery is the same, then the flight of the ball will follow the same path.

In time, Koufax learned to adjust the flight of his pitches subtly; if he stepped an inch or two to his left in his stride, the ball moved four to five inches to the left at the plate. He learned also to follow through completely in the act of pitching, just as he had followed through on his jump shot while playing basketball.

These were things Koufax could have had more time to work out had he been down in the minors; but as Roebuck said, he didn't have that luxury because of his bonus status.

Said Roebuck, "I think his not going to the minor leagues is really a credit to him that he did make it without playing somewhere where he could take a deep breath and relax instead of facing major league hitters every time."

To Roebuck, Koufax's well-documented wildness can also be attributed to his inconsistent starts.

"It's tough enough to be in the regular rotation when you're young like that," he said. "If you took a veteran and said, 'Okay, we're going to start you twice a month,' a veteran would be wild. Walt Alston knew he had to keep him, and we had a pretty good rotation and a real good ballclub and it was just a tough situation for Sandy."

Erskine agreed, saying that Koufax's sub-.500 record in his early years was due to his having to learn on the job. "There are a variety of skills and techniques that have to be honed to be at the major league level," he said, "and Sandy didn't have that advantage. He was still trying to learn how to pitch."

Before the Dodgers broke camp in Vero Beach in '55, they played an exhibition game against the Dodgertown All-Stars, a collection of the organization's best minor leaguers. Given the start for the big club, Koufax struck out five and walked one in three innings of work. He left the game feeling he had done well, and was confident he had shown the team something, which is what he had hoped to do in his first spring training. Looking around the clubhouse, however, and seeing pitchers like Erskine, Don Newcombe, Johnny Podres, Clem Labine, Joe Black, and Billy Loes, Koufax also knew he wasn't going to see much action during the regular season.

Opening week convinced him further. The Dodgers started six different pitchers—Erskine, Newcombe, Loes, Russ Meyer, Podres, and Labine—and only Newcombe had been hit hard. Watching from the bench, Koufax felt he was part of a team that was extraordinary in every way. These were the Dodgers, "Dem Bums" as cartoonist Willard Mullin called them, and the names are legendary—Roy Campanella at catcher, an air-tight infield of Gil Hodges, Junior Gilliam, Pee Wee Reese, and Jackie Robinson, and an outfield of Sandy Amoros, Snider, and Furillo.

Koufax saw that this team could not only hit the ball out of the park, they were slick fielders as well. The Dodgers, he thought, were a confident team; not cocky, but absolutely sure of themselves. Because they had been so successful in recent years—winning pennants in '49, '52, and '53, and finishing second by two games in '50 and one in '51—a calmness filled the clubhouse. There was neither great excitement over winning nor extreme gloom after losing. They expected to win every day; when they lost, they expected to win the next day.

The Bums were a close team, due in part to their having played together for so long. Reese was in his 16th big league season in '55, Furillo his 10th. Snider and Robinson, both graying eagles, were in their ninth seasons, as was Hodges. Campy was in his eighth season; Erskine his seventh.

Walking into the Ebbets Field clubhouse in '55, Koufax felt more like an observer than part of the team. Unlike the custom at other big league clubs, the Dodgers' dressing room was not arranged numerically, nor did it have any sense of order. Close friends like Snider and Erskine occupied opposite sides of the room, completely out of sight of one another because of a large pillar in the middle of the floor. The room was so cramped and crowded that Campanella's locker sat in front of a pillar across from Erskine.

The Dodgers' old breed set the tone for the locker room; but Koufax, whose locker was across from Campy's, felt that Charlie DiGiovanna supplied the spirit. Regarded at the time as "the world's oldest batboy," the 23-year-old DiGiovanna was dubbed "The Brow" because of his bushy eyebrows. Because he was ambidextrous, he became highly proficient at signing the player's names to the boxes of baseballs in the clubhouse every day. Koufax watched with amazement as Charlie the Brow stood and talked with a guest, all the while rolling a baseball in his hands and shifting the pen from his right hand to his left as he forged the name of every player on the team. Snider thought that the Brow could autograph better than the players themselves.

If Charlie the Brow added spirit to the Bums, then John Griffin added flavor. Nicknamed "The Senator" because his paunch and cigar lent him the look of a politico, Griffin had already been with the Dodgers some 40 years as an equipment man when Koufax joined the team. The Senator scared Koufax half to death early in the season. Emerging from the showers, Koufax asked Griffin if there was an extra towel somewhere. The Senator responded with a sharp "No!" But Koufax learned Griffin was gruff rather than mean. Returning to his locker, Koufax found a fresh towel hanging there.

The Senator kept the clubhouse loose with his behavior and his banter. He dressed in outrageous outfits—everything from coonskin hats to cowboy clothes—and was quick on the trigger with his comments. After getting knocked out of the box early in '55, Koufax stormed into the clubhouse and hurled his glove against the wall.

"If you threw that hard out there," the Senator said calmly, "you'd probably still be there."

Along with Charlie the Brow and the Senator, the Dodgers gained additional flavor from their fans, resident characters who regularly showed up at Ebbets Field to cheer for "Dem Bums."

There was Hilda Chester, a leather-throated fan who upon taking her seat at Ebbets Field would bellow "Hilda's here!" and ring her cowbell. Dodger pitcher Ralph Branca said that while fans at Ebbets might have trouble hearing the PA system, they never had trouble hearing Hilda. Eddie Batan blew a tin whistle, and Jack Pierce had balloons bearing the name of his favorite player, Cookie Lavagetto. A TV show for kids, "Happy Felton's Knothole Gang," was broadcast live from the bullpen before each home game, and Tex Rickart, the team's PA announcer, sat in a chair near the Dodger dugout on the first-base side and announced, "Will the fans in the first row along the railing please remove their clothes?"

The Dodgers' band, the "Sym-Phony," played Dixieland music and teased umpires and opposing teams. Major league games in the fifties were played with three umpires, and when a call went against the beloved Bums, the Sym-Phony struck up the tune "Three Blind Mice." When an opposing player made an out, the band played "The Worms Crawl In, the Worms Crawl Out."

Dodger fans lent color to old Ebbets Field, which sat in the heart of Flatbush. With just 32,000 seats, Ebbets Field was the smallest park in either league. Attendance at times swelled to 33,000 as fans paid to stand in the aisles. In a 1947 game against the rival New York Giants, a crowd of 37,512 fans jammed the ballpark.

Like most other ballparks of the time, the outfield walls in Ebbets Field were covered with advertisements promoting local and national businesses—the Brass Rail Restaurant, Gem Razor Blades, Griffin Microsheen Shoe Polish, Van Heusen Shirts, and the ad that stands out in memory—Abe Stark's sign advertising his clothing store. Located in right field at the base of the fence beneath the scoreboard, Stark's ad had a target on it—"Hit Sign Win Suit"—promising a free suit to any slugger who could hit the sign on a fly. Few did, and through the years Stark only lost an estimated five suits. A grateful Stark once gave Furillo a free suit for protecting the sign so well. Stark received so much recognition from his outfield sign that he was eventually elected Borough President of Brooklyn.

Ebbets Field offered an intimate, picturesque setting. Snider thought the field was greener than the grass in the Emerald Isle, and considered the dirt runway leading from the dugout to the field a magic carpet. Like many stadiums of its era, Ebbets Field had been built in the confines of its surrounding neighborhood. Outfield dimensions ran 297 feet down the right-field foul line, a short poke for a left-handed pull hitter except that the wall was 40 feet high. The left-field dimensions were 343 feet down the line, bordered by a nine-foot wall. Dead center field was 393 feet from home plate.

Dodger fans who couldn't make it to games listened to the radio broadcasts of Red Barber. Barber's colorful style, in which he declared the Bums "sittin' in the catbird seat!" when the team won, and "Ohhh, doctor!" when they lost—made him a Brooklyn institution.

But the biggest institution was the Bums themselves: Pee Wee, Campy, the Duke, Oisk, Skoonj, Big Newk, Preacher, and the Reading Rifle. They were Roger Kahn's "Boys of Summer," a collection of athletes who captured the hearts of fans from Coney Island and Canarsie to Flatbush and Red Hook. If the Yankees represented Wall Street with their moneyed wealth, pinstripes, and corporate image, the Dodgers represented Brooklyn neighborhoods where everyone knew everyone else.

Snider compared playing for the Dodgers in the fifties to playing for small towns in the thirties. The Duke was friends not only with players on the team, but people on his block, the people who ran corner candy stores and neighborhood businesses. The same was true of Elmer Valo, an outfielder who was traded to Brooklyn in '57 and moved into the borough a few days before his first game. Walking down the street on his way to the supermarket, Valo was stopped by two guys.

"Hey, you're Elmer Valo. Welcome to Brooklyn!"

The fans recognized Valo from his picture in the paper, and were thrilled he was playing for their team.

The fifties Dodgers were a star-studded team, but also star-crossed. They lost World Series titles to the Yankees in '47, '49, '52, and '53, and were defeated by Bobby Thomson and the Giants in the famous one-game playoff in '51.

Brooklyn finally broke through in '55, winning the National League pennant by 13½ games over Milwaukee. Injuries prevented Koufax from contributing much in the early going. He twisted his left ankle when he stepped on a sprinkler head while running in the outfield and missed 30 days. When he returned on June 8, the Dodgers made roster room for him by sending down Lasorda.

The next day, the Dodgers, who had been carrying ten pitchers and four outfielders, traded Black to Cincinnati for outfielder Bob Borkowski.

As the ninth pitcher on a nine-man staff, Koufax didn't see much action outside the bullpen. When Dodger pitchers began experiencing arm problems in June, however, Koufax finally got the call. During a Friday night game in Milwaukee on June 24, Erskine's elbow began tightening up on him. Alston had Koufax start warming up in the pen, throwing pitches to Rube Walker. Alston had previously used Koufax as a decoy to discourage rival managers from sending up left-handed pinch hitters.

Labine was also loosening up in the pen, throwing to Dixie Howell. When the bullpen phone rang in the bottom of the fifth inning, Joe Becker picked it up, listened for a moment, and then hung up.

"It's Koufax," Becker shouted. "Go get 'em, Sandy."

It was game number 66 of the Dodgers' '55 season, and Koufax was making his major league debut. Walking to the mound with the Braves leading 7–1 and a near-capacity crowd of 43,068 in Milwaukee's County Stadium, the 19-year-old Koufax felt both overjoyed and astonished that he was finally getting into a major league game.

As he made the long walk from the pen in right field to the mound, Koufax suddenly realized he was walking into a wall of sound. County Stadium had few bleachers behind the outfield wall, but it presented a double-decked grandstand behind home plate. As Koufax strode closer to the infield, the grandstand seemed to rise up in front of him, becoming higher and steeper; and the crowd noise grew louder and louder.

Standing on the mound, the young pitcher listened as the PA announcer introduced him as "Koo-fax," and he heard voices in the stands saying, "Who?"

The first batter Koufax faced was Johnny Logan, and his first major league pitch was a called strike. He followed by missing on his next two deliveries, then watched as Logan blooped a hit off the end of his bat, a seeing-eye single that dropped behind first base for a hit.

Eddie Mathews batted next, and Koufax issued another first-pitch strike. Mathews dipped his bat at the next offering, and the ball rolled right back to the mound. It should have been an easy double play, but despite having plenty of time to fire to Reese covering second, Koufax threw the ball wildly into center field.

With men on first and second, Hank Aaron stepped to the plate. In the first meeting of the two future Hall of Famers, Koufax walked the Hammer on four pitches. The bases were loaded, and he still hadn't retired a batter. He walked Aaron after missing with two curveballs, and now that he was in trouble, he decided to go after Bobby Thomson with fastballs. Rearing back and throwing heat, Koufax missed with his first two pitches. Throwing harder, he followed with a strike, a ball, and another strike to run the count full. Staying with the fastball on his 3–2 delivery, Koufax struck Thomson out swinging, his first big league strikeout.

Joe Adcock followed, and he fouled back Koufax's pitch, then took the next two for balls. With the count 2–1, Koufax got Adcock to ground to Reese at short, and the Dodger captain turned the inning-ending double play.

Koufax had survived his first major league jam without yielding a run. In the next inning he retired the bottom of the Braves' order without incident, getting Lew Burdette to end the inning on a called third strike.

His second big league appearance came five days later when he worked the final inning of a game in which the Dodgers trailed the Giants, 6–0. Circumstances were similar to his initial outing against Milwaukee—Alvin Dark greeted Koufax with a single, and Whitey Lockman reached base on a bunt. Willie Mays followed, and in the first meeting between the two, Koufax fell behind 3–0, got a strike over, but then walked Mays. For the second straight game, he faced a bases-loaded no-out situation, and for the second straight game he got out of it. This time it took just five pitches. Don Mueller flied to left, Henry Thompson fouled out to Robinson, and Gail Harris grounded to Reese.

Koufax's success in getting himself out of trouble earned him his first career start a week later in Pittsburgh, against the same Pirates team that had wanted to sign him a year earlier. Falling into a familiar pattern, Koufax quickly got into difficulty by walking three of the first four hitters he faced, then wriggled free. The pattern continued as he issued six bases on balls but still owned a one-hit shutout through four innings.

He surrendered his first run in the fifth inning after giving up a pair of walks and two singles. When Koufax delivered a first-pitch ball to the next hitter, Gene Freese, Alston removed him in favor of reliever Ed Roebuck. In his first start, Koufax's totals showed 105 pitches, with a ball-strike ratio of 52–53. He had faced 26 hitters, going to a 3–2 count on nine of them and 3–1 on two others.

One week after his start against the Pirates, Koufax dropped further in the rotation when the Dodgers called up pitchers Roger Craig and Don Bessent. Seventeen days passed before he got in a game again, working the final two innings in a losing game against Milwaukee. He pitched the final inning in another mop-up performance the next day, then rode the bench for more than a month.

Koufax didn't see game action again until mid-August, when he pitched the final inning of an 8–3 loss to the Reds. He retired the side in order and impressed Alston by striking out the first two hitters on six pitches. The Dodger skipper decided to start Koufax against the Reds the following Saturday. But although his manager had confidence in him, some of his coaches didn't.

As he dressed to start the game, Koufax saw first-base coach Jake Pitler head into Alston's office and overheard the following conversation.

"Well, Skip, who's going to pitch today?"

"Koufax."

"Oh, no."

The Dodgers led the pennant race by 10 games, but with Brooklyn's pitching staff nursing an assortment of sore arms, awful memories of the club's collapse in '51, when they blew a 13½-game lead, remained fresh in the minds of many. Koufax remembered too, so he knew he was pitching a game of some importance.

He started leadoff man Johnny Temple with a ball and a strike, then retired him on a fly out to center field. Smoky Burgess struck out looking, and after Ted Kluszewski punched a first-pitch single, Koufax ended the inning by getting Wally Post to fly out to right.

Koufax's control in the opening inning had been near perfect, and he had thrown just 11 pitches. In the second, he caught Bell looking at a called third strike and retired Rocky Bridges swinging. In the third he whiffed both Roy McMillan and Art Fowler on called third strikes, and ended the fourth by fanning Bell with a 1–2 curve ball. Koufax struck out Mele and McMillan in the fifth to run his strikeout count to eight.

Leading 5–0, he started the sixth by retiring pinch hitter Milt Smith on a called third strike. At that point, however, his control started to desert him; and he was forced to challenge the Reds' sluggers with his fastball. In the seventh, he got Bell looking at a pitch that just nipped the corner of the plate, and ended the inning by striking out pinch hitter Chuck Harmon.

Koufax knew he had no right to expect to pitch nine strong innings after a 50-day layoff, but he was working on sheer adrenaline and excitement. He could actually feel himself getting stronger as the game moved into the late innings.

In the eighth, a tiring Koufax got Temple to fly out on the first pitch, then reared back and struck out Burgess and Kluszewski. Taking the mound for the ninth, Koufax was working on a one-hit, 13-strikeout shutout. He started the final frame by retiring Post on a grounder to third, then struck out Bell for the fourth time and his 14th whiff.

Mele followed with a double into the left-field corner—the Reds' second hit of the game—but Koufax concluded his gem by retiring Bridges on a pop-up to Reese.

He survived against the Reds by relying entirely on his fastball after his curve deserted him in the middle innings. Ten years later, he faced the same daunting task of trying to ride one pitch, his heater, to victory against a team of talented sluggers. The irony could not have been lost on Mele.

Just as the sixth inning had been critical in Koufax's win over Cincinnati, the fifth proved his biggest test in the first half of Game Seven against Minnesota.

Koufax had almost been staked to a larger lead in the top half of the inning. Lou Johnson, whose home run in the fourth was his eighth hit of the series, ripped an Al Worthington delivery deep to right field. Getting a great jump on the ball, Tony Oliva ran it down in the gap in right-center with a tremendous backhanded stab.

Ray Scott, the voice of the Twins, was broadcasting the first half of Game Seven on NBC-TV, and he called the play in his trademark clipped tones:

> Into right-center . . . Oliva . . . and at the end of four-and-a-half innings, the score is the Dodgers two and the Twins nothing.

In the bottom of the fifth, Scott turned the play-by-play announcing over to the voice of the Dodgers, Vin Scully. For fans of classic sports broadcasting, the Scully-Scott pairing, rare as it was, represents nostalgia at its best.

Scully wasted little time getting into Koufax's pitching pattern in Game Seven:

> Koufax through four innings, does not have much of a curveball. He's been doing it with fastballs . . . I think he has thrown one good curve for a strike. He threw it to Tony Oliva. Otherwise, fastball, fastball, fastball. He had one changeup to Bob Allison in the fourth inning, and Allison almost took the hands off Gilliam.

Don Mincher led off the Twins' half of the inning, and Koufax retired him on a first-pitch pop fly to Junior Gilliam at third base.

Frank Quilici followed, and Koufax started him off with a fastball low for strike one. He came back with a fastball high and inside that backed Quilici away, then a fastball low and away. Koufax fired another fastball out over the plate, and Quilici jumped on it, driving it to the base of the left-center-field wall for a double.

Watching Quilici dig for two, *Los Angeles Times* writer Paul Zimmerman thought the ball roped by the Twins' infielder had been a bullet. Since few hitters could get around on Koufax's fastball when he was on his game, a double by the light-hitting Quilici stirred doubts among the Dodgers, and Don Drysdale was up and throwing in the L.A. bullpen.

With a man on second, pinch hitter Rich Rollins, batting for Worthington, represented the potential for a game-tying run. The 27-year-old right-hander was a fidgety hitter, constantly moving in the batter's box, constantly swinging his bat between pitches. A fastball hitter,

Rollins was 0-for-2 in his previous pinch-hit appearances in the Series. He quickly got ahead in the count when Koufax started him off with a fastball outside. Koufax came back with the same pitch in almost the same location to fall behind in the count 2–0. He got a fastball over for strike one, and worked the count even at 2–2 when Rollins fouled the next fastball back.

Koufax followed with his first breaking pitch of the inning, a big curve on the outside part of the plate. He thought he had the strikeout, but home-plate umpire Ed Hurley ruled it a ball. Koufax stared in disbelief and shook his head from side to side as he took a short walk around the mound.

"It was close," Hurley hollered.

Koufax didn't respond, but later he recalled thinking, "At this time of year, I might want a close pitch."

Scully: "Curveball, and he missed with it, and he wanted it. That's the first curve he's thrown in quite some time, and oh, did he want it."

Still visibly upset as he stared in for the 3–2 sign, Koufax backed off the pitching rubber at the top of the mound, grabbed the rosin bag, and slammed it to the dirt. The crowd of 50,596, the largest of the Series, roared as Koufax struggled to gain composure. He seemed dangerously close to falling into his old habit of losing focus and overthrowing the ball in anger.

As Koufax backed off the mound to collect himself, Joe Garagiola, who had replaced By Saam on NBC Radio for the middle innings, told his audience, "This is a big pitch for Sandy Koufax and a big time at-bat for Rollins."

With the crowd roaring, a still-angry Koufax stared in for the sign, then delivered a rising fastball that sailed out of the strike zone. The pitch served three purposes—it sent Rollins to first with a walk; it brought the go-ahead run to the plate in the person of Zoilo Versalles; and it brought Alston striding out of the dugout.

Scully: "Koufax is struggling. It's almost impossible to do it on one pitch in the big leagues, and he does not have a curveball . . . And Walter Alston is going out."

Garagiola thought the Dodgers might be ready to bring in Drysdale to face the right-hand-hitting Versalles: "This could be all for

Sandy Koufax. Don Drysdale has been throwing very hard. There's a meeting at the summit—Alston, Gilliam, Roseboro, and Koufax. Drysdale continues to throw . . ."

Alston reminded Koufax not to try too hard. Seeing that Koufax was worried he was losing his rhythm, the Dodger skipper told him not to try to get anything extra on the ball.

"Just pitch to the spots," Alston said.

With Versalles up, Koufax heard Roseboro shouting above the crowd noise. Twins fans were up and standing; and since he was unable to hear above the din, Koufax headed back towards home to confer with Roseboro.

After Quilici's double, the Dodgers had changed their hand signs from the standard one finger for a fastball, two for a curve. The change to a more complex series was automatic for the Dodgers whenever a runner reached second, since he would be able to see the hand signs Roseboro flashed for each pitch and would be in position to tip off the batter.

To keep the runner at second confused, the Dodgers switched to a new series of signs every two or three pitches, according to a plan agreed upon before the game. Roseboro had already switched signs once during Rollins' at-bat, and he called out to Koufax, "Are you sure you know which ones we're using?"

Against Milwaukee in Koufax's last start of the season, he and Roseboro had mixed signals when the Braves had runners on first and second, and Koufax ended up throwing a pitch Roseboro wasn't expecting. The result was that the ball flew to the backstop, allowing Braves' runners to advance a base.

On NBC Radio, Garagiola, a former catcher for the St. Louis Cardinals, told his national audience it was imperative for Koufax and Roseboro to be on the same page, especially in a Game Seven situation: "You've got to get together, you've got to make sure you're both thinking alike. The last thing you want is a pitcher to say, 'Alright, I'll throw your pitch,' and here comes a big cantaloupe."

While Koufax and Roseboro cleared up their hand signals, Drysdale continued to throw in the pen. Scully remarked that Don was pitching a ballgame behind Sandy, and noted that Dodger bullpen coaches were certainly keeping a close pitch count on Drysdale. By this time, "Twin D" had thrown almost as many pitches as Koufax through four innings, but he sent word to Alston he had good stuff and was ready to go in if needed.

Stepping in to face Koufax with two runners on was Versalles. Minnesota's MVP was hitting .286 against Dodger pitching, and he had singled sharply to center his last time up.

Working from the stretch, Koufax hummed a fastball past the swinging shortstop, who had hit 19 homers during the season and was thinking downtown all the way. Koufax delivered another letter-high fastball that Versalles laid off, then came back with a fastball low and away that Zoilo fouled back. With the count at 1–2, Koufax cut loose with another fastball. Versalles, unable to get his bat around quickly enough, fouled it off again.

Versalles lashed Koufax's next pitch towards third. Guarding the line to prevent an extra-base hit, Gilliam backhanded the hard-hit grounder on one knee, and in one motion, rolled over in the dirt and stepped on third, beating Quilici to the bag for the force-out.

Had Gilliam not made the play, the drive would have gone for an RBI double and put runners on second and third with only one out.

Garagiola: "What a play he made! A back-handed play on a ball that had 'two-base hit' written all over it . . . So far, that has to be the key play of this ballgame . . ."

Koufax considered Gilliam's run-saving stop the biggest defensive play of the game. If that ball had gone through, he said later, the Twins were sure to score one run and might have tied the game up, and that would have finished him for the day.

Koufax had been concentrating so intently on Versalles, he momentarily forgot there were two outs in the inning. When shortstop Maury Wills and second baseman Dick Tracewski approached the mound to make sure Koufax was settled down, Koufax asked, "Who am I supposed to pick up?"

The question shocked Tracewski. If there had been one out and the next batter had hit the ball back to the mound, Koufax would have needed to look for either Wills or Tracewski to cover second. With two outs, however, a ball hit back to the box would automatically be thrown to first.

Seeing Koufax unsettled, Tracewski snapped at him. "Dammit, wake up. There's two out. You throw to first."

Joe Nossek was next, and Koufax delivered a fastball high, then came back with a fastball low. The Dodger ace was clearly straining, and Scully noted that Koufax was no longer pitching, he was throwing: "He's forcing it, high and low, and he's behind two-and-oh . . ."

Koufax delivered a third straight fastball, and Nossek redirected it to Wills at shortstop. Maury flipped to Tracewski, who stepped on the bag for the final out of the inning.

On his best days, Koufax could always count on his fastballs and curves, and an occasional forkball and changeup to tame the other team's hitters. By the fifth inning, however, he relied almost exclusively on fastballs, and the Twins had hit him hard. Quilici's double, and the rocket grounders by Versalles and Nossek, had all been hit off the fastball; and only Gilliam's defensive play at third had prevented Minnesota from a big inning. The Dodgers were fortunate as well that Nossek's hard grounder had been rammed right at Wills.

For the first time in the game, Koufax had gone an inning without registering a strikeout. The Twins put four runners on base in the fifth, yet he somehow escaped without allowing a run. Still, he threw 21 pitches in the inning, two less than his total for the third and fourth frames combined, and his pitch count jumped to 81 through five. He was on pace to throw 162 pitches, an extraordinary amount for an arm-sore pitcher who had already worked 356 innings that season.

Seeing Koufax struggle through the first half of the game, Roseboro thought that it might be only a matter of time before the Twins' big hitters drove the Dodger lefty to cover.

"Get him out of there," Roseboro told Alston, "before someone gets killed."

SEVEN

L os Angeles catcher Johnny Roseboro's concern for Sandy Koufax at the end of the fifth inning of Game Seven was real, and stemmed from the realization that the Dodgers' ace, arm-sore and tired as he was, was trying to get by on just one pitch, his fastball.

"It can't be done," Roseboro said, "unless you're an exceptional pitcher."

In October of 1965, Roseboro considered Koufax the most exceptional pitcher in the game. On most occasions, the Dodgers' confidence in Koufax was so strong Roseboro said that the feeling in the clubhouse whenever he started a game was, "We're gonna kick some ass today."

Part of the reason for the Dodgers' seemingly unshakable belief in their ace was Koufax himself. Whether knocking down Giants' superstar Willie Mays with a purpose pitch or staring in at Yankees' slugger Roger Maris in Game One of the 1963 World Series, Koufax brought a combative nature to the mound whenever he pitched.

Baseball, Koufax said at the time, was a form of warfare. He never believed in fraternizing with opposing players because he saw them as the enemy, and he could see no reason to get to know an enemy well enough to have any feeling towards him other than hostility.

Baseball writer Roger Kahn recalled Koufax striking out the side against the Yankees with hard fastballs in the first inning of Game One of the 1963 World Series, and then fixing the Bombers' dugout with a hard stare that Kahn interpreted as meaning, "I can pitch to your power and I'll still strike you out."

Aggressive as Koufax was on the mound, opposing hitters never considered him a mean pitcher. Duke Snider, who faced an array of Hall of Fame pitchers that included such famous names as Reynolds, Ford, Spahn, Drysdale, Gibson, Wynn, and Marichal in a career that stretched from 1947 to 1964, called Koufax the greatest pitcher he has ever seen. Still, the Duke said Koufax might have been even better had he been as mean as Drysdale.

Even though Koufax's fastball ranged between 95 and 100 miles per hour, hitters weren't afraid to dig in against him because he never threw at them. Dick Groat, an infielder with the Pirates and later the Cardinals in the mid-sixties, didn't mind facing Koufax because his control was so good he could have pitched inside and it wouldn't have made a difference.

Drysdale of course, was a different story. Giants' outfielder Hank Sauer said that if you got a hit off Don, he would knock you down the next time up. Drysdale intimidated hitters with his size, the big, flailing motion of his delivery, and the hard 95-mile-per-hour fastball. From 1958 through '61, Drysdale led the National League in hit batsmen, and Frank Robinson said Drysdale was mean enough to throw at batters, and he did it continuously.

"You could count on him doing it," Robinson said, "and when he did it, he just stood there on the mound and glared at you to let you know he meant it."

Groat said Drysdale's meanness caused hitters to bear down more when they faced him. Everybody in the league, Groat said, wanted to beat Drysdale, and hitters battled him hard when they stepped in against him.

Koufax challenged hitters too; he challenged them with an assortment of four pitches—fastball, curve, forkball, and changeup. But he was primarily a fastball-curveball pitcher. Phils' and Cubs' first baseman Ed Bouchee ranked Koufax, Drysdale, and Gibson as the three toughest pitchers he ever faced. Bouchee, a left-handed hitter who had success against southpaw pitchers, faced Koufax numerous times in a career that lasted from 1956 to 1962. Still, Bouchee could recall getting only four or five hits off Koufax his entire career.

"Who hit Koufax?" Bouchee asked, but he did remember rapping a 440-foot blast off Koufax at the Los Angeles Coliseum. It was just a double, Bouchee said, but it was off Koufax, and that made it memorable.

Koufax went at hitters with his fastball, and players like Bouchee enjoyed batting against him because of that challenge. In a way, Koufax's mound persona contrasted sharply with his manner off the field. Dodger teammate Johnny Klippstein said Koufax was a loner, a noncommittal, private person who never revealed his feelings about baseball or anything else. Klippstein recalled him having a sense of humor in that he appreciated something funny, but joking around wasn't really part of his makeup.

Giants' pitcher Billy Pierce found it interesting that Koufax, so quiet and introverted, was such an aggressive pitcher. Koufax, Pierce said, never tried to nip the corners of the plate with his pitches. He went right at the hitter.

Despite the fact that Koufax was not known as a knockdown pitcher, he did throw purpose pitches inside. Both Drysdale and St. Louis Cardinals' ace Bob Gibson recalled an incident in their respective memories when Koufax threw inside to Lou Brock.

During the '65 season, Koufax shut the Cardinals out the first three times he faced them. St. Louis hitters wanted desperately to find a way to beat him. Brock, the Cardinals' leadoff hitter and superb base-stealer, decided to try to beat Koufax by bunting on him. Brock's plan was successful. The first time he faced Koufax, he bunted for a base hit, stole second and then third, and scored on a sacrifice fly. Later in the game, Brock bunted successfully against Koufax again.

The Cardinals had been trying to figure out for years how to handle Koufax, and they considered Brock's strategy a major breakthrough. They also realized that the next move belonged to Koufax.

Sitting on the St. Louis bench, Gibson knew that Koufax somehow had to stop Brock. The Cardinals' fireballer knew how he would stop someone who was bunting on him, but he also knew that Koufax was not an aggressive man by nature. When Brock returned to bat against Koufax, Gibson watched with interest to see if the Dodger ace, having been bunted into a corner, had it in him to take control of the situation.

Watching from the opposite side of the diamond in the Dodger clubhouse, Drysdale knew what was coming next. The fact that the Cardinals had scored a run without a base hit, Drysdale said, made Koufax irate.

Sitting next to Jim Lefebvre, nicknamed "Frenchy," Drysdale watched Brock dig in against Koufax.

"Frenchy," Drysdale said, "I feel sorry for that man about what he just did."

"Who?"

"Brock," Drysdale answered. "Sandy doesn't appreciate that sort of thing. Sandy gets mad enough when you beat him with base hits. But when you score runs without hits, look out."

Koufax followed by hitting Brock in the left shoulder with his fast-ball. Drysdale thought the thud of Koufax's fastball against Brock was so loud it reverberated throughout the stadium. Brock, he said, fell like a deer that had been shot. Standing up, Brock refused to show he was hurt and would not rub his shoulder until he returned to the dugout. None of the Cardinals charged the mound; in the sixties, players still regarded hit batsmen as an accepted part of the game.

Koufax's message had been sent, and he had done it in a fashion that a fierce competitor like Gibson could appreciate. Koufax, he knew, was the nicest of the Dodger pitchers; but Koufax could not have achieved the success he had, Gibson thought, if he did not assert himself on the mound.

To Gibson, the Brock incident showed how Koufax raised the level of competition by claiming his territory and daring the opposition to take it from him.

When the Dodgers faced the all-conquering Yankees in the '63 World Series, Koufax was named the Game One starter in Yankee Stadium against New York ace Whitey Ford. These were the Bronx Bombers, the Yankees of Mantle and Maris, and they sought a third consecutive world championship. Two years earlier, the Bombers had set a major league record by bashing 240 homers.

The pre-Series articles were a tribute to the Yankee dynasty, and

Koufax geared himself for the showdown. Feeling he had to prove to his teammates and himself that New York was a team of baseball players and not a pride of supermen, he went at them with his moving fastball and corkscrew curve, and struck out a Series record 15 batters.

Pitcher Ed Roebuck, a teammate of Koufax in the early sixties, noticed the same aggressive trait Billy Pierce did. Koufax, Roebuck said, was modest to the point of seeming embarrassed at his own success, yet he never fooled around on the mound. He didn't waste time trying to neutralize batters, and he rarely went to 3–2 counts. "He'd get the batter on three pitches," said Roebuck.

Tim McCarver, a baseball analyst and catcher for the St. Louis Cardinals in the sixties, agreed. When Koufax got ahead of a hitter in the count, McCarver thought, the at-bat was over.

McCarver was Gibson's batterymate during the Cardinals' championship run from 1964 to 1968, and he appreciated the close pitcher-catcher bond between Koufax and Roseboro. The two were a battery with the Dodgers from 1958 to 1966, and Koufax believed that he and Roseboro owned such a complete rapport "it was as if there were only one mind involved."

McCarver could relate, because he maintained a solid relationship with Gibson and later with a young St. Louis southpaw named Steve Carlton. The two were so close that when Carlton was dealt to Philadelphia in 1972, he asked Phillies' management to import McCarver as well.

Carlton preferred McCarver catching him, and in time some called McCarver Carlton's "caddie." McCarver said later that when he and Carlton die, they're going to be buried 60 feet and six inches apart—the distance from home plate to the pitcher's mound.

The bond between pitcher and catcher is one of the most important—and least understood—aspects of baseball.

When Hall of Fame hurler Ed Walsh was asked in 1915 for advice on pitching, he answered, "Hook up with some good catcher." Walsh spoke from his experience with the White Sox, where he worked with catcher Billy Sullivan. From 1899 through 1916, Sullivan batted .212, but he was one of the best defensive catchers of his time.

The pitcher-catcher battery can be found at the core of winning teams throughout baseball history. The term *battery* was initiated in the 1860s by Henry Chadwick, who used it to compare the firepower of his pitching staff to Civil War artillery. Some 20 years later, the term included both pitcher and catcher as standout catchers like Buck Ewing, Wilbert Robinson, and Deacon White gained respect for their position.

In baseball's early years, catchers had little influence on the game's outcome. Their primary duty was to block the ball whenever it passed the hitter. They served as a "backstop" and exerted little influence on the man on the mound.

Roger Bresnahan, who caught for John "Mugsy" McGraw's New York Giants at the turn of the century, changed the way catchers played their position when he introduced shin guards in 1907 and the catcher's mask a year later. From 1905 through 1908, Bresnahan was the battery-mate for the Giants' great one-two combination of Christy Mathewson and Joe McGinnity, and his judgment and tenacity behind the plate not only helped lead New York to the pennant, it also set the standard for future catchers.

Judgment is key, and a catcher must always remain rational, even under the toughest game conditions. In Game Seven of the 1926 World Series between the Yankees and Cardinals, St. Louis catcher Bob O'Farrell skillfully protected a tenuous 3–2 lead by guiding 39-year-old right-hander Grover Cleveland Alexander through the final seven outs against a Yankee lineup of Ruth, Gehrig, Lazzeri, Meusel, and Combs.

O'Farrell's work behind the plate in that seventh game highlighted one of the most important jobs a catcher had as the game evolved in the twenties and thirties, and that was to know the strengths and weaknesses of both his pitcher and the opposing hitter.

Moe Berg, who caught for several major league teams from 1923 to 1939, said that since the catcher is in a position to watch the hitter first-hand, he should recall what kind of pitch the batter likes and doesn't like, to which field he hits, what he did his last time up, and what he's likely to do in his current at-bat.

By the forties, some hurlers were leaving pitch selection entirely in the hands of their catcher. Indians' Hall of Famer Bob Feller believed that if a catcher was intelligent and had considerable game experience, it was best to leave the game almost entirely in his hands. Feller followed his own advice and left the decision making up to Jim Hegan, who played for Cleveland from 1941 to 1957 and proved valuable despite batting just .228.

Bresnahan set the tone for a catcher's tenacity, and later generations followed in his fiery footsteps. Mickey Cochrane, a Hall of Fame catcher in the twenties and thirties, used anger to spur his pitchers on. If Philadelphia Athletics' ace Lefty Grove tired in the late innings, Cochrane called for a mound conference and suggested to the hot-headed Grove that it might be time to give in and take himself out of the game. In an era when pitchers prided themselves on going nine innings, Cochrane's suggestion angered Grove just enough for him to throw harder.

Needing five outs to wrap up a win against the rival Yankees, Cochrane confronted A's pitcher Rube Walberg late in the game and spat, "You remind me more of a gutless, washed-up old bum than a major league pitcher." His biting words energized Walberg enough that the pitcher got the final outs to win the game.

Johnny Bench followed a similar approach decades later when he was behind the plate for Cincinnati's "Big Red Machine" in the seventies. Like Cochrane, Bench knew how to push his pitchers, and Reds' hurler Jim Maloney appreciated it. Maloney said that although Bench treated him at times like a two-year-old, he liked his catcher's ability to take control of the game.

Bench simply followed the edict of his manager, George "Sparky" Anderson. Known as "Captain Hook" for the quickness in which he pulled pitchers, Anderson said the only responsibility a catcher on his team had to have was controlling the man on the mound.

Communication between pitchers and catchers is crucial, and it extends far beyond the signals flashed before each pitch. A casual conversation between Koufax and catcher Norm Sherry in the spring of 1961 had a profound effect on Koufax's career, and may have saved Koufax from early retirement.

Koufax was a 19-year-old pitcher with limited experience when he joined the Dodgers in 1955. Dodger catcher Rube Walker remembered him as being nervous, and that he threw in a style veteran pitchers called "nervous fast."

There were some who thought Koufax would never make it as a

major league pitcher because he would never overcome his speed and wildness. When Herb Olson was a rookie catcher with the Dodgers, Al Campanis told him to catch Koufax. Campanis had been catching Koufax, but he found it difficult to hang onto his fastball. Seeing Olson, Campanis told him to take his place catching Koufax, but he didn't tell him why. Later, Olson approached Campanis and said, "I don't know why it is, but when I catch Koufax, I have a tough time seeing the ball."

Hitters sometimes had the same problem, and in an era before protective batting helmets, when hitters wore only their cloth caps to the plate, batters were reluctant to dig in against a wild kid who reared back and fired fastballs that ranged in the mid- to high nineties. Ed Bouchee said that when Koufax first came up, no one wanted to get in the batter's box against him. Hitters hoped the kid knew where his pitches were going, Bouchee said, but he didn't. Carl Furillo thought that Koufax didn't even know where home plate was half the time.

While some Dodgers resisted taking batting practice against Koufax, Erskine said the widely circulated stories about the team as a whole not batting against him are more legend than fact.

"Hitters only get so many pitches in practice," he said, "and they want them all to be strikes. But there are a lot of pitchers who learned how to control the ball by throwing batting practice. It's required when you're young because most of us have to learn how to control the ball. I don't think Sandy ever had a problem where a hitter said, 'Hey, I'm not hitting today. Koufax is throwing.' They hated to hit against Labine worse than they did Koufax because Labine threw a heavy sinker, and when he'd throw batting practice on a cold day and hit guys on the fists, they would moan."

Hank Sauer of the Giants said that when Koufax first came up, he threw hard, had a good curve and changeup, but could never get anything over the plate.

Koufax's wildness caused a dilemma for both him and the Dodgers. Manager Walt Alston didn't want to pitch him because he was nervous and wild, but Koufax felt he couldn't overcome his wildness until he gained experience.

In a column that appeared on June 14, 1956, Dick Young of the *New York Daily News* wrote that Alston showed little confidence in Koufax:

A pitching pinch has to develop before Walt uses the kid. Then, it seems, Sandy must pitch a shutout or the bullpen is working full force and the kid will be yanked at the first long foul ball.

Young cited two instances in which Alston mismanaged Koufax. The first came in Cincinnati during a game in which Koufax started only because Drysdale had a sore arm. The game was tied 3–3 in the seventh, with Koufax having surrendered a solo home run to Frank Robinson in the first inning and a two-run triple in the fifth that was a catchable ball. Despite walking just one batter through six innings, Sandy was lifted for a pinch hitter in the seventh and replaced by Clem Labine. Labine pitched the next two innings, yielded three runs, and was tagged as the losing pitcher.

Against St. Louis on the same western road trip, Koufax took a 3–1 lead into the fourth when he walked the leadoff hitter and went to a 2–0 count on the next batter. Rather than let Koufax try to pitch his way out of the inning, Alston took him from the game and brought in reliever Carl Erskine, who allowed seven hits over the next four innings. After the game, Alston told reporters that Koufax, who had given up just three hits in three innings, didn't have good stuff, but Erskine did.

Erskine recalled Koufax's inconsistencies as a young pitcher.

"Sometimes he had real problems early and just couldn't get with it," Erskine remembered. "But if he got into a groove early, he was awesome. He was just not polished enough or refined enough to be consistent. Sandy's struggles were with himself, to bring himself to a major league level as a pitcher. He had spurts (of greatness) in those early years, and that's why they stayed with him. On any given day, he was awesome. But then two outings after that, he'd have trouble getting out of the first inning. But the potential was definitely there.

"Sandy and I used to talk some and he would ask me questions about various things. He was always very congenial, never made any waves, never saw Sandy upset about a game or a play. He was just real cordial, a real gentleman. He was well liked. Everybody kidded him a little bit being a younger player."

In his first three seasons in Brooklyn, Koufax pitched in just 62 games and compiled a 9–10 record. His wildness was evident his first two years when he struck out just three more than he walked.

"When I was a young pitcher, I came up in '48, all the coaches and managers were position players other than pitchers," Erskine said. "You seldom saw a pitcher coach. So Sandy came looking to me or to others to gain something from an experienced head. I don't think any of us ever took Sandy aside and said, 'Look, son, let me show you a couple of things.' And he never asked. It wasn't his personality to come and say, 'Hey, I need help.'

"I don't know if Sandy ever felt like he didn't get the kind of help he needed. He kind of had to learn like the rest of us. It obviously was not the best way for that talent to develop. The right way would have been for him to pitch at least a year in the minors. And when he came to the major leagues after that I'm sure he would have mastered enough of those skills because he's a very smart individual."

Despite being a raw talent, Koufax still flashed signs of his enormous potential. Pitching against the Cubs on June 4, 1957 in Ebbets Field, Koufax dominated. He struck out the side in the second inning and fanned six of the first eight batters he faced.

By the fourth inning, he had seven strikeouts and was ahead of the pace he had set when he whiffed 13 Cubs. On WOKO Radio out of Albany, Dodger announcer Vin Scully elaborated on Koufax's strikeouts:

> I said earlier that Koufax did not appear to be loose, but now he is firing . . . Eight men have come to bat and only one of them has hit the ball. Koufax is remarkable with his strikeouts this year. If you figure out how many innings he's pitched and how many strikeouts he has, you really start to shake your head. He's worked 44-and-a-third innings and has struck out 53 men.

Koufax eventually struck out 12 in 7-plus innings, and went on to compile his best stats in the team's final year in Flatbush, posting his first winning record at 5–4 and striking out 122 hitters in 104 innings.

It was said at the time that Koufax owned "a Rex Barney fastball." Barney was a Dodger fireballer whose career was curtailed in 1948 when he slid into second base and broke his leg in two places. Had he not been injured, some believe Barney might have taken his place alongside the great fastball pitchers in the game. Koufax later became friends with Barney, and he told him that since people had always told him he had a "Rex Barney fastball," he was curious.

"I always wanted to know what that was," Koufax told Barney.

Koufax owns the distinction of throwing the final pitch for the Brooklyn Dodgers when he entered the '57 season finale in Philadelphia in the sixth inning of a 2–1 loss. In the bottom of the eighth Koufax struck out Willie Jones, and a short time later, the era of the Dodgers in Brooklyn officially came to an end.

The move to Los Angeles marked a bittersweet time for Koufax and the Dodgers. Koufax's best game to that point was the first one he had pitched at old Ebbets Field, and now he was part of a team undergoing a gradual youth movement and a changing of the guard. The Boys of Summer—Robinson and Reese, Newcombe and Erskine—had become the men of winter, and were giving way to Gilliam and Wills, Koufax and Drysdale.

Infielder Randy Jackson was acquired from the Cubs to replace Jackie Robinson at third, and he could see right away when he joined the Dodgers that Koufax, despite not pitching much, had potential.

Koufax wasn't always so sure. His three years in Brooklyn had seen him start 28 games but go the distance only four times. The Dodgers' move west to L.A. in '58 did little to improve his situation. He went 11–11 in '58 with a 4.47 ERA and improved only slightly the next season by going 8–6 with a 4.06 ERA. The '59 season was a roller-coaster ride for Koufax. In one relief appearance in April, he surrendered four hits, four walks, and five runs in two-thirds of an inning. During one 11-inning stretch, Koufax gave up 15 runs on 19 hits and 17 walks to run up an ERA of 12.27.

He struggled to find his rhythm on the mound, and Dodger pitching coach Joe Becker could see his frustration. "He has no coordination," Becker told confidants, "and he has lost all his confidence. His arm is sound, but mechanically, he is all fouled up."

When writer Roger Kahn asked veteran Dodger pitcher Joe Black about Koufax's problems, Black pointed to his temple. "Up here," he told Kahn. "The problem has to be up here."

Privately, Koufax felt the Dodgers were ready to give up on him, and his only thought was that if he was put on waivers, whoever claimed him would keep him in the big leagues and not send him to the minors.

Alston, however, refused to quit on Koufax. The skipper's attitude towards his young lefty had changed since '56, and despite Koufax's control problems, Alston gave him three straight starts in mid-June.

"You can't give up on him," Alston told reporters, and Koufax responded to the vote of confidence with a career-first three complete games. Included in that was a 16-strikeout performance against the Phillies, at that point a record for a night game.

Koufax's performance earned him an August 31 start in a crucial three-game series against the rival Giants. San Francisco entered the L.A. Coliseum with a two-game lead over the Dodgers, and maintained that slight edge by splitting the first two games.

Alston started Koufax in the third and final game of the series on a Monday night, and 82,794 fans packed the Coliseum, the largest crowd of the year. Koufax struck out the first two hitters he faced, then gave up back-to-back doubles to Willie Mays and Orlando Cepeda as the Giants took a 1–0 lead. Of the first 10 outs he recorded, Koufax had just three strikeouts. In the fourth inning his fastball began exploding on the hitters, and as the game wore on, his curveball was exploding as well. By the ninth inning, Koufax had 15 strikeouts, two short of Dizzy Dean's National League record and three shy of Bob Feller's major league record.

Koufax set the side down on just 10 pitches. He started Eddie Bressoud off with a curveball for a called strike, got Bressoud to foul off a fastball, then fanned him with another fastball. Danny O'Connell looked at a fastball for a strike, swung and missed on the curve, and was called out looking at another fastball.

Realizing Koufax had just tied Dean's league record of 17 strikeouts in a game, the crowd cheered on every pitch as he faced Jack Sanford. Throwing nothing but fastballs, Koufax struck Sanford out swinging on four pitches.

The Dodgers won the pennant in '59 by defeating defending league champion Milwaukee two games to none in a best-of-three playoff series. Koufax pitched in relief in the second game, but worked just two-thirds of an inning after retiring the first two batters and then walking the bases full.

In the World Series, the Dodgers faced one of history's most colorful teams, the "Go-Go" White Sox and their high-octane offense of Luis Aparicio, Nellie Fox, Jim Landis, and Ted Kluszewski.

Koufax was still so little known that Series announcer Mel Allen referred to him as "Koo-fax" when he entered Game One in the fifth inning of a White Sox romp: "He had an 8–6 record in the regular season and of course, turned in a magnificent performance this year when he struck out 18 men to tie Bob Feller's record. He's got a good curve but his control is sometimes erratic."

Koufax was anything but erratic in his first Series appearance. He pitched two perfect innings of relief in the Series opener, and then was named the Game Five starter in L.A. Owning a 3–1 Series lead, Koufax was in position to pitch the Dodgers to a world championship. A standing-room-only crowd of 92,706 packed the Coliseum on October 6, and Koufax pitched well, allowing just one run, an RBI groundout from Sherm Lollar that scored Jim Landis in the fourth. Duke Snider pinch-hit for Koufax in the seventh in a game L.A. eventually lost, 1–0. The Dodgers wrapped up the Series two days later with a 3–0 win, and Koufax finished with nine innings pitched over two games, seven strikeouts, five walks, and a 1.00 ERA.

Koufax's control problems resurfaced the following season, however, and they almost drove him from the game. His win-loss percentage dipped to .381, the lowest of his career, and he went 8–13 with a 3.91 ERA. Actually, Koufax had to rally to get even eight wins. At one point during the '60 season, his record stood at 1–8. His 100 walks in '60 were the second highest total of his career—he walked 105 in '58—and his first three seasons in L.A. saw him issue 297 free passes.

Pitching infrequently, he pressed whenever he entered a game. He overthrew and seemingly tried to strike out every batter he faced. Lacking knowledge of his craft, he was still more of a thrower than a pitcher. Lacking maturity on the mound, he let his emotions get the better of him whenever he allowed a hit or a walk. Frustrated, he would overthrow again, eventually giving in to wildness and lack of control.

"I had a lot of faults," he said. "I'd get mad at myself every time I made a mistake, and it seemed like I made a mistake every time I threw the ball. So then I'd try to throw a little harder, and I'd get a little wilder, and then I'd finally get the ball over, and they'd get a hit."

Tired of his infrequent starts and upset by the Dodgers' wavering confidence in him, Koufax asked to be traded.

"I want to pitch," he told team president Buzzie Bavasi, "and I'm not going to get a chance here."

"How can we pitch you," Bavasi countered, "when you can't get anyone out?"

"How can I get anyone out when I'm sitting around in the dugout?" Koufax retorted. "If I can't do the job for you, why don't you send me somewhere where I can get a fresh start?"

Privately, Koufax considered quitting. He had seen fringe players hang on as long as possible because they had a family to support, but since he was still young and unmarried, he felt he could afford to give up his baseball paycheck and take a chance on another profession. He had already gone into business as a manufacturer's representative for electrical lines, and he contemplated devoting his next few years to building up that business.

Seeking advice from friends, Koufax sought out teammate Carl Erskine.

"He said to me, 'You know, Carl, I have a chance to buy into a radio station, and I'm really thinking about leaving the game,'" Erskine said. "He was seriously thinking about leaving baseball with a record of under .500. But he said to me that he felt like he had been paid for six years and had never really been a good producer. He had never felt like he had pulled out all the stops.

"He said, 'I've got to go back to spring training one more time and do that. If I still feel the same way, I think I'm going to get out.'

"At that pivotal point, his sensitivity caused him to say, 'I can't quit. I've been paid, they've expected a lot out of me. And maybe I need to go back and really open it up the best I can and if I still feel the same way, I think I'll probably retire from the game.'"

The thought of walking away from baseball before achieving any measurable success bothered him, as did the realization that he had not yet worked as hard as he could have or learned as much as he could have. Believing he had not yet given himself every possible chance of succeeding in baseball, Koufax decided he would give the '61 season an all-out effort.

Koufax's career turnaround began gradually in the off-season, and was sparked by three sources: catcher Sherry, pitching coach Joe Becker, and club statistician Allan Roth.

During the off-season, Roth showed Koufax numbers that revealed he was less effective against left-handed hitters than right-handers. Traditionally, southpaw pitchers do well against lefty hitters, and one of the reasons is the way a left-hander's curve breaks on the hitter. Koufax's curve was breaking in a way that prevented him from exploiting what should have been a natural advantage against lefties. Working with Becker, Koufax discovered that by altering his grip on the curve and moving his fingers slightly, he could throw a curve that at times dropped down and away on lefties.

Becker also got Koufax to tighten the windup on his delivery, a slight mechanical adjustment aimed at both helping his control and hiding his pitches. When Wally Moon joined the Dodgers the season before, he told Koufax that the Cardinals picked up tips from Koufax's delivery from the stretch, that he brought his hands up higher for the fastball than the curve. By unknowingly tipping his pitches, Koufax was giving the hitter a chance to gear up for either the fastball or the breaking ball.

Scout Kenny Meyers worked with Koufax on pitching to spots, but soon noticed that Koufax's motion obstructed his vision. How can you hit that spot," Meyers asked, "when you can't even see it?" By tightening his windup, Koufax was able to pick up the catcher's mitt easier.

It was Sherry, however, who provided the biggest impetus for Koufax's career turnaround in the spring of '61. The two roomed together in spring training, and while the Dodger regulars were playing Detroit in Lakehurst, Sherry was scheduled to catch Koufax in a B-squad game in Orlando. Ironically, the opponent was the Minnesota Twins.

On the bus ride to the game, Sherry and Koufax went over the signs and pitches Koufax would work on. The two men had a rapport, not only because of their catcher-pitcher relationship, but because they roomed together on the road.

"He was a good guy," Sherry said. "He was easy to room with; we got a lot of room service. For the most part, he kept to himself. Everybody liked him. On those Dodger teams, 99 percent of the guys got along.

"He worked hard, and he's a perfectionist. He dressed well and he always looked good. He used to carry a kit around with him and he'd try to fix things. If the TV in the room wasn't working, he'd try to fix it. When he couldn't do things the way he'd like, he'd get upset about it. He wanted to be successful and pitch well, and when it didn't happen, it bothered him.

"When I came up in '59, he was just another one of the pitchers. He had a good arm and at times he showed he could pitch real good, but he had problems with his control.

"He gave me a lot of credit for changing him around. It was a B-squad game in Minnesota. We left Vero Beach and headed over to Orlando, and we were short-handed because we were missing a couple of guys and one of our pitchers had missed the trip.

"On the way over Sandy mentioned that he wanted to work on certain pitches, like his changeup and his curveball. He wanted to throw a lot of those; in spring training a lot of pitchers like to work on those things.

"When we started that ballgame he went out for the first inning and I said, 'We'll start off with some curveballs and changeups and see what happens.'

"Well, he had trouble finding home plate. It was ball one, ball two, and he'd shake me off and want to throw the fastball. And he'd throw it and it was high, and that was his problem. He threw a lot of fastballs up and out of the strike zone and guys wouldn't swing at them. That happened with the first two guys and then he started shaking me off and trying to throw the fastball each one harder than the one before, and now he had the bases loaded.

"I went out to the mound and said, 'Sandy, you know we're short-handed. We don't have a lot of pitchers here. Why don't you take something off the ball and just let them hit it? We can get the outs and get out of this inning, because nobody's going to swing at the rate you're going.'

"I went back behind the plate and he just wound up and said, 'Here, hit the ball,' and struck out the side. When he walked off the field, I said, 'I'll tell you something. You just now threw harder trying not to than when you tried to.'

"His bell or light, or whatever you want to say, went off, and he got it into his mind, 'That's all I need to do.'"

Sherry had offered similar advice to Koufax before, but Koufax had tuned him out. This time he listened, and facing a Twins' lineup that featured many of the same names he would face in the '65 Series— Killebrew, Allison, Battey, and Rollins—he pitched without pressing. When he got ahead of the hitter, Koufax aimed for the spots, and hit them with regularity. He faltered in the fifth after walking two batters and began overthrowing again. He quickly walked the bases loaded, bringing Sherry back out to the mound.

"Think about what you're doing," Sherry said. "Pick me up. Watch my glove. Be a pitcher. Make them swing the bat."

Facing Killebrew and Jim Lemon with the bases loaded, Koufax regained control and struck out the side. He finished with a seven-inning no-hitter in which he struck out eight and walked five.

Later, Koufax said that there is nothing like instantaneous success to let you know you are on the right track. And he credited Sherry with helping him find that success.

"I told him, 'I'm not blowing smoke up your rear end, but you threw harder trying not to than when you were trying to,'" Sherry recalled. "And that evidently struck home. Here's a guy who since '55 has been trying to make it in the major leagues and always had the same problem. And what, a couple of words like, 'Don't try to throw so hard,' is going to change him? It hit home, but it takes time for pitchers to find themselves. But he did it, and he became dominant."

By fate or coincidence, the Minnesota Twins were the opponents in the two signature games of Koufax's baseball life. Four years following his career-turning outing against the Twins, Koufax faced Minnesota again. The stakes, however, were infinitely higher. This was no relaxed spring training game in March; the season had grown late, and October baseball is always fraught with sudden danger.

Still nursing a 2–0 lead into the bottom of the sixth inning, Koufax prepared to meet the heart of Minnesota's power attack—Tony Oliva, Harmon Killebrew, and Earl Battey. The trio had reached Dodger pitching for a combined 13 hits and six RBI in the Series.

On NBC-TV, Vin Scully sized up the situation facing Koufax:

Bottom of the sixth, and the big boys come up for the Twins . . . And so far the question is, "Just how long can a pitcher go with one pitch?" Koufax has allowed two hits, walked three, struck out six.

The Twins were getting to him in the fifth except for the great play by Gilliam.

The play by Gilliam was on the minds of the Minnesota hitters in the sixth inning. Oliva later recalled the feeling of the Twins that they had Koufax on the ropes but failed to knock him out.

"When you have a guy like Koufax pitching, throwing 100 miles an hour, that play was huge," Oliva remembered. "We had an opportunity to score runs but we couldn't get the big hit."

Oliva was 0-for-1 with a walk and a strikeout in Game Seven, and Koufax started him off with a fastball high. Tony O. cut and missed at a fastball low, and his swing sent the bat flying into the Twins' dugout along the first-base line. Oliva was known for letting his bats fly, and this one led Scully to say in an aside to broadcast partner Ray Scott, "No wonder they don't play him to pull."

Koufax followed with a fastball in the dirt, then came back with another fastball that Oliva fouled back. Koufax to this point had thrown just one changeup in the game—to Bobby Allison back in the fourth inning—a half-dozen curves, and the rest of his pitches had been fastballs.

With a 2–2 count on Oliva, Koufax came in with another fastball that was again fouled away. He went to a 3–2 count on the two-time American League batting champ when he flared a high fastball that Roseboro had to stab at. With the count full, Koufax threw another fastball. Oliva swung and missed, and Koufax had his sixth strikeout of the game and 26th in less than 22 innings of the Series.

"It got to be amazing," Sherry said. "Here's a guy that went from having an idea of where he wanted to throw the ball but would never go there to a guy who could put it wherever he wanted to."

Sherry saw Koufax at spring training in the mid-sixties go to the Dodgers' pitching strings in Vero Beach and say, "Cover up the plate and give me a line on each corner." The plate would be covered, the lines would be strung on the black fringe of the plate, and Koufax would hit the strings all day.

Killebrew followed. The big slugger was 0-for-1 on the afternoon with a walk and a groundout back to the box. Koufax started the Killer off with a fastball off the plate for ball one, then came back with another fastball that Killebrew fouled off. Having just missed getting around on Koufax's fastball, Killebrew was assured he could do it next time.

"I wouldn't say it was unhittable," Killebrew said. "But if he put it in the right spot it was tough to hit."

Koufax put his fastball in the right spot on the next offering, and Killebrew lifted it into a high foul down the third-base line. Gilliam, shortstop Maury Wills, and left fielder Lou Johnson all gave chase, and Johnson pulled the ball in near the left-field boxes.

With two outs, Battey stepped in to face Koufax for the third time in the game. The Twins' catcher had struck out in the first inning and flied deep to right-center in the fourth. Jumping on a first-pitch fastball, Battey hit the ball hard again, but lined it directly at Wills for the third out.

Watching from the press box, Scully found it interesting that the Twins, knowing that Koufax was working on two days' rest, were going after his first pitch. Scully wondered whether the Twins would make Koufax throw more pitches as the game rolled along.

Returning to the Dodger dugout, Koufax was grateful for any assistance the Twins were providing him. Recalling that Roseboro had told him three innings earlier that his curveball *had* to improve, Koufax approached his batterymate.

"You lied to me," he said, and it was clear that both pitcher and catcher knew by now that the curveball that had devastated the National League in 1965 would not be of any use this day.

As Scully had noted, Koufax would have to continue to challenge the Twins with "fastballs, fastballs, fastballs."

EIGHT

During the bottom half of the seventh inning, NBC cameras panned the commissioner's box, where Ford Frick sat along the third-base line, watching Sandy Koufax finish his warmup pitches.

Game Seven of the 1965 World Series was historic in that it represented a changing of the guard in baseball's hierarchy. The 69-year-old Frick, who had been commissioner since 1951, was stepping down following a season in which baseball had added several significant footnotes to its history. A free-agent draft had been instituted in an effort to equalize the allotment of talent among clubs. Casey Stengel, baseball's "Ol' Perfessor," retired as manager of the New York Mets after breaking his hip on the eve of his 75th birthday, and the Houston Astrodome opened in the spring, marking the arrival of the first multipurpose stadium to feature artificial turf, enclosed ceiling, and climate control.

Frick passed baseball's torch to General William Eckert, a man who soon became known for his lack of decisive leadership and poor public image. Eckert lasted just two seasons on the job before being fired by club owners and replaced by a 42-year-old Wall Street attorney named Bowie Kuhn.

As NBC cameras focused on Frick, it was clear his departure after a lifetime in baseball was not the only thing that made this final game of the 1965 season special in baseball annals. Throughout the sport's long history, Game Seven of the World Series has represented a magical event. It is a single showdown for baseball's world championship, and that do-or-die aspect has always sprinkled stardust on a Series, turning the ordinary into something extraordinary.

No one among the more than 50,000 in Metropolitan Stadium and the millions watching on NBC-TV knew that better than the man who had been baseball's czar since the Truman era. From Billy Martin's mad dash across the infield to grab a Jackie Robinson pop-up in 1952 to Bill Mazeroski's bottom-of-the-ninth home run in '60 to Bobby Richardson's snare of Willie McCovey's liner in '62, Frick had seen Game Seven theatrics before.

As a baseball writer in the twenties and thirties and later a National League publicist, Frick knew Koufax's mound appearance in Game Seven wasn't historical because the Dodger ace was working on two days' rest. He had seen other pitchers do that. The year before, Bob Gibson worked Game Seven for St. Louis against the New York Yankees on two days' rest, and survived three late home runs to win, 7–5. In 1957, Lew Burdette led the Milwaukee Braves to a 5–0 victory over the Yankees on two days' rest. Twelve years earlier, Detroit's Hal Newhouser defeated the Chicago Cubs, 9–3, and in 1940, Cincinnati pitcher Paul Derringer tamed the Tigers, 2–1.

Pitching and winning on two days' rest in the World Series was extraordinary. But what separated Koufax from the game's other iron arms was that he was pitching with a painful arthritic left elbow, one that *L.A. Times* columnist Jim Murray said could end his career in the next 10 pitches or the next 100.

Despite pitching in pain and with only a fastball remaining in his repertoire, Koufax stood just nine outs away from recording his second shutout in three days, which would make for a modern Series record. That he was shutting down a Minnesota Twins' team that had been held scoreless just three times during the entire '65 season made Koufax's work through six innings all the more amazing. It also left observers like Frick wondering whether even Koufax could continue to silence the Twins' big bats.

Koufax enjoyed pitching in big, high-pressure games. He found the finality of the situation comforting. He was prepared to go all out this one last time, give it his best, and—win or lose—relax as the long winter stretched out before him.

The first six innings had been a struggle for him, and he had momentarily lost his cool with home plate umpire Ed Hurley back in the fifth. Standing on the mound in the seventh, Koufax twitched his shoulders to loosen the thickly corded muscles in his back. His gray uniform jersey smelled of Capsolin, and sweat beaded above his dark eyebrows and streaked the shiny black hair beneath his sky-blue Dodger cap.

Koufax was thankful for the cool Twin Cities temperatures. Against Milwaukee late in the regular season, he had worked nine innings in 90-degree weather, and the torturous exercise had drained him physically over the final innings.

By his own admission, Koufax actually began to feel stronger as Game Seven wore on. The cool weather energized him, and knowing that he had a good fastball and good control gave him added confidence. Everything, he felt, was falling slowly into place, just as it had for him career-wise back in 1961.

Entering the '61 season, Koufax's career record stood at 36–40. He posted just one winning season in his six-year career, and was known mostly as a scatter-armed fireballer. Following the advice of catcher Norm Sherry, pitching coach Joe Becker, and team statistician Allan Roth, Koufax pitched well enough in spring training to earn an early-season start from manager Walt Alston. He responded by defeating Cincinnati 5–2 to earn the first April win of his career. Pitching regularly in the Dodgers' rotation, Koufax thrived on the steady work and won six straight starts from mid-May to mid-June.

"If there was any magic formula," he told a reporter, "it was getting to pitch every fourth day."

Koufax's win streak ended when he was outdueled in the L.A. Coliseum by the Braves' Lew Burdette, who was working on an eight-game win streak himself. Koufax hurt his chances of winning when he reverted to old habits in the top of the seventh. After walking Gino Cimoli and Frank Bolling, he stamped around the mound in anger. Overthrowing his fastball, he walked Eddie Mathews to load the bases. Hank Aaron was up next, and Dodger stats showed the Hammer had hit Koufax at a .475 clip in his career. In 1960, Aaron reached Koufax for four hits, including a home run and a double, in six at-bats. Aaron hit Koufax so well the Dodger star began referring to him as "Bad Henry."

Alston pulled Koufax in favor of reliever Larry Sherry, and Sandy angrily strode off the mound, realizing that by reverting to what he called the "Old Koufax," he had lost the game.

Keeping his composure in his next start, Koufax shut the Cubs out on two hits while striking out 14. After 64 games, his record stood at 10–3, and he looked forward to reaching the 20-win plateau for the first time in his career. But he struggled the second half of the season, losing 15 of his next 22 decisions.

In a matchup of two 25-year-olds who would dominate their sport by the mid-sixties, Koufax defeated Bob Gibson of the St. Louis Cardinals, 1–0, in a classic decided by Tommy Davis's homer. Koufax seemed set to snap out of his slump when he outdueled Braves' southpaw Warren Spahn on September 15. Amid a light drizzle that began falling in the fifth inning, Koufax pitched the Dodgers to within four-and-a-half games of the league-leading Cincinnati Reds and broke a 50-year-old league strikeout record. Fanning 15 Reds in a lineup that included National League MVP Frank Robinson, Koufax increased his season's total to 243 strikeouts, blowing away the mark of 237 set by Rube Marquard of the old New York Giants in 1911.

Koufax's 10 K's against Milwaukee marked the 10th time he had reached that total in a game in '61. Since giving up his athletic scholarship at the University of Cincinnati, Koufax had struck out 925 hitters in 922 innings. Just as importantly, he had limited the powerful Braves' lineup of Aaron, Mathews, Frank Thomas, and Joe Adcock to only five hits, and outpitched the veteran Spahn, who was gunning for his 11th straight win and would eventually win 21 games that season.

Despite the Dodgers' late challenge, the Reds kept them at arm's length the rest of the season. Part of the reason the Dodgers failed to gain ground on the Reds was that they lacked any real home-field advantage when playing in the L.A. Coliseum. The Dodgers abhorred playing in the spacious, 92,000-seat stadium, which was more suited for football than baseball. The left-field wall stood just 250 feet from home plate—a freakish distance that made it the shortest porch in the majors. When Don Drysdale saw the Coliseum for the first time, he was shocked.

"I gotta change my style of pitching," the Dodger right-hander told teammate Duke Snider. "My knuckles are scraping that left-field wall every time I throw a pitch."

The left-field porch was so close, writers were hitting baseballs over it in batting practice before a game against the Cubs. Seeing right-handed power hitters Ernie Banks and Ron Santo striding by, Drysdale thought, "What chance do I have getting these guys out if the writers are clearing that fence?"

Drysdale's concern was realized during the Dodgers' first season in the Coliseum in 1958. His earned run average, a respectable 2.69 the year before, shot up to 4.16, and his record went from 17–9 to 12–13.

If the Coliseum was death to right-handed pitchers like Drysdale, it was equally tough on left-handed power hitters like Snider. The right-field wall stood 402 feet from home. Snider had been used to taking aim on the 296-foot distance in Ebbets Field, and when Giants' slugger Willie Mays saw Snider for the first time at the Coliseum in '58, he kidded the Duke.

"Look where that right-field fence is," Mays said to Snider. "You couldn't reach it with a cannon. You're done, man! They just took your bat away from you."

Snider, who saw his home run and RBI totals plummet from 40 and 92 his final season in Brooklyn to just 15 and 58 his first year in L.A., later called the Coliseum "a nightmare."

Outside of right-handed power hitters like Gil Hodges and Wally Moon, whose "Moon Shots" over the left-field wall became legendary, the Dodgers were glad to be moving to Chavez Ravine in '62. Koufax, who had thrown the final pitch by a Dodger in Ebbets Field in '57, earned another historical distinction when he was named the starting pitcher for the Dodgers' final game at the Coliseum.

It was a memorable event. Throwing a staggering 205 pitches over 13 innings, Koufax struck out 15, walked just three, and pitched hitless ball over the final five innings for his 18th win of the season.

With nine road games left, Koufax still had a chance to reach 20 victories, but he was routed by St. Louis in three innings in his next start, then dropped a 2–1 decision in Philadelphia on September 27 when he came back on two days' rest.

Frank Finch, writing in the *L.A. Times,* blamed the Dodger defense for the loss:

PHILADELPHIA—Sandy Koufax threw bullets at the Phillies Wednesday night and set a modern National League record of 269 strikeouts, yet saw his chance to become a 20-game winner go down the drain.

Seeking his 19th victory, and assured of another start Sunday if he achieved it, Koufax was the victim of two unearned runs that gave the impossible Phillies a 2–1 nod.

Koufax's performance against the Phils was an historic one, although only 4,166 fans were in attendance at Shibe Park. When he blazed a fastball past Pancho Herrera in the bottom of the sixth inning, he recorded his 268th strikeout of the season, one more than the National League record of 267 set by Christy Mathewson of the New York Giants back in 1903. Koufax struck out seven Phillies to push his season strikeout mark to 269, a record made more remarkable by the fact that he achieved it in just 256 innings. Mathewson had needed 366 innings—110 more than Koufax—to strike out two less batters than Koufax had.

The '61 season was one for the record books, but Koufax's pitching accomplishments were overshadowed by the bat of a Yankee slugger 3,000 miles away. Roger Maris captured the imagination of the sports world by belting 61 home runs and eclipsing the hallowed 60-homer mark set by Babe Ruth in 1927.

Stan Hochman, a columnist for the *Philadelphia Daily News,* felt the lack of attention paid to Koufax's record was an injustice. "Nobody called from Cooperstown to ask for the baseball that blurred past Pancho Herrera," Hochman wrote. "A guy breaks a record that has stood for 58 seasons, and he gets treated as if he has German measles."

The '62 season saw Koufax sidelined by an ailment more mysterious than measles. His first start in the regular season came against the Reds in the second game in new Dodger Stadium. Alston had declined to start him in the opener because he felt Koufax would be too nervous. Naming him the starter on a special "Chinatown Night" promotion, Alston watched as Koufax was carried onto the field in a rickshaw as part of the celebration.

Looking around the stadium, Koufax thought it was one of the prettiest ballparks in the league. The first baseball field ever sunk into the earth, Dodger Stadium was graced with soft pastel-colored seats. Beyond the bright pavilions and swaying palm trees bordering the outfield, purple mountains were visible.

Unlike the grotesquely configured Coliseum, Dodger Stadium had a symmetrical shape. Left and right fields owned equal dimensions of 330 feet, and curved outward to 410 feet. Submerged as it was into a ravine, the stadium was cloaked in part by a haze of smog from nearby Los Angeles. The combination of the ravine, the nearby mountains, and the gauze-like layer of smog contributed to the "dead air" over the stadium. Realizing that flyballs at Dodger Stadium were slowed by the dead air, Koufax soon found the best way to pitch at Dodger Stadium was to keep the ball away from the hitter, so that if he did hit it, he hit it out to the spacious air over center field.

Impressed by the picturesque, pastel setting of Dodger Stadium and its pitcher-friendly dimensions, Koufax opened the game by allowing a soft fly by Eddie Kasko, who reached base when the ball was lost in the lights. That was the last hit the Reds would get until the ninth, and Koufax walked off the mound with a four-hit victory. He cruised through April, winning four games. On April 24, he took the mound in Wrigley Field for a Tuesday afternoon game against the Cubs. Against a Chicago team featuring Banks, Santo, Billy Williams, and Lou Brock, Koufax tied the major league record he shared with Bob Feller by striking out 18 batters in a 10–2 win.

Koufax's performance before 8,939 vindicated his 18-strikeout game against the Giants on August 31, 1959, a mark some writers were critical of because it happened in a night game. The doubts angered Koufax, because they came at a time in his career when he was struggling to make it in the majors and was still seeking positive reinforcement.

Koufax's record against the Cubs came under what Banks liked to call "the best lights in baseball," meaning Chicago sunshine. He struck out the side in the first, third, and ninth innings and fanned at least one batter in every inning but the sixth. After enduring a brief wild streak in the fifth, Koufax settled down in the sixth and seventh innings. Needing four strikeouts in the final two innings to tie the all-time record, he whiffed Ken Hubbs with one out in the eighth, and Bob Will,

Sandy Koufax prepares to let go with a pitch against the Minnesota Twins' Tony Oliva in Game Seven of the World Series, October 14, 1965, at Minneapolis's Metropolitan Stadium.
(AP/Wide World Photos)

Above: An eight-year-old Koufax gets some batting practice.
(National Baseball Hall of Fame Library, Cooperstown, New York)

Below: The future Dodger in his University of Cincinnati baseball uniform.
(AP/Wide World Photos)

As a rookie left-hander for Brooklyn, Koufax puts in some time at the drafting board as a Columbia University student in the winter of 1955.
(AP/Wide World Photos)

Jay North, star of *Dennis the Menace*, joins Koufax in a 1962 publicity shot for an episode in which Koufax made an appearance.
(AP/Wide World Photos)

In this study of his pitching style, Koufax shows his form. (Bettman/Corbis)

Koufax lets fly in the eighth inning of his first no-hitter on June 30, 1962.
(Bettman/Corbis)

Dodger teammates mob Koufax in celebration of his 5–0 no-hitter against the
New York Mets.   (AP/Wide World Photos)

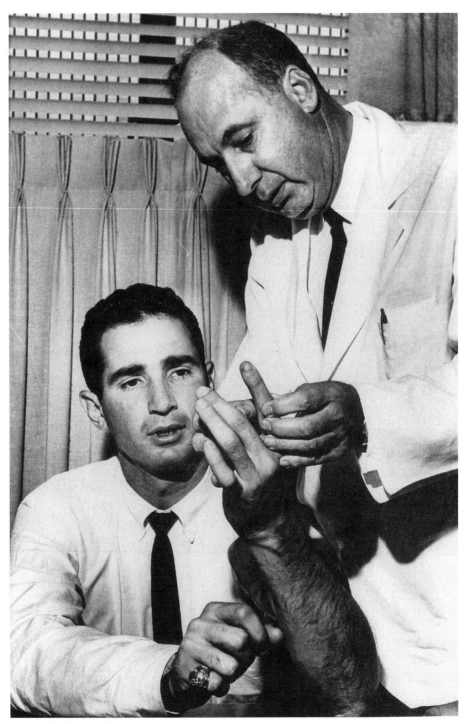

Dr. Robert Woods examines Koufax's injured finger in July 1962.
(AP/Wide World Photos)

Koufax displays his patented long stretch in the first game of 1963's World Series against the New York Yankees. In the 5–2 win, he set a Series record by retiring 15 batters on strikeouts. (AP/Wide World Photos)

Enjoying a glass of champagne after pitching the Dodgers to a 2–1 victory over the Yankees, Koufax savors his team's four-game sweep of the '63 Series. (AP/Wide World Photos)

After hurting his elbow in a 1964 game against the St. Louis Cardinals, Koufax has his swollen arm treated in an ice bath. (AP/Wide World Photos)

Koufax backs away as an umpire restrains San Francisco Giants' pitcher Juan Marichal, who had just clubbed Dodgers catcher John Roseboro in the head during the 1965 National League pennant race. (Bettman/Corbis)

Koufax winds up to fire a strike en route to his fourth no-hitter on September 9, 1965. (AP/Wide World Photos)

Leaving the mound after his perfect game against the Chicago Cubs, Koufax is rushed by his jubilant teammates. (AP/Wide World Photos)

Koufax holds up baseballs representing his four no-hit games.
(AP/Wide World Photos)

Following the Dodgers' 1965 World Series championship, Koufax receives a
Corvette convertible from *Sport Magazine*. (AP/Wide World Photos)

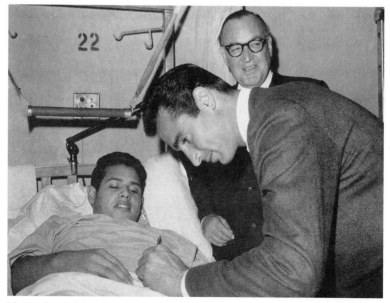

The Dodger left-hander signs an autograph for Vietnam veteran Ramon Olayo as
California Governor Edmund G. Brown looks on. (AP/Wide World Photos)

Following a 32-day holdout, Koufax and fellow Dodger pitcher Don Drysdale (*far left*) smile for the cameras as club general manager Buzzie Bavasi meets their salary demands for the 1966 season. Actor and former baseball player Chuck Connors, who acted as intermediary, joins them for the March 30 announcement. (AP/Wide World Photos)

Koufax announces his retirement from baseball on November 18, 1966. (AP/Wide World Photos)

Fellow Dodger Don Drysdale presents Koufax with his third Cy Young Award. In 1963 he had become the first to win it by unanimous vote, then was again chosen unanimously in both '65 and '66. (AP/Wide World Photos)

Following his retirement, Koufax participates in 1967's Bob Hope Desert Golf Classic. (AP/Wide World Photos)

Koufax and wife Anne, daughter of actor Richard Widmark, gaze fondly at one
another at their wedding on New Year's Day, 1969. (AP/Wide World Photos)

In his role as an NBC sport commentator, Koufax prepares to pay tribute to former teammate Don Drysdale, who was being honored prior to a Giants-Dodgers game. (AP/Wide World Photos)

Koufax poses with Roy Campanella and Dodger president Peter O'Malley in 1979 during a press luncheon in which it was announced that the former pitcher would rejoin the team as a pitching instructor during spring training. (AP/Wide World Photos)

Donning a Dodger uniform, Koufax takes up his duties as pitching coach.
Joining him are (*left to right*) Burt Hooton, Don Sutton, Andy Messersmith, Rick
Rhoden, Doug Rau, and manager Tommy Lasorda. (AP/Wide World Photos)

Koufax (*center*) is honored as a pitcher for the All-Century team, along with (*left
to right*) Roger Clemens, Bob Gibson, Nolan Ryan, and Warren Spahn. The living members of the All-Century team were honored in Atlanta prior to Game
Two of the World Series on October 24, 1999. (AP/Wide World Photos)

Elder White, and Moe Morhardt in the ninth. His control had been impeccable; of his 144 pitches, 96 were strikes.

In addition to tying the major league mark he shared with Feller, Koufax established a National League record by a left-hander for strikeouts in a day game with 17. It was a record shared by right-handers Dizzy Dean and Art Mehaffey.

Asked after the game about the differences between the record he set against the Giants in '59 and the game he had just pitched against the Cubs, Koufax cited the crowd size.

"The first time there were 83,000 fans at the Coliseum and I knew right along I was shooting at the record," he said. "This time there were only 8,938 fans. I lost track of how many strikeouts I had today. I didn't know I'd tied the record until the game was over and everybody came off the bench to shake my hand."

In his *L.A. Times* article the next day, Finch called Koufax "the Dodgers' human strikeout machine" and noted that he had rung up 41 K's in just 32 innings, and was averaging better than one strikeout per inning pitched (993–980) in his career.

Five weeks after pitching one of the best games of his career, Koufax returned to the Polo Grounds in New York to pitch in what he later called one of his most exciting games. Formerly the home park of the Dodgers' biggest league rival, the New York Giants, the Polo Grounds in '62 had become home to the fledgling New York Mets. In near-perfect weather on Memorial Day, Koufax was named the starter for the Dodgers' first game back in New York since the '57 season. Having thrown the last pitch for the Dodgers before they left New York in '57, he was now throwing their first upon returning.

Scoring 10 runs over the first four innings, L.A. staked Koufax to an early lead. Pitching from the same mound on which he had exhibited almost uncontrollable wildness in a tryout with the Giants eight years earlier, Koufax struggled to keep the Mets in check. With a holiday crowd of 55,704 fans jamming the old ball park and providing a steady chorus of "Let's go, Mets!" New York stroked 13 hits off Koufax. Four of those came in the ninth, and Alston walked to the mound and asked Koufax if he wanted to be taken out.

"No," Koufax said. "I want to finish it."

His reasoning was simple. Having left New York before as a hanger-on, he wanted to show in his return that he was now a pitcher. It was important to him, Koufax said later, that he go the distance.

He did, getting the last out in a wild 13–6 win.

"It was the most exciting game I ever pitched in my life," he told reporters. "That crowd was unbelievable. It never stopped cheering."

Koufax rematched with the Mets one month later in a Saturday night game at Dodger Stadium. Before the crowd of 29,797 fans were even settled in their seats for the first inning, Koufax opened the game by blazing three straight strikes past leadoff hitter Richie Ashburn, a .333 hitter. A veteran of 15 years in the majors, Ashburn couldn't believe the speed of Koufax's fastball, and later called it the fastest pitch he had ever seen.

Facing the Mets' number-two batter Rod Kanehl, a .339 hitter, Koufax threw his entire repertoire at him—fastball, changeup, curve—and struck him out on three pitches. Felix Mantilla followed, a former Milwaukee Brave who had always hit Koufax well. Koufax struck him out on three pitches as well. Registering three strikeouts on the minimum nine pitches, Koufax called it the best inning he had ever thrown. "Every pitch," he said, "went exactly where I wanted it to."

Following the inning, Mets' third-base coach Solly Hemus walked past Koufax and kiddingly said, "You know something? You've got a no-hitter."

Said Koufax, "I've had 'em later than this and lost them."

The Dodgers backed Koufax with four runs in the bottom of the first off Mets' starter Bob Miller, and he still owned a no-hitter heading into the eighth. He started the inning by firing a called third strike past Cliff Cook on a 3–2 pitch, retired Jim Hickman on a fly to center, and after a walk to Elio Chacon, struck out Chris Cannizzaro swinging on a 2–2 count.

Armed with a 5–0 lead in the ninth, Koufax walked pinch hitter Gene Woodling to start the inning, then induced Ashburn to bounce to shortstop Maury Wills for a fielder's choice. With each out, Dodger radio announcer Vin Scully reported the precise time the out was recorded. Scully made it a habit to record every out of the final inning of a Dodger no-hitter for posterity, and then present a tape of the game to the pitcher afterwards.

Kanehl followed with another fielder's choice, this to third baseman Jim Gilliam. One out away from baseball immortality, Koufax faced Mantilla, who had beat him with a ninth-inning single to left in an exhibition game that spring. With the count at 2–1, Koufax got Mantilla to bounce to Wills for the forceout, bringing a shower of seat cushions from the stands as Koufax was mobbed on the field by teammates and fans.

Hemus, who had kept reminding Koufax of his no-hitter throughout the game, trotted past him at game's end. "Congratulations," the Mets' coach whispered.

Throwing 138 pitches, Koufax struck out 13, the 10th time that season he had reached double figures in strikeouts. He struggled with his control, however, walking five and going to a 3–2 count nine times.

In the *L.A. Times* the next day, Finch wrote:

Magnificent Sandy Koufax scaled one of baseball's highest peaks Saturday night in Dodger Stadium when he hurled a no-hit, no-run game against the New York Mets.

There was only one tough play for Sandy's Dodger teammates to make as he struck out 13 Mets in scoring a 5–0 triumph before 29,797 starry-eyed fans.

The Dodgers' only difficult play had been a backhanded stop by Wills on Frank Thomas's hard grounder in the second inning.

The victory improved Koufax's record to 11–4, and with the season not yet at the halfway mark, there was speculation he might become baseball's first 30-game winner since Dizzy Dean went 30–7 in 1934. But a numbness in the index finger of his pitching hand began to develop in mid-May. Though Koufax realized that the loss of circulation is not unusual for a pitcher, over the next two weeks he saw the digit grow numb and cold. The finger whitened, and when Koufax pressed the nail of his thumb into it, the impression remained, as if the finger was made from wax.

Everyone on the team agreed that the finger looked nasty; they also thought it would eventually go away. With Johnny Podres, the Dodgers' only other lefty starter, sidelined by a sore shoulder, Koufax felt obligated to pitch through the injury. Since he used the index finger merely to hold the ball—he spun the curve and fastball off his middle finger—he experienced little problem with his control. From mid-May through late June, Koufax threw complete games in which he struck out 10, 16, 10, and 13 hitters—a total of 49 in all—and walked a combined total of just eight.

Ironically, as his index finger worsened, Koufax's pitching improved. He embarked on the hottest win streak of his career to that point. It started with a 2–1 win over Spahn, in which Koufax caught hold of a screwball and drove it to left field for his first career homer. As he ran around the bases, Koufax could hear someone shouting at him. Turning around, he saw Spahn yelling at him. As Koufax rounded third, Braves' third baseman Eddie Mathews also had some words for him.

"What are you trying to do," Mathews asked. "Make a joke out of the game?"

After defeating Spahn 2–1, Koufax came back in his next start to beat Gibson, 1–0. It was the second time in as many years that Koufax had outdueled the Cardinals' right-hander by a 1–0 score. Koufax went on to pitch his no-hitter against the Mets at the end of June, and one week later beat the Phillies, 16–1, in the first game of a July 4 doubleheader. The win highlighted a four-game holiday sweep in Dodger Stadium.

His next start was July 8 in San Francisco, the third game of an important three-game series and the final game before the All-Star break. Warming up before he faced the Giants, Koufax saw that his index finger had turned red and grown sore and tender. When he pressed his finger against the ball to hold it, it felt like a knife was cutting into his finger. To make matters worse, he was unable to control his curveball.

Turning to catcher John Roseboro before the game, Koufax said, "No curves, John."

Giants' skipper Alvin Dark, who had been able to tip off Koufax's pitches four years earlier when he was playing for the Cubs, watched Koufax warming up and noticed how the Dodger lefty kept looking at his finger.

"Maybe he's got a blister," Dark told his team. "He won't be able to throw anything but fastballs today."

Even though the Giants were sitting on Koufax's fastball, they still didn't hit him in the first two innings. By the third inning, he had lost his changeup as well. But his fastball was popping and his control was good, and through six innings he was working on another no-hitter. By the ninth Koufax had allowed just one hit, but his pitching hand had gone numb through the fleshy webbing between his index finger and thumb.

Leading 2–0, he surrendered a leadoff single to pinch hitter Bob Nieman. With 41,717 fans roaring for a Giants' rally, Koufax battled veteran Harvey Kuenn, who worked the count to 3–2 and then fouled off four straight pitches. Koufax followed by nicking the outside corner of the plate with a called third strike, but the effort seemed to exhaust him. With each pitch, he was working in a lather of sweat.

Because this was the final game before the three-day All-Star break, Alston could afford to pitch Drysdale in relief since the players would have several days off. With Koufax ailing and tired and unable to throw anything but the fastball, Alston felt it would make sense to bring the right-handed Drysdale in to face the Giants' string of righties due up in succession: Jim Davenport, Willie Mays, Orlando Cepeda, and Felipe Alou.

Facing Davenport, Koufax struggled to another 3–2 count, then lost him to a walk. When he issued two straight balls to Mays, Alston replaced Koufax with Drysdale. "Big D" retired Cepeda and Alou to nail down an important win.

As one of several Dodgers chosen to represent the National League in the All-Star Game in Washington's Griffith Stadium, Koufax was supposed to fly back to Los Angeles with the team and then catch a connecting flight to D.C. He made arrangements instead to see Dr. Robert Kerlan, the Dodgers' club physician, and then catch a later flight to Washington. After examining the finger, Dr. Kerlan advised Koufax to see a vascular specialist who could properly test the blood flow through his pitching arm.

The Dodgers contacted the league office to obtain permission for Koufax to miss the All-Star Game, but the league refused. In years past, other clubs had tried to rest their stars over the break by getting them excused absences for injuries. League officials noted that since Koufax had just pitched a two-hit shutout through eight innings against the Giants, how injured could he be?

Disappointed as he was, even Koufax recognized the league's position. Whenever a starting pitcher on a contending club comes up with a "disabling" injury on the eve of the All-Star Game, he said, it's easy to suspect that they may be trying to protect their rotation.

Alston asked National League manager Fred Hutchinson not to use Koufax in the game because of his injured finger, and Hutchinson graciously agreed. With President John F. Kennedy watching from a box seat, Wills scored two runs to pace the National League over the American League.

The Dodgers' claim that Koufax was injured looked even more suspicious when he was given the start in the team's first game following the All-Star break. The color in his index finger by now had gone from red to blue, and the skin was more tender than before. Complicating matters further was a blood blister that was forming on the tip of his finger.

Facing the Mets in New York, Koufax pitched six scoreless innings before the blood blister broke, and pale red blood seeped out. Since the blood wasn't colored the normal deep red, it was another sign to Koufax and the Dodgers that something was seriously wrong with his finger. Still unable to grip the ball properly to throw his curve, Koufax worked a scoreless seventh inning, shutting the Mets out with a fastball dotted by the blood of his finger.

By the end of the seventh, Koufax had lost his feel for the ball and was forced to leave the game. In his New York hotel room during the Mets' series, Koufax pondered his problem. Pitching with a steadily worsening finger ailment, he had won his last four games, three by shutout. Over the past eight games, he had allowed just four earned runs and owned an ERA of 0.53. In 67⅓ innings, he had struck out 77 batters.

Yet his finger had turned a deep reddish-blue and grown more swollen. When his uncle, Sam Lichtenstein, visited him in New York, he was startled at the condition of Koufax's finger.

"Sandy, your finger looks like a grape," Lichtenstein said. "How can you pitch with that? Are you crazy?"

Lichtenstein insisted Koufax visit another of his uncles, an osteopath whose practice was in New York. Koufax's condition was finally diagnosed as a loss of circulation, most likely caused by a blood clot, and he was warned to get it treated as quickly as possible.

Koufax traveled with the club to Philadelphia and then Cincinnati. Warming up to face the Reds, Koufax realized his finger was so sore he could barely grip the ball. A teammate watched him struggle and said, "Forget it, Sandy. Don't even try it."

Koufax did try to pitch, however, and in the first inning the finger finally split wide. The blister was open and raw, but strangely, no blood came out. Just as he had done against the Mets, Koufax delivered fastballs splattered with blood. The Reds reached him for two runs on three hits, and as he walked back to the dugout at the end of the inning, Koufax told Alston he didn't think he could go any further. Dodger trainer Bill Buhler called Buzzie Bavasi, who was in New York with Dr. Kerlan. Bavasi told Buhler to have Koufax fly to Los Angeles the next morning to see Dr. Robert Woods, the club's other doctor. Woods then sent him to a cardiovascular specialist, Dr. Travis Winsor.

An arteriogram was ordered, and doctors tracked Koufax's flow of blood with a machine that takes readings from point to point. A strip of rubber was wrapped around his arm at various points along his forearm and wrist, and a cup was placed at the tip of his finger. Tests revealed that while the flow of blood was normal through his arm, it decreased 15 percent below the palm in the finger itself.

Since there was no bruise on the palm, doctors wondered if Koufax had Raynaud's Phenomenon, a rare and incurable blood disease that causes a narrowing of the artery. Doctors gave him an assortment of injections and medications to dissolve the blood clot, widen the artery, and allow blood to flow freely into the finger. Koufax's finger remained blue, however, and the dying tissues and lack of circulation led doctors to consider amputation to prevent gangrene.

Though the press reported that Koufax was suffering from Raynaud's Phenomenon, doctors eventually ruled it out. But they kept after him in trying to get him to remember if he had suffered any recent trauma to the hand. Finally, Koufax recalled a late April game against Pittsburgh in which he had switched from batting righty to lefty. Since as a righty hitter he exposed his left arm, his pitching arm, to the opposing pitcher, he felt he was risking injury if he was ever hit by a pitch. By batting lefty, he protected his left arm from an errant pitch by shielding it with his body.

Batting against the Pirates' Earl Francis in the third inning, Koufax was jammed by a pitch but managed to hit it off the handle of his bat and back through the middle for a single. The bat handle pinched the middle of his hand, and he spent the rest of the game checking his palm for bruises.

Whether the pinched nerve caused Koufax's mysterious ailment was unknown at the time; certainly it contributed to his condition. Gradually, the medication he was taking began to have a positive effect on him, and the blood flow returned to the index finger. An infection grew around the cuticle, and Koufax was sent to see a hand specialist. The concern was that the infection might spread to his finger bone and cause osteomyelitis. Just like gangrene, it would have forced doctors to amputate Koufax's index finger.

"I didn't mind when the finger was just numb," Koufax told his teammates. "But this is intolerable. I can't touch anything. It's like I'm touching fire."

At one point, a despondent Koufax looked at his miscolored finger and told reporters, "It looks like it might have to come off." Within weeks, however, Koufax's condition improved; when he saw Dr. Kerlan again in Cincinnati, the infection and blood clot were both clearing up.

"You're very lucky," Kerlan told Koufax. "You don't know how close you came to losing the finger."

Kerlan compared Koufax's condition to a car and a train racing to a crossing. The car was Koufax's blood circulation, the train was the spreading infection. The crossing was the tissue, which needed the blood to feed it and carry away the infection.

"You don't know which is going to get there first," Kerlan told Koufax. "In your case there were trains coming from both directions, and you had to squirt through the middle."

Koufax was 14–7 and led the league in strikeouts and earned run average when he left the Dodger lineup on July 17. Opponents immediately took aim on L.A.'s lead atop the league. San Francisco's Willie Mays thought that with Koufax out, there was no question that the Giants could make a run at the Dodgers.

By late September, L.A. owned an eight-game lead with nine games remaining. But the absence of Koufax had thinned their pitching. Recognizing his team's plight, Koufax volunteered to pitch the Dodgers' September 21 game against St. Louis. It was the 154th game of the regular season, and two years earlier, that would have marked the season finale. But the '61 season had expanded the scheduled to 162 games, and the additional games put the Dodgers' lead in peril.

Pitching against the Cardinals with two months' worth of rest, Koufax loaded the bases in the first and then issued a high fastball that Charlie James drove on a parabola to the top of the pavilion in right field. When he walked the next batter, Koufax was lifted from the game. He pitched two days later in a relief role, then was named the starting pitcher against Houston.

Owning a two-game lead with three to go, Koufax could clinch a tie for the pennant with a win against the Astros. For four innings he appeared to be on his way. He retired the first 11 hitters he faced, four of them on strikeouts, then tired in the fifth and gave up two runs. Believing the two months of inactivity had robbed Koufax of his stamina, Alston lifted him with the Dodgers leading 4–2 at the end of the fifth. L.A. went on to lose the game, then dropped their final two to fall into a tie for first with the surging Giants.

Faced with a three-game series to decide the National League pennant, Alston called Koufax over to his seat on the plane ride to San Francisco.

"How do you feel?"

Koufax, knowing Alston was asking if he could pitch the opener, replied, "I can try."

Knowing the Dodgers didn't have anybody else to use in the play-off opener, Koufax agreed to take the ball in the hopes of giving the team four or five good innings before giving way to a reliever.

Before the opener in Candlestick Park, Alvin Dark ordered the groundskeepers to water down the area around first base. By making the ground between first and second base wet and heavy, Dark figured to slow down Dodger speedster Maury Wills, who had swiped a major league record 104 bases in 1962. Dark also had the grounds crew water down the infield grass on the left side of the diamond. Since the Giants had two slow fielders in shortstop Jose Pagan and third baseman Jim Davenport, by watering the field they were looking to slow down the speed of the grounders hit to the left.

Jocko Conlan, who was in charge of the umpiring crew for the first game, saw what Dark was doing.

"Now, Alvin, that's enough water," Conlan said. "You have the field too wet as it is."

The remark angered Dark, who believed the Dodgers doctored their home field and fixed the baselines so their bunts would stay in fair territory.

"Jocko, I don't know what you're talking about," Dark said. The Giants' manager, though, was well aware of Conlan's concerns. The day before, the Giants had held Fan Appreciation Day at the ballpark, and were giving away cars. Before the ceremonies began, the head grounds-keeper approached the master of ceremonies and told him not to park any cars on the left side of the infield.

"The cars," he said, "will sink to their hubcaps."

When Conlan told Dark to call the groundskeeper to dry out the basepaths, Dark replied, "Call him yourself."

It was tactics such as these that gave Dark the nickname of "Swamp Fox." But the Giants knew before the first playoff game that none of Dark's schemings would work against Koufax. To beat Koufax, they knew they were going to have to make contact with his fastball and try to scratch out runs whenever they could.

"You don't try for big innings against Sandy Koufax because you're not going to get them," said Dark, recalling the Giants' strategy. "He was one of the most dominating pitchers in all of baseball, and I had great admiration for his ability."

Koufax retired the first two batters he faced, then surrendered a double to Felipe Alou, who roped his drive just past Andy Carey at third base. Mays was up next, and Koufax fell behind 3–1 before coming in with a fastball. Mays caught all of the pitch and drove it over the right center-field fence for a quick 2–0 lead. Koufax, by his own admission, had nothing on his pitches. In the second inning he gave up a solo homer to Davenport to fall behind 3–0. When Ed Bailey followed with a single, Koufax was lifted from the game. The Giants went on to win Game One, 8–0, and took the playoff series in three games.

When a writer wrote the next day that Koufax had tried to decoy the Giants by deliberately serving up slow pitches, Koufax laughed. That wasn't a decoy, he thought. That was the best fastball he had that day.

Facing the Twins in the seventh game of the '65 Series, Koufax's decoy wasn't the fastball, but the curve. He had thrown 92 pitches through six innings, but no more than a half-dozen had been breaking balls. So it was surprising to see him start Minnesota leadoff man Bob Allison with a big curve. Allison had struck out swinging on a backdoor curve in the second inning, and smashed a breaking pitch that almost tore the hands off third baseman Jim Gilliam in the fourth. Allison jumped on Koufax's first-pitch curve in the seventh, pulling another hot grounder to his left. Maury Wills made a nice stop on the ball deep in the hole, and gunned the ball across the diamond to Wes Parker at first for the out.

On NBC-TV, Scully made another reference to the Twins' over-anxious hitters, jumping on the first offering from an arm-sore pitcher. It would serve Minnesota well, Scully seemed to be saying, to make Koufax work harder for his outs.

Don Mincher followed, and the big lefty swung wildly and missed Koufax's first two fastballs. Joe Garagiola, broadcasting the game on NBC Radio, was impressed watching Koufax challenge the Twins with his fastball: "Koufax really rearing back. You can see it, he's just lettin' out . . . He's throwing as hard as he can."

Mincher, who was 0-for-2 and struck out on a checked swing in the second, checked his swing again on two more Koufax fastballs. Both of Mincher's cuts were dangerously close to strikeouts, and his whipping bat seemed to clearly go around on the second checked swing, but umpire Ed Hurley called both pitches balls. Koufax again seemed upset by Hurley's non-call on a seeming strikeout, and he looked away in exasperation.

With the count at 2–2, Koufax and Mincher settled into a duel of power pitcher versus power hitter. Three times Koufax reached back and fired his fastball, and three times Mincher fouled it off. As the tension mounted with each pitch, Koufax was a man in motion between pitches as well.

Garagiola: "Koufax constantly removes his cap, wipes his brow, takes a pinch of the rosin bag, gets his sign, ready . . ."

Having retired Allison on one pitch to lead off the inning, Koufax was now in the seventh pitch of Mincher's at-bat. Mincher was getting his cuts, and Billy Martin shouted encouragement from the third-base coaching box. Refusing to compromise, Koufax rocked and hummed yet another fastball. Mincher again swung late—he was having difficulty with the speed of Koufax's pitches—and again fouled it off. This time the ball went high in the air between home plate and first base, and catcher John Roseboro settled under it to record the second out of the seventh inning.

Frank Quilici, who had popped out to left in the second and doubled to left-center in the fifth, was next, and he swung and missed at a first-pitch fastball. Having thrown nine straight fastballs, Koufax followed with an outside curve. Looking to drive the ball the opposite way to right field, Quilici instead fouled it off.

Recalling perhaps that Quilici's extra-base hit in the fifth had come off a high inside fastball, Koufax stayed with his breaking pitches in this at-bat. He issued two high, looping curves that Quilici took for balls, then came back with the fastball. Quilici cut and missed, and Koufax walked off the mound with his eighth strikeout of the game.

His lead, spare as it was at 2–0, was still intact through seven.

NINE

O ne hundred and fourteen silent screams a game.

That, Jim Murray wrote, is what Sandy Koufax endured to pitch for the Los Angeles Dodgers in the mid-sixties. The famed *L.A. Times* columnist compared the Dodger southpaw to a diamond cutter working with cataracts. Pain and Koufax, he said, were like peas in a pod. Wrote Murray:

> You shouldn't have to earn your living at something that makes you scream. Or cough. Or bleed. You shouldn't have to sign for your paycheck with "ouch!"
>
> Sandy Koufax does . . . A curve ball is as big a thrill as swallowing iodine. A fast ball is merely like tightening your arm in a vise by comparison—a down-right relief.

Through seven innings against Minnesota, Koufax endured 106 silent screams. He endured the iodine of throwing a curve 10 times, and tightened his arthritic arm in the vise of the fastball on 96 other pitches. Working on two days' rest, Koufax and his aching arm had survived the Twins' big hitters, and he owned a two-hit shutout with eight strikeouts and three walks. Minnesota, by contrast, had trotted out four pitchers through seven innings—Jim Kaat, Al Worthington, Johnny Klippstein, and Jim Merritt.

Merritt, a 21-year-old southpaw, had been a part of the Dodgers' minor league organization, and he flashed the promise L.A. scouts had seen in him years earlier by retiring the National League champions on a handful of pitches in the top of the eighth.

For large portions of the game, Metropolitan Stadium's record crowd of 50,596 sat quietly, almost pensively, as if awed by the finality of a World Series Game Seven. Gone were the lighthearted and raucous celebrations of the first two Series games in Minnesota, when the Twins' big hitters knocked out Don Drysdale and Koufax on successive days. In the course of a week, the game had grown grim and dangerous, and the fate of the Series now hung on every pitch.

On NBC Radio, Joe Garagiola noted the quietness of the big crowd in the bottom of the seventh inning, and told listeners it was because Koufax had taken complete control of the game. Koufax too was struck by the fact that for much of the afternoon, the game had been played in almost absolute silence.

Shadows creeping across the infield in the bottom of the eighth signaled the lateness of the 1965 baseball season. In mid-October, the Twins shared the Met with their NFL counterparts, the Vikings. The stadium grass was already scarred from home dates against Detroit and the New York Giants, and Minnesota's sports fans looked forward to a Western Conference home date against the rival Chicago Bears on the coming Sunday.

With the Twins facing the final six outs of their great season, the Met crowd came to life in the bottom of the eighth. As Vin Scully plugged NBC's coverage—"live and in color"—of that coming Saturday's college football showdown between undefeated Texas and unbeaten Arkansas, he noted the sustained hand-clapping as the Twins came to bat.

Scully: "Two-to-nothing Dodgers, and Minnesota, with the Twins' fans doing a little hand-clapping to music, trying to shake something loose . . ."

Garagiola also took note of the crowd's stirring, and told his NBC Radio audience that Minnesota fans "want some action" from their powerful lineup.

Pinch hitter Sandy Valdespino, who was batting for Merritt in the number-nine spot, dug in against Koufax to lead off the Twins' half of the eighth. A 26-year-old lefty, Valdespino seemed a curious choice by Minnesota manager Sam Mele to bat against Koufax, since conventional baseball strategy calls for matching righty hitters against southpaw pitchers and lefty swingers against right-handed pitchers.

A .262 hitter during the regular season, Valdespino had three hits in 10 at-bats against Dodger pitching. He had singled off Koufax in Los Angeles, one of only four hits he allowed in the complete-game shutout just three days earlier. It was for that reason that Mele sent Valdespino to the plate in the eighth, setting up a matchup of Sandy versus Sandy.

Koufax started Valdespino off with a hard fastball for a called strike, then came back with a second fastball for another called strike. Pitchers like Koufax approached an 0–2 count in a way that was vastly different from his predecessors. In earlier years, pitchers were told to waste a pitch or knock a batter down with an 0–2 delivery. New York Giants' manager Mel Ott fined one of his pitchers, Bill Voiselle, a then-hefty sum of $500 for allowing a batter to hit an 0–2 delivery. Voiselle made only $3,500 that season, and Ott told him it would be another $500 fine if he ever threw the ball over the plate again on an 0–2 count. When Voiselle later struck a hitter out looking on an 0–2 pitch, he railed against the umpire. "What are you trying to do?" Voiselle yelled. "Ruin me?"

By the sixties baseball wisdom had changed, and pitchers like Koufax and Bob Gibson went for the jugular on 0–2 pitches. Both strikes against Valdespino had come off of Koufax's over-the-top delivery; but he delivered his next pitch, a curve, with an odd, almost side-arming motion that sailed out of the strike zone and left him leaning towards first base. It was the first time in the game he had altered his release point so dramatically, and it may have been a concession to his tired arm.

With the count 1–2, a Koufax fastball sailed very high over the plate, and he shook his head in disgust. As the crowd roared its approval, Scully noted that the pitch had gotten away from Koufax, and that in the Dodger bullpen, Drysdale and Ron Perranoski were up and throwing.

Koufax came back with another fastball, this one letter-high and almost level with the "Twins" stitched in script on the front of Valdespino's uniform. Whipping his bat around, Valdespino arced the ball to left field, a slicing fly that curved towards the seats along the foul line. Racing over from his left-field position, Lou Johnson crossed the white-chalked foul line and backhanded the ball at the wall for the first out. It was a fine defensive effort by Johnson, the second time in the game he had run down a fly ball in the left-field corner.

Stepping to the plate for perhaps the final time in the season, Zoilo Versalles received a rousing ovation from the crowd. Scully called him "the most electrifying of the Twins." Versalles had struck out in the first inning, singled in the third, and apparently stolen second base, but was sent back to first when umpire Ed Hurley ruled that Joe Nossek had interfered with Dodger catcher John Roseboro. He was later robbed of an extra-base hit and RBI by Junior Gilliam's great play at third in the fifth inning.

As Drysdale and Perranoski warmed up beyond the outfield wall behind him, Koufax started Versalles off with a curve for ball one. He evened the count at 1–1 on the next pitch by blowing a fastball past the swinging Versalles, then ran it to 1–2 when Zoilo dipped his bat and bunted a fastball foul outside the first-base line. Another fastball followed, and Versalles—for the third time in the game—hit Koufax hard, driving the ball deep to left field. For a split second it appeared that the ball was on its way out of the park, but Johnson backtracked and caught up with it on the warning track for the second out.

Nossek stepped to the plate, and Koufax came in with a curveball high. He had now thrown 10 pitches in the inning, and almost one-third of them had been curves, though none for a strike. After going through the middle innings—the third through the sixth—throwing 90 percent fastballs, he had resorted to breaking pitches on seven occasions in the seventh and eighth innings combined.

Returning to his 95-mile-per-hour fastball, Koufax hummed a letter-high offering that Nossek fouled back. He came back with another high fastball, this one so fast and so hard that Roseboro stabbed at it only to see the ball explode out of the webbing of his catcher's mitt. For the third time in the inning and fifth straight time overall, Koufax was ahead in the count against a Twins' batter. His next pitch, another fastball, was a grounder that shortstop Maury Wills fielded cleanly and fired to Wes Parker at first for the final out of the eighth.

Koufax by now was a pitching machine. He worked fast between pitches, though not as fast as his contemporary, Gibson. Yet compared to some of the living statues taking the mound in the late nineties, Koufax worked at almost warp speed. He averaged just 11 seconds between pitches, and occasionally snapped off a delivery in as little as eight seconds. A review of his brisk work proved refreshing, especially when pitchers in the nineties have been timed at a lengthy 28 seconds between pitches.

To the millions of viewers watching NBC's broadcast in 1965, Koufax's mound style and mannerisms had become one of the ornaments of modern baseball. His ritual between pitches was always the same—a slight tug on the bill of his sky-blue Dodgers cap, a touch of the rosin bag, a quick tug on the back of his cap and wipe of the brow, the stare-in for the sign, and then the classic, over-the-top motion with the high leg kick that ended with his left arm slamming across his body and his hat slightly askew.

Rocking and throwing, Koufax had regained the pitching rhythm that eluded him in the early innings. It was the same rhythm he had settled into when he exploded upon the baseball world in 1962 before being sidelined by the circulatory problem in his left index finger.

The injury forced Koufax to spend the winter months taking inventory on his baseball life. He told a reporter that he didn't know if his career was over or not. He didn't know for sure if his finger would hold up for a full season. Scar tissue had developed in the tip of his finger; and though it hardened, it did get tender at times, and there was a sore spot inside.

There were other things to think about, too. Sometimes he felt as if he lived in a dream world. He had everything a man could want, but who knew what would happen in the future, when his career would end? If it ended the next season, then what would he have? The money he had saved could be spent in a short time; and though he had some schooling, by his own admission he was not prepared to do anything but pitch.

"I remember too many great arms," he said, "too many great

pitchers that everybody thought were going to be great—and all of a sudden it was over."

It was a realistic, thoughtful appraisal of his life as the '63 season approached. Koufax, however, felt that if he could pitch until he was in his mid-thirties—he had just turned 27—he would have everything he wanted.

In February of '63, he joined fellow Dodgers Willie Davis, Don Drysdale, Frank Howard, Duke Snider, and Maury Wills in a comedy skit with Milton Berle on stage at the Fountainebleau Hotel in Miami Beach. During one part of the skit, Berle stopped and ask Koufax, "How's the finger?"

"It's coming along fine," Koufax answered. "I've been to the doctor, and he says it shouldn't bother me at all."

With that, Koufax took his left hand from behind his back and laughingly showed the audience a huge plastic finger.

With his injury behind him, Koufax enjoyed himself as the '63 season approached. A callous covered the tip of his left index finger and allowed him to regain the proper grip on his pitches. He struck out 13 Chicago White Sox in a spring training outing, and was again given the start in the second game of the season. Facing the Cubs, Koufax five-hit Chicago in a 2–1 win. Just over a week later he faced the Cubs again and proved even tougher, striking out 14 in a two-hit, 2–0 shutout.

"He's sound again," Dodger manager Walt Alston smilingly told reporters.

In truth, Koufax's arm was far from sound. He sat out the next two weeks with a sore shoulder. Because throwing a baseball is an unnatural motion, Koufax had stretched and torn the muscles in his left arm. By '63, scar tissue surrounded the muscles, and over the winter months these adhesions tightened. Normally, the adhesions broke loose during the course of throwing in spring training, but in '63 they didn't tear until early May, leaving Koufax with a tender arm.

Returning to the mound against the St. Louis Cardinals, Koufax also returned to form, five-hitting the Cardinals in an 11–1 win. The Dodgers, however, were struggling. Following the team's near-pennant in '62, most observers were sure the Dodgers would have won if Koufax had been healthy, and L.A. was picked by many to win the pennant in '63. The Dodgers stumbled out of the gate instead. Hitters and pitchers alike struggled, and in early May, the team favored to win the pennant sat mired in sixth place.

The Dodgers were in desperate need of a wake-up call, and on May 11, Koufax provided it. The mound matchup for a Saturday night game against rival San Francisco was classic—Koufax versus Giants' ace Juan Marichal. It was Koufax's sixth start of the season, and warming up in the bullpen before the game, he realized he didn't have overpowering stuff. Walking through the infield on his way to the mound to start the game, Koufax yelled to third baseman Tommy Davis, "Hang loose!" It was a warning that he didn't have his best fastball and that Davis should expect to have hits rocketing at him all game. Koufax was half kidding; he didn't have his best fastball and curve, but he felt his stuff would be good enough to get by.

His first pitch of the night was a fastball that Harvey Kuenn rammed to center field. Willie Davis made the catch, and turning to watch, Koufax realized that 20 feet in either direction and the Giants would have started the game off with a hit. Having taken his normal treatment of Capsolin before the game, he stood on the mound straining to loosen up his thick back and shoulder muscles.

Watching Koufax doing what Dodger Stadium fans called mound "dancing," Vin Scully told listeners, "I keep telling Sandy he's got to stop wearing those cheap undershirts."

With transistor radios held to their ears, many in the packed house of 55,530 sent a ripple of laughter through the ballpark. Koufax retired the side in order, then was given a 1–0 lead in the second when Wally Moon smashed one of his towering "Moon Shots" into the foul-pole screen in right field. Moon and Roseboro combined to drive Marichal from the mound as the Dodgers scored three runs in the sixth.

Koufax continued to hold the defending National League champions hitless, even though they had packed their lineup with right-handed hitters against him. Through seven innings he worked on a perfect game, and was so dominant that the Dodger defense had just three tough fielding chances behind him. The first came in the fifth inning, when Dick Tracewski charged Orlando Cepeda's slow roller and made an off-balance throw to first for the out. In the seventh, Felipe Alou backed Tommy Davis, who had been moved from third to left—against the railing in front of the stands with a tremendous drive.

Koufax, watching, thought, "It's a home run," but Davis made the play. Willie Mays then followed with a scorching liner that Jim Gilliam snared at third.

Koufax lost his perfect game in the eighth when Ed Bailey, the lone left-handed hitter in the Giants' lineup, led off the inning and took a fastball low for ball four. Bailey was removed from the bases when Jim Davenport grounded into a double play, and Koufax closed out the inning without further incident and carried his no-hitter into the ninth.

With the Dodgers leading 8–0, the game was no longer in doubt; but the fate of Koufax's bid for an historic second no-hitter still was. To that point, only 12 other pitchers in major league history had ever thrown more than one no-hitter in their career.

Relying on his hopping fastballs, Koufax fell behind Joey Amalfitano 2–0 and then jammed him with an inside fastball that Amalfitano popped up. A veteran hitter, Amalfitano seemed stunned by the speed on Koufax's ninth-inning fastball.

"I thought I was going to hit it squarely," he said, "but it just seemed to run up my bat."

With one out, Jose Pagan flied out to Willie Davis in deep center. Facing pinch hitter Willie McCovey, one of the top home-run hitters in the game, Koufax issued a two-out walk to McCovey on four pitches. Koufax got ahead of Kuenn, who had led off the game with a hard liner to center, with a called strike, then got him to top the ball back to the mound. Fielding it cleanly, Koufax started running to first to make sure he didn't throw the ball away. He then carefully flipped it underhand to Ron Fairly for the final out.

Koufax leapt joyously into the air in celebration of his second no-hitter, and *L.A. Times* sportswriter Frank Finch watched as Dodger Stadium fans showed their approval by showering the field at what he called "Taj O'Malley" with seat cushions. Later, Finch tapped out the following lead to his next-day story:

> Sandy Koufax, just about the best pitcher extant when he's on his stick, silenced the big boppers from San Francisco with his second no-hit, no-run game Saturday night before a turnaway crowd of 55,530.

Koufax was more than happy to "settle" for the no-hit shutout, and told reporters afterwards that the win was more special because it had come against the same team that had driven him from the mound in Game One of the three-game playoff the previous season.

"I'd have to say there was a greater thrill in pitching this one," he said. "People said the first one was against the Mets. This one was against the Giants. There's not a weak spot in their lineup."

Koufax's point was well taken. His no-hitter against the Mets in '62 had seen him walk five and fan 13. Against the Giants, who were leading the National League pennant race, he struck out four and walked only two. Of his 112 pitches against 'Frisco, 73 were strikes. In picking up his fourth win of the season and second shutout, Koufax had lowered the opponent's team batting average against him to a miniscule .122.

Pitching superbly through the first half of the season, Koufax carried a 14–3 record into the All-Star break. It was the same mark he had in '62 at the season's halfway point, but the difference in '63 was his health; there were no circulatory problems holding him back for the stretch run.

A healthy Koufax gave the Dodgers a Big Three rotation that included Don Drysdale and Johnny Podres, and L.A.'s pitching advantage signaled a shift in the balance of power in the National League. Spurred by Koufax's no-hitter, the Dodgers began their climb in the league standings. By late June, L.A. was battling both San Francisco and St. Louis for top spot in the National League; by July the Dodgers had moved into first place, albeit barely.

San Francisco's big bats—Mays, McCovey, Cepeda, Alou—kept the Giants in the pennant race until late August; but the pitching staff, which was thin outside of Marichal, dropped them to third in the league.

Taking 'Frisco's place as the Dodgers' prime contender was the St. Louis Cardinals. Rallying from an eight-game losing streak just before the All-Star break, the Redbirds won 19 of 20 games in September. By the time the Dodgers arrived in St. Louis's Busch Stadium on September 16 for a crucial three-game series, L.A.'s lead had been pared to one game.

The memory of the Dodgers' collapse the year before was fresh in everyone's mind, and while the writers focused on the "choke of '62," L.A.'s veterans welcomed the challenge. Koufax felt his teammates were almost rooting for the Cardinals to keep winning until the Dodgers could get at them. Everyone on the team had a bad taste in his mouth from losing the pennant in '62, and they looked forward to vindicating themselves. With 12 games remaining in the regular season, the Dodgers knew they had to defeat the Cardinals at some point to win the pennant. The club attitude was, "Let's go out and beat 'em and get it over with."

The Dodgers' tough-minded attitude in '63 reflected the maturity of their top players. Gilliam was 34 years old, Moon 33; Podres, shortstop Maury Wills, and catcher Johnny Roseboro were all 30; Koufax was 27; Drysdale and Frank Howard were 26. Together, they represented a second generation of Dodger stars following the aging of Robinson, Reese, Campanella, and Newcombe; and they had become seasoned by the pressures of the pennant race.

The Dodgers-Cardinals series dominated the nation's sports news. Each game sold out, and reporters from around the country surrounded St. Louis manager Johnny Keane before the opener.

"Boys, I know why you're here," Keane smiled. "And I'm glad to see you here, because you go where the action is."

Podres cooled the Cardinal attack on the opening night of the series, limiting them to three hits in a 3–1 win. The second game matched Koufax against St. Louis's ace southpaw, Curt Simmons, who had been with the Phillies. The last time the Dodgers and Cardinals played, Koufax and Simmons had locked up in a mound duel that stood at 1–1 after 12. Koufax left the game for a pinch hitter, but Simmons pitched 16 innings before eventually dropping a tough 2–1 decision.

A 34-year-old veteran, Simmons had not lost since the defeat against the Dodgers, and when he took the mound against the Dodgers on the second night of the series, he had not been scored on in 27 consecutive innings. Koufax, having won 20 games in a season for the first time in his career, began the game gunning for his 24th win of the season. He had thrown 10 shutouts, including the no-hitter against the Giants, and in July had pitched three straight shutouts and 33 straight scoreless innings.

Koufax noted with a certain wryness that the even more conservative writers were hyping his matchup with Simmons as the latest "game of the century."

To Keane, beating Koufax was key to beating the Dodgers. All the Cardinals had to do to win the pennant, Keane said optimistically, was beat Koufax. Cardinals' ace Bob Gibson said Keane made beating Koufax a personal mission. Keane finally determined that the way to beat Koufax was to refrain from trying to pull his pitches. He announced before one game that anyone who tried to pull Koufax would be fined $500. The Cardinals still ended up with only one hit that night—a double that Dick Groat pulled past third.

Staked to a 1–0 lead in the first, Koufax dominated the early innings, holding the powerful Cardinals' lineup of Stan Musial, Bill White, Ken Boyer, and Tim McCarver hitless through six innings. The big defensive play for the Dodgers came in the third inning. Koufax accidentally hit McCarver with a pitch, then followed by fielding Simmons' sacrifice bunt and throwing the ball wildly over second base and into center field for an error. With runners on second and third and one out, Koufax induced Julian Javier to ground to shortstop Maury Wills.

The play was strikingly similar to one in the fifth game of the 1959 World Series against the White Sox. With Chicago runners on first and third and no one out, Wills had gone for the double play and Chicago scored their only run in a 1–0 win against Koufax. Against the Cardinals, Wills threw home to protect the 1–0 lead, and catcher John Roseboro applied the tag on McCarver.

Koufax carried a no-hitter and a 1–0 lead into the seventh. Facing the legendary Musial, who would retire at season's end, Koufax's thoughts centered on pitching "The Man" outside to prevent him from pulling the ball. Musial was 42, and Koufax knew that at this stage of his career, some pitchers were tempted to try overpowering him with fastballs. It was a dangerous misconception, and one Musial did not discourage. Koufax had seen pitchers try to throw the fastball past him, and had watched as Musial uncoiled and his bat flashed quick as ever.

Facing Koufax, Musial took a called strike, then went with an outside pitch and broke up the no-hitter by roping the ball the opposite way to left-center for a single. Koufax stranded Musial by shutting down the Cards in the seventh, getting Boyer and White on first-pitch fly outs.

Koufax gained insurance runs in the eighth when Howard, the Dodgers' 6' 7", 275-pound first baseman, hammered a three-run home run. Backed with a 4–0 lead, Koufax surrendered three singles over the final two innings before wrapping up his shutout. In boosting L.A.'s lead over the Cards to three games with a four-hit, 4–0 win, Koufax had thrown an economical 87 pitches—his lowest ever for a nine-inning game—and did not walk a batter. From the fifth through the ninth innings, he did not go to more than a one-ball count to any Cardinal hitter, a remarkable statistic, and he threw just two balls to the final 14 batters. In a string of 12 straight batters from the sixth through the ninth innings, Koufax threw just one pitch that was not a strike.

"I probably had the best control of my life," he said later.

The Cardinals actually helped Koufax's cause by attacking his pitches early in the count. The Redbirds took just 13 pitches in the middle innings, and just five over the final three. Of the final 10 hitters Koufax faced, nine swung at the first pitch.

He left the team following the game, having gained the club's permission to return to Los Angeles to spend Yom Kippur with his father. The final game of the series saw Gibson carry a 5–1 lead into the eighth, but the Dodgers fought back with three runs in the inning, and tied the game in the ninth on a solo homer by rookie first baseman Dick Nen, who was playing in his first major league game. L.A. eventually won the game 6–5 in 11, dropping St. Louis into a four-game hole from which they never recovered. By season's end, the Dodgers finished six games ahead of the Cards and 11 ahead of the Giants.

Koufax finished the season leading the majors with a 25–5 record. His 306 strikeouts in 311 innings broke his own league record, and his 11 shutouts set a new record for southpaws. Combining a dazzling fastball with a graceful curve, he posted a 1.88 earned run average that was the major league's best. Koufax's pitching excellence, coming as it did just one season after he had almost lost the index finger on his throwing hand, impressed observers.

Dodger pitcher Ed Roebuck felt Koufax had become the best pitcher in baseball, and Cincinnati Reds' manager Fred Hutchinson told reporters it was getting to the point that the league's best right-handed hitters actually bragged in the dugout about getting a hit off a Koufax curve. Writers began calling him "Special K."

As good as Koufax was in '63, Dodger coach Leo Durocher told reporters that he could get even better. "Koufax wins with speed and power," Durocher observed, "but he may get clever yet. It took Warren Spahn about ten years to add cunning to his pitching."

Tris Speaker, a Hall of Fame outfielder with the Cleveland Indians in the 1920s, believed that good pitching can carry a ball club to a pennant. "Even," Speaker said, "a weak-hitting club."

Speaker's words echoed through time and perfectly fit the '63 Dodgers. Despite the presence of power hitters Frank Howard and Tommy Davis, L.A.'s total of 110 homers ranked fourth lowest in the 10-team National League, and was 30 homers lower than their '62 total. It also ranked considerably lower than the 188 homers hit by the American League champion New York Yankees, whom they would face in the World Series.

Experts pegged the Dodgers as certain underdogs for the Series opener on October 2 in Yankee Stadium. Most observers figured the '63 edition of the Dodgers was not even as strong offensively as their '62 team, and the numbers backed them up. L.A. scored fewer runs, posted a lower team batting average, and stole fewer bases in '63 than they had the season before.

The Dodger offense looked overmatched against the Yankees, who were making their third straight Series appearance and were two-time defending world champions. L.A. won 99 games in '63; the Yankees 104. New York had eight hitters reach double figures in home runs; the Dodgers had three. Led by heavy hitters Mickey Mantle, Roger Maris, Joe Pepitone, Elston Howard, Tom Tresh, and Johnny Blanchard, the Bronx Bombers owned a team slugging average of .403. The Dodgers' was .357.

New York newspapers played up the Yankee infield of Pepitone, Richardson, Kubek, and Boyer as the "two-million dollar infield." The Dodger infield of Fairly, Gilliam, Wills, and McMullen? Koufax thought they were being portrayed in the press as a band of ragamuffins worth 50 cents.

The '63 Series renewed the famed Yankee-Dodger Series rivalry— but on a transcontinental, rather than subway, level. New York had won six of the seven previous matchups, and only the presence of L.A.'s fantastic array of starting pitching—Koufax, Drysdale, and Podres—gave Dodger fans any semblance of hope.

Still, the Yankees countered with a rotation of 20-game winners Whitey Ford and Jim Bouton, and 17-game winner Ralph Terry, the hero of the '62 Series.

The opening game of the Series offered a not-to-be-missed collision between Koufax, who led the National League with 25 wins, and Ford, who topped the American League with 24. Asked about the prospect of facing Koufax and his blazing fastball, Tresh, who had hit 25 homers that season, told reporters, "We don't know how fast he is. We can't tell from the newspapers."

Other Yankees were less diplomatic. Writers around the batting cage heard Yankee players downplaying the stories they had heard about Koufax's pitching dominance. "He's only human," one Yankee said. "He doesn't throw that hard."

A crowd of 69,000 crammed into sun-drenched Yankee Stadium for the expected Game One pitching classic. Looking around the banner-bedecked stadium, with the red, white, and blue bunting flapping in the soft sunshine, Koufax could feel the difference in atmosphere between the '59 Fall Classic against the Chicago White Sox and the '63 Series against the Yankees in New York. Considering its trademark latticework facade, "Death Valley" outfield in left-center, and monuments of Ruth, Gehrig, and Huggins in distant center field, Koufax realized why many baseball people felt that a World Series is something less if the Yankees aren't in it.

To Koufax, every stadium had its own unique personality. Ebbets Field had been a ramshackle stadium perfectly suited to "Dem Bums." Dodger Stadium in Chavez Ravine was a colorful, friendly park that fit with the casual, sun-spangled atmosphere of Los Angeles.

Yankee Stadium, Koufax thought, stood forth as a monument of a ballpark. Big and green and aristocratic, it resembled something official, something with the Presidential Seal upon it, like Arlington National Cemetery.

On the field before the game, cameramen got Ford and Koufax to pose for photos and film shots. Koufax felt uncomfortable at the constant comparisons between himself and Ford. It seemed to be less a game between the Dodgers and Yankees, he felt, than between Koufax and Ford.

The two had been compared to each other as far back as 1961, when Koufax was beginning to blossom into the National League's best pitcher. At the time, reporters asked Ford if Koufax's career turnaround was due to his becoming a smarter pitcher.

"Koufax isn't any smarter than he ever was," Ford said. "He's got better control, that's all. He doesn't make as many mistakes as he did."

Because he was still developing as a pitcher in '61 and Ford was recognized as baseball's "Chairman of the Board," the best clutch pitcher in the game, Koufax had downplayed the comparison.

"I still need better control," he said. "Sharp pitchers like Ford can shoot for the outside corner of the plate. I'm lucky to hit the outside half."

Two years had passed since, and the game's two best pitchers were now together for the first time, with baseball's world championship as their stage.

Joe Garagiola told his radio audience before Game One that while Ford specialized in this kind of big-game atmosphere, Koufax's win-loss record that season showed he had become more than just a strike-out artist:

> You try to figure out the big difference in Koufax and he says that when he realized he didn't have to try and throw every pitch with all his might, he became a pitcher. Up until the last couple of years, Koufax would just rear back and throw that real hard fastball into the strike zone. But now, he can spot that fastball.

A review of the Series film illustrates the classic matchup between the two future Hall of Famers. Standing stock-still on the mound between pitches, Ford personified the big-city, businesslike approach of the Yankees. Street-smart and cocky, Ford was a bantam rooster in pin-stripes, frustrating hitters with an assortment of curves and scuffed balls.

Koufax was all motion on the mound, lightly touching his hair or his hat and working his back muscles loose before rocking and delivering the high fastball and low curve.

Ford opened by striking out two of the first three Dodgers he faced, and in the bottom of the inning, Koufax took the Yankee Stadium mound for the first time.

Facing leadoff hitter Tony Kubek, who had struck out just 68 times in 557 at-bats in '63, Koufax opened up with a fastball on the inside corner. Kubek cut at it and missed. Koufax came back with an outside fastball for a called strike, jammed Kubek inside for ball one, then snapped off a curve that rolled down and over. Kubek swung and missed, and Koufax had struck out his first Yankee hitter on four pitches.

Bobby Richardson followed. In the Dodger scouting report from Al Campanis, the Yankee second baseman was regarded as being very important to his team as a player and a leader. Richardson was also the toughest Yankee to strike out; he had batted a league-leading 630 times that season and struck out just 22 times, lowest among New York's regulars.

L.A.'s scouting report warned against throwing Richardson high fastballs on the first pitch, but Koufax started him off by firing a high heater that Richardson swung at and missed. The pitch was important to Koufax, because discovering that he was able to rifle it past Richardson—a high fastball hitter—made Koufax realize he had tremendous stuff that day. Koufax could actually see his fastball rise an inch or two above Richardson's bat. He came back with a big curve that Richardson missed for strike two, then cut loose with another high fastball. Richardson swung and missed, and Koufax had struck out New York's best contact hitter on three pitches.

Stories circulating later said the Bombers were demoralized by Richardson's strikeout. Koufax dismissed the notion, but Richardson related a story involving his second at-bat against Koufax that revealed the Yanks' thoughts that afternoon.

"The second time I batted against Sandy, he struck me out again," Richardson said. "And I remember as I was walking back to the dugout I passed Mantle. He shook his head and said, 'I might as well not even go up there.'"

Because it was the World Series, fans filled the backdrop behind centerfield. Their light-colored clothing made it difficult for hitters to pick up the flight of the baseball. That was one of the reasons Ford and Koufax had combined to strike out five of the first six batters they faced. While Dodgers hitters eventually adjusted to Ford's pitches, the Yankees had their problems catching up with Koufax.

"His fastball took off pretty quick," Richardson recalled. "He just threw it by us. And his curveball was dropping like it was rolling off a cliff."

Some of the Yankees felt Koufax had deliberately challenged Richardson with high fastballs to prove a point to the Yankees. Koufax followed by freezing Tresh with a curve for a called third strike. Sandy walked off the mound knowing he had struck out the American League champions on just 12 pitches. Those strikeouts, he thought, drove home the point to his teammates that they were not going up against a club of supermen.

The Dodgers scored four quick runs off Ford in the top of the second, and Koufax, armed with a big lead, settled in to face the heart of the Yankees' order—Mantle, Maris, and Howard. Facing Mantle for the first time, Koufax started him off with a low, outside curve that he swung at and missed. Ahead in the count, Koufax challenged the Yankee slugger with fastballs. In a classic matchup of power pitcher versus power hitter, Koufax ran the count to 1–2 and struck Mantle out looking with a waist-high inside fastball.

Having retired Mantle on four pitches for his fourth straight strikeout, Koufax got Maris swinging on an outside curve on a 2–2 count for his fifth straight strikeout. The Yankee Stadium crowd buzzed, but Koufax's strikeout streak ended when he retired Howard on a high foul that catcher John Roseboro grabbed at the lip of the Yankee dugout.

L.A. reached Ford for another run in the top of the third, and Koufax cruised through the middle innings with a 5–0 lead. He retired the first 14 hitters he faced before Howard stroked a two-out single the opposite way to right in the fifth. New York scored two runs in the eighth on Tresh's homer to trim their deficit to 5–2, but Koufax fanned Richardson for the third time to tie former teammate Carl Erskine's single-game Series record of 14 strikeouts. With two outs and Pepitone on, Koufax was still one strikeout away from a new series record. He was also one pitch away from a possible 5–4 game, so Dodger manager Walt Alston made a trip to the mound when New York announced pinch hitter Harry Bright, a veteran right-hander who had seven homers in '63 and would be aiming at the short porch in right.

Out on the mound, Alston asked Koufax if he knew anything about Bright. "I remember him from Pittsburgh," Koufax said. "He likes the off-speed pitch."

Throwing outside fastballs, Koufax ran the count to 2–2. Bright fouled off another fastball outside, topping it down the third-base line. Koufax was on the brink of baseball history, and many of the 69,000 fans jammed into the stadium were cheering him on. Bright, who had dreamed his entire life of playing in the World Series, listened to the crowd and thought it strange that hometown fans would be rooting against a Yankee.

But the big crowd wanted to witness history. Koufax cut loose with another fastball.

On radio, Garagiola called the historic pitch:

Koufax has struck out 14, that ties Erskine's record . . . The left-hander gets a pinch of the rosin bag, takes a look down at Roseboro, checks the base runner Pepitone . . . At the belt . . . here's the two-two pitch to Bright . . . Struck him out!

Erskine, who was in attendance, congratulated Koufax in the locker room on his record-breaking 15 strikeouts. "I suppose," Erskine said smiling, "I should thank you for letting me hold it four more years."

Koufax didn't immediately know what Erskine meant, but he found out later. When Koufax had struck out two of the first three batters he faced in his only previous Series start in '59 against the White Sox, Erskine had turned to his wife on that occasion and said, "You don't mind losing that record today, do you?"

More than 30 years later, Erskine recalled the conversation he had with Koufax in the Dodgers' locker room after the game.

"I told him that I felt good that a teammate had broken my record and kept it in the Dodger family," Erskine said. "You know what he told me? He said in the eighth inning, he was thinking, 'It would be nice to tie Carl.' Why would he even think about that in the middle of the game? That shows what a very sensitive person he is."

The Yankees, meanwhile, seemed awestruck. Mobbed by reporters in the clubhouse, Mantle said everything he had read about Koufax's fastball was true. "He threw me five, six pitches right down the middle and I was sure I could hit them," Mantle said. "But I kept tipping them off."

Tilting his hand at a 45-degree angle to imitate a jet taking off, Mantle said, "I guess his pitches must go up. He let me get away twice. Otherwise, he would have struck out 16 or 17."

Richardson asked reporters how Koufax won "only" 25 games. "If he's this consistent, I've never seen anything like him. It's a good thing I walked. He might have got me four times if I didn't."

Looking back at Koufax's Game One performance, Richardson recalled the effect it had on the Yankees.

"We had been the World Series champions two years in a row," he said. "But to see Sandy pitch the way he did, that took some of the wind out of our sails."

Yankee skipper Yogi Berra, a veteran of 11 World Series, sounded just as amazed as his players. "I can see how he won 25 games," Berra said of Koufax. "What I don't understand is how he lost five."

Podres and Drysdale continued the Dodgers' mound mastery the next two games, winning by scores of 4–1 and 1–0 respectively.

Game Four on October 6 in L.A. offered a Koufax-Ford rematch, and fans crowded into Chavez Ravine. Koufax registered four strikeouts in the first three innings, but Ford matched him in scoreless ball through four innings. L.A. scored in the fifth when Howard hammered his second Series homer off Ford, but Mantle tied it in the seventh with a monstrous homer off a Koufax fastball. Watching Mantle's blast sail deep into the left-field pavilion, Koufax realized that after getting away with several pitching mistakes against Mantle in the Series, it was only fair that Mickey would catch up with one.

L.A. got its lead back in the bottom of the seventh, when Pepitone lost a throw to first in the bright background of Dodger Stadium and Gilliam scored an unearned run. Leading 2–1 in the ninth, Koufax was just three outs away from a four-game sweep of the Yankees.

Richardson led off with a single to put the tying run on base; but Koufax struck out Tresh looking on a curve, then faced Mantle again. Throwing fastballs, Koufax got ahead in the count 0–2 when Mantle fouled off his first pitch and swung and missed at the second. Koufax followed with perhaps his best pitch to Mantle, a change-of-pace curve that so froze Mantle he barely took the bat off his shoulder as the ball dropped in for strike three.

With two outs, the Yankees' last hope was Howard, and Koufax got him to ground to short. Wills flipped the ball to second baseman Dick Tracewski for the force on Richardson. As the second-base umpire's hand began to go up signaling the final out, Koufax began his victory leap; but the ump reversed his call when he saw Tracewski didn't have the ball.

The Series wasn't over yet: Koufax was now looking at a first-and-second situation. Staring in at Hector Lopez, who had 14 homers on the season, Koufax kept reminding himself "Concentration. Concentration." Rather than being distracted by the missed opportunity at second, Koufax was grateful the Series hadn't ended on a disputed play. He didn't want fans to think he had benefited from a bad call just when the Yankees were rallying.

Koufax's first pitch to Lopez was a low, tight fastball, and Hector fought it off his fists. Ironically, the ball headed straight toward Wills again, virtually identical to Howard's grounder a moment before. Wills again flipped the ball to Tracewski, and this time he made the final out.

Roseboro rushed to embrace Koufax, who was named Most Valuable Player of the Series. Facing a Yankee team some considered one of the greatest in franchise history, Koufax went 2–0 with two complete games, struck out 23 in 18 innings, walked just three, and posted a stunning 1.50 ERA.

Jim Murray wrote in the *L.A. Times* that Koufax pitched against the Yankees as if he had been double-parked:

> I'm not sure, but I think he got the first three guys out before he got into his uniform. He could have struck out the side from his whirlpool bath.

In the Dodgers' champagne-sprayed dressing room, Koufax told reporters that he had two great thrills in the ninth inning. "One, when I thought the Series was over," he explained. "Two, when I knew it was over."

Koufax's MVP performance against the Yankees completed a season in which he was named MVP of the National League, Player of the

Year by *The Sporting News*, Pitcher of the Year by *The Sporting News*, and Cy Young Award winner at a time when the honor was given to just one pitcher in the majors.

It had been nine years since Koufax had joined the Dodgers as a hopelessly wild kid pitcher, three years since he had almost quit baseball out of frustration, and one year since his career had come close to ending because of an amputation.

One by one, Koufax had overcome the obstacles in his career to become the dominant pitcher in the game. By 1963 the Jewish kid from Brooklyn was the best pitcher in the game—a fact the Twins were well aware of as they approached the final inning of Game Seven.

TEN

s the late afternoon shadows stretched across the green infield of
Metropolitan Stadium, Vin Scully checked his game statistics in
the NBC-TV broadcast booth. The totals through eight innings showed
the Los Angeles Dodgers with two runs, seven hits, no errors, and nine
men left on base. The Twins had no runs, two hits, one error, and five
left on.

Scully took a breath, and as the broadcast resumed following a
television commercial, he leaned towards his microphone to address
his viewing audience of more than 50 million: "So, we're finally face-to-
face with the ninth inning of the seventh game of the 1965 World Series . . ."

Jim Perry, a 29-year-old right-hander, was on the mound for Minnesota—the Twins' fifth pitcher of the day. His first batter in the ninth
was the man who had been the Dodgers' only pitcher of the day—
Sandy Koufax.

As Koufax approached the batter's box on the right side of the
plate—Sandy threw with his left hand but batted from the right—the
PA announcer intoned, "Number 32, Sandy Koufax."

Many in the sell-out crowd of more than 50,000 reacted with sustained applause. Koufax struck out; and if it seems strange that Twins

fans were cheering the enemy pitcher in the climactic game of base-ball's world championship, simply recall the belief of *Newark (N.J.) Star-Ledger* sportswriter Moss Klein that there always seemed to be a certain atmosphere in the stadium when Koufax pitched; the fans al-ways seemed a bit more respectful, like music lovers at a Sinatra con-cert.

Koufax's refusal to pitch a World Series opener on Yom Kippur, his quiet nature, and his classy mannerisms gave him a gentlemanly air. He seemed to be the living embodiment of a baseball poem describing those players who, wearing uniforms designed for an era past, were gentlemen meeting of a Sunday on the grass.

Baseball writer Roger Angell said once that Jim Palmer, a Hall of Fame pitcher for the Baltimore Orioles in the seventies, pitched with such elegance that he seemed somehow to be above the game. Koufax, whose final game would ironically be against Palmer and the Orioles in the '66 World Series, provoked the same kind of sentiment.

With his raven-colored hair and dark good looks, with his classic pitching style and personal charisma, Koufax too seemed above the game. Trimmed in Dodger blue, he had a star quality about him that perfectly fit the Dodgers' Hollywood trappings. He did indeed, as Mets' Hall of Fame pitcher Tom Seaver said once, seem to have come down from another league, a higher league.

Having humbled the Yankees twice in the '63 World Series, Koufax transformed in the off-season from athlete to celebrity. Few remem-bered the nine seasons of control problems, career-threatening injuries, and chronic self-doubt he had endured to become an "overnight" suc-cess. He lived in a $50,000 two-bedroom home that overlooked the pic-turesque San Fernando Valley, and also bought a house for his parents and moved them from Brooklyn to Southern California. He equipped his home with a state-of-the-art, hi-fi stereo system and padded around the place working on odd jobs to the accompaniment of Frank Sinatra music or show tunes. Modern paintings adorned the walls of his home, and his picture window looked out upon the lights of the valley. The house had a large-beamed living room, a wood-burning fireplace, a kitchen, dining area, den, and utility room. It sat on an acre lot that included a small swimming pool, a sheltered terrace, and a rising rock garden. *Sport* magazine writer Milton Gross took a look around

Koufax's house for a November 1964 story on the Dodger star and thought it seemed to be built for repose and relaxation.

Some reporters tried to make Koufax into a deep thinker who spent his leisure time listening to classical music and studying philosophy. "They tried to make him out to be everything but a violin player," author Ed Linn remembered with some distaste. Koufax disputed such lavish reports by quietly insisting his tastes in music and books were the same as the everyday person. "I'm very normal," he said, and went on to mention that he took particular delight in reading the comic strips in L.A.'s daily papers.

Former Dodgers' general manager Buzzie Bavasi said that while Koufax's interests were normal for an everyday person, they differed from those of other ballplayers. Many ballplayers were interested only in talking about their conquests on the field and off. A standing joke in major league clubhouses was how the players were going to explain to their wives why they needed to get a penicillin shot for a kidney infection.

Koufax, however, wasn't one to speak of his dating life. He maintained his privacy, prompting some reporters to call him "reclusive" and to make him into more of a mystery than he was.

"I think few players had the same interests as Sandy," Bavasi said. "I don't think too many players had an interest in music, in lectures, or doing some work around the house. Sandy was a loner in that respect. And you never wanted to pry with Sandy, so I never got too close to him. But I'm sorry I didn't. I always thought he was smarter than I was."

Koufax relaxed with music and books, and tried to get in extra leisure time by golfing. His competitive nature, however, still occasionally got the best of him—just as it used to on the mound—and he would heave his club following an errant shot, sheepishly retrieving it moments later when he calmed down. Asked about his golf game at the time, Koufax told a visitor he was indeed improving. "Now," he said, "I'm just terrible."

He invested his money carefully—stocks, a 64-unit motor hotel on Sunset Strip, a piece of "The Tropicana," an interest in FM radio station KNJO in Thousand Oaks, California. He was just as careful choosing among the numerous endorsement opportunities presented to him in the '63 off-season. He agreed to endorse a boys' baseball game, but turned down lucrative offers to lend his name and face to beer and cigarette ads because he refused to promote drinking and smoking among young people.

Intent on preserving his privacy, Koufax changed his unlisted phone number numerous times, to no avail. Business agents and celebrity hunters harassed him, and he received voluminous mail from fans—300 letters a week—some of them lengthy and expecting equally lengthy responses. In one such instance, a woman complained in the fall of '64 that she had written a letter to him months before and had yet to receive a response. She wanted nothing from him, she said, just the courtesy of a response. Has he, she asked, become so big and stuck up that he won't even bother to reply to his fans?

Koufax had been trying to answer his letters in turn, and he did send her a written response. Unlike some ballplayers, who routinely allowed locker-room attendants to forge their autographs on mail items, Koufax personally handled his own picture and autograph requests from fans. The only help he asked from the Dodgers was in addressing the envelopes.

As the world's most eligible Jewish bachelor, he sometimes received letters and phone calls from mothers wanting to introduce him to their daughters.

At 28, Koufax still wasn't sure he knew what qualities he wanted in a woman with whom he expected to spend the rest of his life. Ever the realist, he knew there were aspects of his baseball life that could make married life difficult, in particular the spring training season and lengthy road trips that required long stays away from home.

"A ballplayer's life," he said, "isn't stable . . . He works weekends and nights when other people are home."

Even before his awesome dismantling of the Yankees in the '63 Series, *Life* magazine pictured Koufax on its August 2 cover. The photo was a closeup of Koufax pulling on his Dodger cap, with the heading: "The Mostest Pitcher: Most Wins, Most Shutouts, Most Strike-outs." After the Series, *Sport* magazine honored him as the Most Valuable Player of the '63 Series, and awarded him a new Corvette. As photographers snapped pictures of Koufax in jacket and tie holding the keys to his car aloft in his now-famous left hand, he shyly issued the obligatory smile.

Though he shared friendships with individual members of the media—including *L.A. Times* columnist Jim Murray—Koufax still felt uncomfortable with the mainstream media. Bavasi watched him deal with mobs of reporters, and while patient and polite, Koufax was clearly uneasy. Bavasi always had the feeling that Koufax would have squirmed less while enduring a dentist's drill then he did when enduring a drilling by reporters.

When Milton Gross approached him in 1964 for his *Sport* magazine piece, Koufax was wary of yet another article being written about him.

"I wish you wouldn't," he told Gross, "although I realize this is the way you earn your living."

"Why," asked Gross, "don't you want the article written?"

"I've seen my name and my picture in magazines so often now," Koufax said, "it's become embarrassing."

With the Dodgers having swept the '63 Series, and with Koufax and Don Drysdale forming the most formidable one-two pitching combination in baseball history to that point, experts picked L.A. to repeat as National League champions in 1964.

Spring training indicated otherwise. Slugger Frank Howard reported to camp overweight, and Koufax grumbled that his $70,000 salary was too little. Plagued by distractions, the Dodgers went 9–16 in Grapefruit League games. L.A. took another hit once the regular season started when veteran lefty Johnny Podres, who had won 14 games as the third starter in '63, was hit by a pitch that chipped a bone and sidelined him for the season.

L.A.'s power production fell from 110 homers in '63 to just 79 in '64, and the anemic offense failed to support the stellar work of Koufax and Drysdale.

Unlike past seasons, when manager Walter Alston would start him the second game of the season, Koufax was on the mound when the world champions took the field at Dodger Stadium on Tuesday, April 14, against the St. Louis Cardinals. A Koufax start had become an event, attracting celebrities like John Wayne, Cary Grant, and Frank Sinatra. A crowd of 50,451, the largest opening-day crowd in the majors in that season, crammed into Dodger Stadium.

Koufax had beaten the Cardinals four straight times, and shut them out in 15 consecutive innings, including a key win in the heat of the previous season's pennant race. The Cardinals hadn't beaten Koufax in more than a year, since September 21, 1962.

Backed by a typical Dodger offensive showing, Koufax continued his mastery over the Redbirds. Wrote Frank Finch in the *L.A. Times:*

> Using their favorite formula—pitching, the single, the bunt and the steal—the Dodgers got off on the right foot Tuesday night as Sandy Koufax hurled a six-hit, 4–0 shutout over the St. Louis Cardinals.

The Dodgers scored in the third when Willie Davis singled off Ernie Broglio, stole second, and scored on Tommy Davis's groundout. Ron Fairly followed by slashing a single up the middle for a 2–0 lead. The Dodgers padded their lead in the eighth when Howard hammered a two-run home run off reliever Ron Taylor, the ball landing halfway up the pavilion 400 feet from home plate.

It was the 100th career homer for Hondo, but the night belonged to Koufax. He allowed just one Cardinal—Bill White in the fourth—to get as far as second base, and it was the ninth time he pitched a complete game without walking a batter.

The victory was Koufax's 10th in a row, dating back to seven straight wins in '63 and two Series starts against New York; he hadn't lost since dropping a decision against Cincinnati on August 11, 1963. The shutout was the 21st of his career, and came one season after he had set a major league record for lefties with 11 shutouts.

As was his custom by then, Koufax missed time during the early weeks of the season, tearing the adhesions in his pitching arm loose and sitting out 12 days. He struggled to regain his rhythm following the layoff, and by the end of May his record stood at just 4–4.

Heading east for a road trip, Koufax struggled through a 5–4 win over the Pirates in Forbes Field. Despite gaining the decision, he had been roughed up, surrendering a home run to Roberto Clemente that was hit so hard the ball was still climbing when it struck a light tower in left-center field, 450 feet away from home plate. Koufax knew there was no embarrassment in yielding a home run to Clemente, even though it was a fastball and it came on a 1–2 count. Clemente, he knew, could hit any pitch, anywhere, anytime.

After allowing the homer to Clemente, Koufax was knocked out of the game in the eighth. The Dodgers next traveled to Philadelphia, and as Koufax sat in front of his locker in Connie Mack Stadium, he began flipping idly through back issues of *Sport* magazine. Seeing an article on his no-hitter against the Giants the season before, he noticed something in the photos taken of his delivery in that game. The pictures had been shot from behind home plate by Dave Sutton, and as Koufax looked at them, he noticed his front foot was positioned more to the right side during his throw home. His form was wide open, the ball almost in back of his ear before being released.

After Dodger pitching coach Joe Becker saw the photos, he and Koufax immediately began working on the mechanics of Koufax's motion, getting him to open up. Two nights later on Thursday, June 4, Koufax took the hill at historic Connie Mack Stadium, confident his rhythm was back and his fastball was moving the way he was accustomed to. Warming up, he knew he had tremendous stuff.

He had defeated the Phillies six straight times since losing in Philadelphia 2–1 on September 27, 1961. But he took the ball knowing he could not afford to give the Phillies too many run-scoring chances. His opponent, 26-year-old southpaw Chris Short, owned the lowest earned run average in the majors, and the Dodgers' offense had been struggling. He had received no run support in a 1–0 loss to the Reds, and he had watched Drysdale victimized by an unearned run in a 1–0, 11-inning decision the night before.

Just over two hours later, pinch-hitter Bobby Wine flailed and missed at a fastball, and Koufax walked off the field with the third no-hitter of his career and a 3–0 victory. Throwing just 97 pitches, he had been behind on only three batters all evening. Striking out 12, Koufax faced the minimum 27 batters and came within one pitch of a perfect game. Only a walk to Phils' slugger Richie Allen on a 3–2 pitch in the fourth spoiled his bid for perfection. Moments later, Allen was thrown out while trying to steal second.

Allen also figured in the Dodgers' toughest fielding chance of the night. Third baseman Jim Gilliam, who had committed an error the night before that allowed the Phillies to score their only run in the win over Drysdale, redeemed himself by cleanly fielding Allen's slow roller and firing to first for the out.

In the history of the major leagues to that point, only three other pitchers had thrown as many as three no-hitters in their career. Two of those came before, or at, the turn of the century. The Cubs' Barry Corcoran recorded no-hit games in 1880, 1882, and 1884. Cy Young of the Red Sox did it in 1897, 1904, and 1908. Only Bob Feller of the Cleveland Indians had thrown three no-hitters in an era that even slightly resembled Koufax's, and his were spaced out in years—1940, 1946, and 1951.

Koufax was the first pitcher in major league history to throw a no-hitter in three straight seasons. Recalling his no-hitting the Mets on June 30, 1962, and the Giants on May 11, 1963, Frank Finch wrote in the *Times* that his performance against the Phillies was "easily the best of Koufax's three gems."

Koufax agreed. In the jubilant clubhouse after the game, he told reporters, "This was the best of them," he said, smiling, "the best of them all."

A crowd of 29,709, the Phils' largest of the season to date, had turned out for the expected mound showdown between Koufax and Short. The two matched scoreless innings through six before L.A. broke through in the top of the seventh. Following singles by Gilliam and Tommy Davis, Frank Howard launched a long homer to left-center, giving the Dodgers a 3–0 lead.

By the final inning, the fans were rooting for Koufax as he faced Tony Taylor leading off the bottom of the ninth. After trying to bunt his way on, Taylor struck out swinging on a 2–2 pitch. Ruben Amaro followed, and Koufax retired him on a first-pitch foulout to first baseman Ron Fairly.

With the crowd rocking the old stadium in anticipation of the no-hitter, Koufax cut loose with a fastball that Wine tipped foul. He followed with two more fastballs, Wine swung and missed at both, and the Dodgers rushed to the mound to embrace their ace.

Drysdale, who had gone to Washington the night of the game to take care of a personal legal matter, didn't learn about the no-hitter until he was told by a reporter.

Asked Drysdale, "Who won?"

Drysdale's remark was a pointed reference to the Dodgers' struggling offense. Koufax, however, didn't seem fazed by the lack of run support.

"I always go for a shutout," he said. "Then one run is all I need."

The no-hitter improved the Dodgers to 22–25, but they remained in eighth place. Koufax went on a personal streak of excellence, winning 10 of his next 11 games, but the Dodgers failed to gain any ground. The loss of Podres to injury had robbed the team of a reliable third starter, and with their starting corps depleted, L.A. lingered in eighth place.

Obviously, the Dodgers knew by midsummer that they were not going to repeat as pennant winners in '64. Their disappointment deepened in early August, however, when Koufax endured another mysterious arm ailment. Pitching in Milwaukee against the Braves on August 8, Koufax was losing 2–1 to Tony Cloninger when he came to bat in the fifth. Koufax, who was one of the worst-hitting pitchers in baseball, stroked a single off the Braves' right-handed ace and took second on a single by Maury Wills.

Attempting to pick Koufax off, Cloninger wheeled and threw to second. Koufax dove back in safely, a four-point landing on elbows and knees, but a hard tag shocked his left elbow. Despite a stinging pain, Koufax stayed in the game, and eventually scored on a two-run triple by Ron Fairly that gave the Dodgers a 3–2 lead. An RBI single by Tommy Davis drove in Fairly to make it 4–2. The Dodgers pushed across another run, and Koufax gave up a two-run homer to Dennis Menke in the seventh before walking off with a hard 5–4 win.

Awakening in the Schroeder Hotel the next morning, Koufax realized his left elbow was swollen. Though there was no discoloration on his arm, the arm ached. Four days later, Koufax ignored his aching elbow and shut out the Reds for seven innings before allowing a homer to Deron Johnson. He finished with 10 strikeouts and just one walk, and despite the on-again, off-again swelling and soreness, Koufax started four days later against the Cardinals on a Sunday afternoon in Los Angeles. Striking out 13 and again walking just one, he earned his 15th win in his last 16 starts. His record was 19–5 and he had a league-best 1.74 earned run average; but when he awoke the next morning, he realized his season was in jeopardy.

The swelling in his pitching arm was no longer confined to his elbow; it now extended from wrist to shoulder. The arm was locked in a hooked position; he couldn't bend or move it more than an inch in any direction. When he tried, he could literally hear liquid squishing inside.

It was, he said later, as if he had a wet sponge inside his arm. Looking at his swollen limb, he thought, "I have a knee for an elbow."

More surprised than frightened, Koufax hoped the swelling would reduce itself over the course of a day or two, as it had previously. Since Monday was an off day, Koufax waited until his return to Dodger Stadium on Tuesday to show his swollen arm to Dr. Robert Kerlan. The Dodgers' team physician took one look at Koufax's pitching arm and sent him to his office for treatment and x-rays.

Tests showed that Koufax's left arm had passed beyond the irregularities most veteran pitchers have, the pulls and nicks that wear down the protective cartilage covering the elbow joint. Past x-rays of Koufax's arm revealed numerous chips and tears that had occurred from thousands of pitched balls, but the x-rays taken August 17, 1964, showed the arm had undergone a traumatic blow. The damage to his arm, Dr. Kerlan told him, was no longer temporary. It was permanent.

"Sandy," he said, "you have arthritis."

Dr. Kerlan was familiar with the condition. A former athlete, his own back was bent by arthritis and he walked in a crouched manner. Koufax had traumatic arthritis, brought on by the chipping away through pitching of the cartilage around his elbow. The hard tag at second base in Milwaukee might have been the hit that accelerated the arthritis. But the condition had already been developing in his pitching arm for years, the result of a delivery that slammed his left arm across his body with each pitch.

When the lining in his arm became inflamed, it "weeped" excess fluid into the hinge at the joint of his elbow. Water on the knee is a common condition for NFL running backs who take repeated hits to their legs, but Koufax may have been the first pitcher in major league history to suffer from water on the elbow. He called his left arm "the weeping hinge." Needles were plunged into his arm to draw out the excess fluid, and the condition was treated with cortisone and oral medication. He took two weeks off, then tried to return against the Cardinals in St. Louis. After throwing three or four warmup pitches, Koufax could actually see the arm begin to swell up again. Within minutes, he could hear the liquid squishing inside, and he was sent back to L.A. for further treatment.

Two weeks later he tried again, throwing batting practice at Dodger

Stadium. His elbow remained sore and swollen, and that finished him for the season. The National League pennant race by then was in full fury; four teams eventually finished within five games of pennant winner St. Louis. The Dodgers were 13 games off the pace, and with L.A. not in contention, club officials decided to rest Koufax over the winter and look ahead to '65.

Koufax looked ahead to an arthritic condition for which there was no cure, which could only get worse every time he pitched.

Koufax approached the '65 season with cautious optimism. Because he had not thrown a ball all winter, and had not taken any treatment for his arthritic left elbow, he didn't know what to expect from his pitching arm once spring training opened in March.

He was convinced that if he hadn't tried to rush his comeback the previous August, he might have been able to pitch down the stretch. Now, with a winter-long rest, he was hoping that what he referred to as the "healing touch of winter" would allow him to resume his career. Indications in early spring were that Koufax's hopes would be realized. The arm had responded to rest, and he was loose and strong in the early weeks of the grapefruit season at the Dodgers' camp in Vero Beach, Florida.

Coming along faster than usual for him, Koufax worked nine innings earlier than he had ever done since joining the Dodgers ten years before. On March 30, a week before the club was set to break camp, Koufax faced the Chicago White Sox in Sarasota and threw another complete game. The next morning, he awoke to find his arm swollen again, though not to the tree-trunk size of a year before. He showed his blown-up arm to roommate Dick Tracewski, and the Dodger second baseman responded with a sad shake of his head.

Rather than panic or become discouraged, Koufax attacked the problem by analyzing his performance against the White Sox the day before. Since he had not experienced previous arm trouble this far into the spring, he believed the swelling must have occurred from his pitching style against the Chisox.

Recalling that Chicago's lineup had a high number of lefty hitters, Koufax had subconsciously adjusted his pitching motion by going to a sidearm motion with his slider. He had thrown sidearm the year before when he aggravated his elbow against St. Louis, and he estimated that he threw sidearm on as many as 12 to 14 pitches against the White Sox.

Koufax made a decision from that moment on to scratch the slider from his pitch selection. He also decided to hide his injury by wearing a heavy sweater, believing he could hide the swelling until it reduced in a day or two. When the arm remained swollen the next day, he approached Buzzie Bavasi in the club dining room.

"It looks like I'm in trouble," Koufax said. "There's no way I'm going to be able to pitch with this for awhile."

Bavasi arranged for Koufax to return to L.A. to see Dr. Kerlan, and the two also realized that since the press would be wondering why Koufax was leaving camp, the time had come to tell the media about his arthritic condition.

The next day, newspapers across the country carried bold headlines declaring, "Koufax Has Arthritis." Drysdale brushed off talk of his 29-year-old counterpart being forced into early retirement.

"I know Sandy," Drysdale said. "He'll be back if he can pitch at all."

Alston tried to downplay Koufax's condition by telling reporters he couldn't believe his ace would be out for any length of time.

"There may be medical things I don't know," Alston said, "but from what I've seen of him this spring, I have to be optimistic."

Dr. Kerlan was less so. Though cortisone treatments reduced the swelling in Koufax's arm, Kerlan didn't like the idea of injecting him with shots twice a week during the regular season and then sending him out to pitch. The Dodgers' team physician didn't believe the arm would hold up to that kind of wear and tear, and was doubtful that Koufax could even be a "Sunday" pitcher, the baseball term for pitchers who throw once a week.

Again, Koufax's resolve to pursue his baseball career led him to explore every possibility short of retirement. Doctor and patient discussed having him pitch every fifth day instead of every fourth, but over the course of a 162-game regular season that meant Koufax would make 34 starts instead of 41. Dr. Kerlan wasn't convinced that a mere seven fewer starts would dramatically improve Koufax's condition.

Wrestling with his dilemma, Koufax came up with an idea that prolonged his career. Rather than reduce the number of starts he would make, why not eliminate the throwing he did on off days? "I won't throw on the second day," Koufax told his doctor. "I won't pitch any batting practice. I won't pick up a baseball at all between the time I finish one game and the time I begin to warm up for the next one."

If that didn't work, Koufax said, he would try to pitch every fifth day, or even every sixth day. If all else failed, the game's best pitcher would consider becoming a Sunday pitcher.

As the club headed north to Washington for an exhibition game against the Senators—before opening the National League season in New York's Shea Stadium against the Mets—Koufax hoped his arm would hold up long enough for six or seven starts before it swelled up so bad he would be forced to miss a start. It was, he realized, the best he could hope for.

Alston and Koufax agreed that the Dodgers' ace would loosen up for the season by throwing in the bullpen during the Senators' game. If the arm responded, Koufax would pitch two innings against Washington. Entering the game in the seventh, Koufax worked the final three innings, striking out five and surrendering just one hit. The last batter he faced was Doug Camilli, an ex-roommate who had been sold to the Senators in the off-season. Camilli had caught Koufax's no-hitter against the Phillies the year before, and expected him to be weakened by his much-publicized arthritic condition. Popping out when he couldn't get his bat around quick enough on a blazing fastball, Camilli shouted over at Koufax, "Sore arm, my eye!"

The Senators' game signaled the start of what would become a regular routine for Koufax in '65. He took phenylbutazone alka, a drug that attacks inflammation but can carry a weighty side effect—a reduced red blood cell count. Koufax also soaked his left elbow for 45 minutes in a tub of near-freezing water. To help him cope with the cold water, team trainer Bill Buhler cut a length of rubber from an inner tube, then fashioned it into a "sleeve" to protect the skin on the arm from exposure to water whose temperature climbed no higher than a frigid 35 degrees.

Early-season rainouts delayed Koufax's first start of the regular season to the second week. On a rainy Sunday in Philadelphia, he defeated the Phillies 6–2. He struck out seven, but walked five and scattered six hits. Koufax worked out of a late-inning jam and threw a lot of pitches, and by his own admission had pitched what he later called a "ragged" game. Yet it was the kind of game he had expected after throwing just three innings over the previous 18 days.

The best news came the next morning, however. The left elbow was sore and a little puffy, but that was all. Koufax had been curious to see how the elbow would be affected after the game. If it continued to swell, he was sure Dr. Kerlan could handle the inflammation. To Koufax, it was a matter of finding out if he was going to go through the season the hard way or the easy way.

Koufax was 4–2 at the end of April, and in his eighth start of the season pushed himself and his arthritic elbow through 11 innings in a 5–3 win over Houston. Widespread attention had been paid to his condition, and people responded by mailing him remedies that included exercises, magic charms, and prescriptions. Author George Vecsey called him "America's favorite medical project." Frank Finch of the *L.A. Times* labeled him "America's most prominent arthritic patient."

Throughout the season, Koufax's arm would swell the day after he pitched, feel better the second day, then begin to swell again the third day. By the fourth day, his arm would be back to normal size as he took the mound again to pitch. Koufax discovered as the season went on that there were neither rules nor guarantees to his condition. Some days the arm didn't bother him at all between starts. On other days it hurt so much he was ready to concede to the pain and miss a start.

He never did. Resisting cortisone shots and cutting down on his medication, he pitched through the swelling and the pain and didn't miss a turn the entire season. By the end of the season, he had started 41 games and pitched a league-high 336 innings, the most by a left-hander since 1906 and more than anyone since Robin Roberts threw 337 innings in '54. Koufax's total in '65 was also 45 innings more than the 291 thrown by American League leader Mel Stottlemyre of the Yankees.

By the midsummer All-Star break, questions concerning Koufax changed from early retirement to whether he would become the first major league pitcher to win 30 games since Dizzy Dean of the Cardinals did it back in '34. He won his 20th game on the remarkably early date of August 10 when he beat the Mets 4–3. Combining with Drysdale, who threw 308 innings, and lefty Claude Osteen, who worked 287 innings after being acquired over the winter from Washington to fill the need for a third starter, L.A.'s workhorse pitching staff carried the weak-hitting Dodgers in the pennant race.

Setbacks and frustrations filled the Dodgers' drive to the pennant. They lost their best hitter, Tommy Davis, on May 1 when he broke his right ankle sliding, and starters Willie Davis, Ron Fairly, John Roseboro, and Maury Wills were all sidelined at times by injuries. They were embarrassed by the Reds 18–0, and on Labor Day, the traditional start of the final push for the pennant, they lost three leads and eventually the game itself against the Giants. They also dropped three straight decisions to the last-place Mets.

As late as September 16, the Dodgers stood four-and-a-half games behind the Giants and felt the pressure of the pennant race. Koufax felt the pressure as well. In early September, after going five starts without a win and seeing the pennant slipping away, he stormed into the Dodger clubhouse following a no-decision against Houston, overturned a rubbing table, and threw it against a wall.

The tension of the pennant race engulfed the Dodgers and Giants. Age-old rivals in New York, they had transplanted their fearsome battles to the West Coast in '58. In the six years since, they had combined to make three World Series appearances and were perennial contenders for the National League pennant. In late August, the two teams locked up in a four-game series in San Francisco's Candlestick Park, and the final game on August 22 offered a dramatic Sunday afternoon showdown between Koufax, an eventual 26-game winner, and Giants' ace Juan Marichal, who would go on to win 22 games.

A crowd of 42,807 crammed into Candlestick to see two of the game's best pitchers go head to head. With Koufax firing fastballs to sluggers Willie Mays and Willie McCovey, and with Marichal keeping the Dodger jackrabbits off-balance and off base with his high leg kick, the pitching matchup lived up to its billing. L.A. gave Koufax a 2–1 lead in the early going, and Marichal responded by dusting Dodger hitters with inside pitches. Koufax was confident he could get hitters out without intimidating them and was fearful, like Walter Johnson before him, that his fastball could seriously injure an opponent. But Dodger catcher John Roseboro decided to take matters into his own hands.

When Marichal batted in the bottom of the third, Roseboro approached the mound and told Koufax, "I'm going to take care of this guy."

Roseboro's intent was to throw close to Marichal when he returned Koufax's first pitch. He did, but Marichal, believing the ball ticked his right ear, turned and screamed at Roseboro, "What'd you do that for?"

What happened next shocked the baseball world. Film of the game shows the Giants' pitcher exploding in rage and clubbing Roseboro over the head with his bat, opening a bloody two-inch gash on the left side of his scalp. Koufax can be seen rushing to Roseboro's aid and attempting to separate the two men as Marichal's bat flailed wildly in the air. Players from both sides vaulted from their dugouts as baseball's most infamous fight escalated into a bench-clearing brawl.

As San Francisco stadium police rushed towards home plate, Mays put his arms around Roseboro. A photographer rushed in and snapped one of baseball's most famous photos—an anguished Mays leading the blood-drenched Roseboro away from the melee. Seeing that his friend had blood streaming down his face, Mays screamed, "John, you're hurt! You're hurt bad!"

"I need one more shot at him!" an angry Roseboro spat through blood-streaked lips.

The Dodgers took their catcher to the clubhouse to repair the cut in his scalp, and Marichal was ejected from the game. The fight followed Marichal and Roseboro for years. Marichal continued to claim Roseboro had hit him in the ear with his return throw, a claim Roseboro has always disputed. If he had wanted to hit him, Roseboro said, he would have hit him in the damn head.

Marichal's attack on Roseboro remains baseball's most infamous brawl, and baseball observers believe it kept Marichal out of the Hall of Fame for years. Not until Roseboro and Marichal ended their feud in recent years was the Giants' ace finally voted into Cooperstown.

Shaken by the events on the field, Koufax tried to settle down. He struck out Bobby Schroder, who was batting for Marichal, then retired Tito Fuentes on a fly ball. He followed by walking Jim Davenport and McCovey on eight straight balls, then watched as Mays crushed his first pitch for a three-run homer.

"I knew Sandy was shook up," Mays said. "After what happened, Sandy didn't have his real good stuff."

The Giants won 4–3, frustrating Koufax and the Dodgers even further. Having won 20 games by August 10, Koufax won only one more game through September 8. He broke his personal five-game losing streak in history-making style in Dodger Stadium, on September 9 against the Chicago Cubs.

Koufax matched up against Bob Hendley, a tall, 26-year-old southpaw. The two lefties matched no-hit ball through the first four innings. In the bottom of the fifth, L.A. scored in typical fashion. Lou Johnson, a 30-year-old outfielder called up from the minors to replace the injured Tommy Davis, drew a walk and was bunted to second by Ron Fairly. When Jim Lefebvre dipped his bat and dropped another bunt, Johnson headed for third, then scored when rookie catcher Chris Krug's throw headed into left field for an error.

Hendley held L.A. scoreless the rest of the way, allowing only one hit, a double by Johnson. Koufax nursed his slim 1–0 lead through the middle innings, pitching a perfect game and allowing just seven balls to be hit out of the infield. As he stood on the mound in the eighth, he sweated beneath the glare of the Dodger Stadium lights. Heaving fastballs, Koufax struck out Ron Santo, Ernie Banks, and Byron Browne swinging.

Watching Koufax work, Hendley knew the Cubs were in trouble. "Around the seventh inning or so, we knew Sandy wasn't going to give us a hit," Hendley said. "He was just unbelievably fast."

In the top of the ninth, Koufax struck out Krug and Joey Amalfitano. One out away from witnessing an historic perfect game, the Dodger Stadium crowd of 29,139 cheered on every pitch. Having struck out Amalfitano swinging on three straight fastballs, Koufax prepared to face veteran pinch hitter Harvey Kuenn. As Amalfitano walked back towards the dugout, he passed Kuenn, who was walking towards home plate.

"It's not worth it, Harvey," Amalfitano whispered. "You might as well not even bother coming to the plate."

Rocking and throwing, Koufax fired three fastballs towards Kuenn. Three times the former American League batting champion swung and missed.

"Great, oh great!" Koufax shouted happily as teammates rushed to congratulate him. In the Cubs' clubhouse, Banks approached a pair of dazed rookies. "Are you sure," he asked, "you kids want to play in the National League?"

Santo, who would hit 33 homers that season and drive in 101 runs, seemed stunned. He had never seen Koufax throw as hard as he did when he struck Santo out in the eighth. The Cubs' slugger had been waiting for the fastball, but Koufax still threw it past him.

Banks, en route to a 28-homer, 106-RBI season, tipped his cap to Koufax. "He was getting the curve over real good the first five innings, then he got tremendous momentum."

In the Dodger locker room, reporters surrounded Koufax, whose perfect game was just the eighth in major league history. Incredibly, the no-hitter was his fourth in as many seasons.

"You know, as much as I wanted the no-hitter and the perfect game, I was just as pleased that I won my twenty-second game," he said. "I had five starts at it before getting the win and guys were beginning to think there was something wrong with me.

"I got stronger as I went along and that's something that had not happened to me before this year. In the last three innings, I had my best fastball in a long, long time. Early in the game, I had a great curve."

Koufax lost his next start, a return match with Hendley, then came on in relief two days later to earn a save, one of two he had on the season. The following week, L.A. launched a 13-game win streak that carried them past the faltering Giants and into first place.

In the September heat of the pennant race, Koufax keyed the Dodgers with a white-hot streak of excellence:

On September 18, he shut out defending world champion St. Louis, 1–0.

On September 25, he shut out the Cardinals again, 2–0.

On September 29, he shut out the Reds, 5–0.

On October 3, the final Saturday of the regular season, he took the mound with two days' rest and held the Milwaukee Braves to four hits while striking out 13 in a 3–1 win that clinched the pennant.

After Johnson gloved Dennis Menke's lazy fly ball to left for the final out of the game, Finch crafted the following lead for his story in Sunday's *Times:*

Those unbelievable Dodgers made believers of everyone Saturday, and they did it in their typically unbelievable style to win the National League pennant.

They scored three runs with the benefit of only one base hit and made them stand up—rather, magnificent Sandy Koufax did—in defeating the Milwaukee Braves, 3–1, before 41,474 ulcer and coronary cases at Dodger Stadium.

It was Los Angeles' 14th win in its last 15 games, climaxing one of the great stretch drives in the history of the game. . . .

Next Stop: Minnesota.

Finch's story was topped by a boldface headline that read: "It's All Over. The Dodger Way: 2 Hits Plus Sandy Equals Flag."

Beneath it ran a smaller head that read: "Mr. K (26–8) Sews Up L.A.'s Third Pennant—and Alston's Fifth."

Finch wrote that Koufax had unintentionally wrung every last ounce of suspense out of the clincher as fans endured a thousand deaths. It was, he wrote, a nerve-wracking case of Koufax protecting his small lead because everyone knew the Dodgers weren't going to score another run.

"After all," wrote Finch, "it isn't every day their pitchers can enjoy the luxury of three runs."

Finch's words about the pennant clincher were just as applicable to the situation Koufax and the Dodgers found themselves in two weeks later in Game Seven of the Series. After Koufax struck out to start the top of the ninth, Wills tried to ignite a ninth-inning rally when he worked Jim Perry for a walk. The uprising ended when catcher Earl Battey gunned out Wills trying to steal second, and Perry followed by getting Jim Gilliam to ground out to Zoilo Versalles at short.

Clinging to a bare 2–0 lead, Koufax headed to the mound for the bottom of the ninth. In the NBC broadcast booth, Scully had remarked minutes earlier how long ago the first day of spring training now seemed, and how everything these two teams had labored months for was at stake here in the ninth: "What makes this Series end up on some kind of a high note is in the ninth inning, all the Twins have to come up: Tony Oliva, Harmon Killebrew, and Earl Battey."

As the Twins came to bat in the bottom of the ninth, Scully left the broadcast booth to make his way to the locker rooms to prepare a postgame broadcast. Taking over at the NBC mike was Ray Scott, the voice of the Twins:

> The man recognized as baseball's greatest pitcher, Sandy Koufax, in the last of the ninth, must face one of the fine hitters in the game, two-time American League batting champion Tony Oliva; one of the premier long-ball hitters in the game, Harmon Killebrew; and another long-ball threat, Earl Battey.

The millions listening on NBC Radio could hear the sustained roar of the 50,000-plus at Met Stadium, the background noise very nearly drowning out the words of play-by-play announcer Joe Garagiola: "Two-to-nothing the Dodgers lead . . . bottom of the ninth . . . And the crowd wants action. A very partisan crowd here . . ."

As Koufax stood on the mound, his gray uniform, dampened by the mix of sweat and Capsolin, rippled in a crisp fall wind. Rolling his shoulders to loosen his thick back muscles, he waited for Oliva to take his position in the batter's box.

Garagiola:

> Sandy Koufax has to get the three toughest outs in baseball. Three outs to nail down a victory, and how much tougher can it get than this? This is the seventh game of the World Series, he's got a two-run lead, and he's got the American League's leading hitter, a home-run hitter in Killebrew, and Earl Battey. That's the story as Koufax gets set.

Through eight innings, Oliva was 0-for-2 against Koufax with two strikeouts and a walk.

"Sandy was throwing hard that day," Oliva recalled, "and there's not too many guys who can hit a fastball that's moving like that. We knew he had elbow problems, but after he warmed up, he was throwing better on two days' rest than most pitchers do on four days' rest. He didn't try to trick you. He would just throw strike after strike after strike. He won 26, 27 games back then, so he knew what he was doing."

Koufax started Oliva off with a fastball, and Oliva flung his bat down the first-base line after swinging at strike one. Koufax came back with an inside fastball, and Oliva swung and missed for strike two. With the count 0–2, Koufax delivered an outside fastball that Oliva punched the opposite way to backup third baseman John Kennedy, who had replaced Gilliam at the start of the inning for defensive purposes. Fielding the ball cleanly, Kennedy threw to first baseman Wes Parker for the first out.

Koufax had now retired 12 straight Twins. Facing the powerful Killebrew, he bounced a curve in the dirt for ball one. Koufax came back with a high fastball. Killebrew, who was also 0-for-2 with a walk, swung and missed to even the count at 1–1. Koufax delivered another fastball that sailed high for ball two, but the Killer jumped on the next pitch, a fastball, and singled sharply to left.

The hit was just the third of the game for the Twins, and it roused the Met Stadium crowd. Killebrew's hit meant Minnesota now had the tying run at the plate—the powerful Battey. At third, Kennedy took up a position practically astride the white-chalked foul line; the Dodgers were desperate to prevent an extra-base hit down the line. As if the baseball gods were trying to add more suspense to an already tense situation, the October wind suddenly picked up and began blowing towards left—an unmistakable aid to a right-handed pull hitter like Battey.

Drysdale, who had thrown nearly a full game in the bullpen, was throwing hard and with purpose, just in case Koufax faltered. In the Dodgers' locker room, Gilliam sat on a trainer's table puffing nervously on a cigarette as he watched the game on TV.

"Sandy's pitching on instinct," Gilliam told Scully, who had just arrived from the booth. "He's like a fighter on the ropes trying to survive."

NBC cameras focused in on the tiring Dodger superstar. Koufax seemed to be aging on every pitch. He was just 29 years old, but he said later that he felt 100 years old by game's end. His coal-black hair was streaked with sweat and glints of gray, and his two-day stubble had grown darker in the late afternoon shadows.

Throughout the '65 season, whenever Koufax had been in a jam, Roseboro would ask him what he wanted to throw. The answer was always the same.

"Heat," Koufax would say.

As beads of sweat glistened on his dark stubble, Koufax got set to pitch from the stretch for the first time since the fifth inning. Arm-sore and bereft of his curve, he was throwing nothing but fastballs.

Battey, who owned a .409 slugging percentage during the season, swung and missed at strike one. Koufax fired another fastball and Battey swung through it again. With the count 0–2, he rocked and flashed an inside fastball that froze Battey for a called third strike.

Koufax now stood just one out away from pitching the Dodgers to their second world championship in three seasons and their third since '59. Allison, 0-for-2 with a strikeout, fouled a fastball straight back for strike one, then bent backwards to avoid an inside riser. Koufax was high and tight with his next fastball to run the count to 2–1.

Scott: "Koufax reaching back. So far today, every time he has to reach back, he has found what he needed."

With 23 homers on the season, Allison was a legitimate long-ball threat, and fans on both sides knew that with Killebrew at first, one swing could tie the game. Allison was a fastball hitter, Koufax a fastball pitcher, and the confrontation stirred the crowd.

Garagiola: "Koufax comes down the stretch . . . Bottom of the ninth, two men out, Killebrew at first . . . Bob Allison, big powerful right-hand hitter. He had a big home run yesterday. Koufax looks down for his sign . . . Allison waits . . ."

Reaching back, Koufax rocked and cut loose with a fastball so hard he almost fell off the mound, staggering to his right with the force of his follow-through.

Garagiola: "Koufax at the belt . . . delivers . . . Swung on and missed and it's strike two. Koufax really turned one loose. It actually knocked him to one side as he really came following through . . ."

Now one strike away from the Series title, Koufax reached over again and pinched the rosin bag. He had thrown 106 pitches this day, 17⅔ innings in three days, and 360 innings dating back to April—exhausting work for a man with an arthritic elbow.

Now, seven months after having thrown his first pitch in spring training, he was one strike away from final victory. Scudding clouds passed in front of the sun and turned the color of the outfield grass from the emerald green of the early innings to a darker, winter green. Outside the stadium, the cool October wind rustled treetops, loosened the grips of leaves, and left the trees bare.

Summer, it seemed, had finally run its course.

Tugging on his cap, Koufax stared in for the sign, set himself, checked Killebrew at first, and with arm and elbow aching, fired one final fastball.

Allison whipped his bat through the strike zone, and 50,000 Twins fans roared at the anticipation of a hit that could rescue their dream season.

With his bat flashing in the fall sunshine, Allison swung viciously. And missed.

The crowd hushed; suddenly, the skies over Minnesota had the hazy look of winter.

Scott: "He did it! Sandy Koufax gets his tenth strikeout, his second consecutive shutout of the Twins. On Monday on a four-hitter; today on a three-hitter.

"Every pitcher likes to finish a game with a strikeout. This, of course, was not 'a' game.

"This was the seventh game of the World Series."

ELEVEN

J im Gilliam mashed out his cigarette in the visiting clubhouse and grinned at the television monitors showing his Dodger teammates mobbing a weary Sandy Koufax out on the field.

Overextended by his tremendous effort, Koufax looked both exhausted and exhilarated as he smilingly shook hands with teammates.

As the jubilant Dodgers rushed joyously into the clubhouse, outfielder Lou Johnson beamed. Exhibiting the smiling exuberance that led teammates to call him "Sweet Lou," Johnson shouted, "All the way with Sandy K!"

In the press box, veteran reporters were convinced they had just witnessed one of the most courageous clutch performances in sports history. Jim Murray of the *Los Angeles Times* thought that Koufax in his painful condition shouldn't even be throwing a baseball for a living, never mind a three-hit shutout in Game Seven in an enemy ballpark that's hitter-friendly. Murray later likened Koufax's assignment to a guy with silicosis going back down into the mine, the tubercular seeking out a cold, damp climate.

Leonard Koppett of the *New York Times* thought Koufax had to survive a shaky beginning before he simply began overpowering the Twins. Koppett called it a performance that involved determination and response to pressure as much as sheer talent and skill. The fact that Koufax shut out the champions of the American League on two days' rest, one less than healthy pitchers usually need, made Koufax's Game Seven even more memorable for the *Times* reporter.

Praise for Koufax filled both locker rooms. In the Twins' quiet clubhouse, manager Sam Mele sat behind his neatly organized desk as reporters crowded in to speak with him. Mele's dark blue Twins' cap rested on his lap, and a cigarette sat in a black plastic ashtray; smoldering but within reach, it symbolized perfectly the Twins' plight in Game Seven.

"Koufax," Mele said, "is great. The best I believe I have ever seen."

As Mele talked, he kept running his fingers through his graying hair, and he spoke of Koufax in tones *Sports Illustrated* writer William Leggett felt reflected a mix of frustration and appreciation.

"You hate to lose," Mele continued, "but we didn't disgrace ourselves. We were beaten by the best pitcher that there is, anywhere."

Leggett felt that if baseball's world championship had to be decided by one game, it should be decided by a Game Seven as magnificent as this. Baseball is fun, he thought, when the best meets the best, when strength faces strength; and the strengths in this World Series were Koufax and the Twins' hitters.

Leggett thought that Koufax had seemed unsure of himself when he struggled and fidgeted through the early innings. But after surviving the difficult fifth inning, he seemed to grow stronger and stronger. By the time the Twins got a runner on in the bottom of the ninth and had the tying run at the plate, Leggett thought the entire 1965 baseball season had come down to the strength of Koufax against the strength of Earl Battey and Bob Allison.

Koufax struck them both out, and as Leggett noted, this Series proved beyond a doubt that he did indeed "belong in a higher league."

When Leggett's cover story appeared in the October 25 issue of *Sports Illustrated,* it ran beneath the headline "The Final Strength Was Sandy." Beneath it ran a smaller head declaring, "The best pitcher in baseball proved to be the difference between two very different ball clubs."

As champagne sprayed freely around the Dodgers' lathery locker room, Koufax was brought to the center of the room, where he joined

Vin Scully on top of a trunk serving as a makeshift podium to be interviewed for NBC TV and radio.

"Sandy, in Los Angeles, when you pitched your seven-to-nothing shutout, you were quoted as saying after the game, 'I feel a hundred years old.' So today, how do you feel?"

"A hundred and one," Koufax laughed. "I feel great, Vinny. I know I don't have to go out there anymore for about four months."

When Scully remarked that it appeared as if the fastball was really the only pitch he threw for quite some time, Koufax nodded.

"Yes it was," he said. "I don't know what it was today. I didn't have the curveball at all, I wasn't getting it over. I just stayed with the fastball and tried to get it to pretty good spots. When I got the lead, I tried to keep them from pulling the ball if I could.

"I felt like my fastball the last three or four innings was as good or better than it was early in the ballgame, which I really didn't expect."

Wrapping up the interview, Scully listed Koufax's accomplishments—four no-hitters, a perfect game, 18 strikeouts in a single game, a World Series record of 15 strikeouts in a game. Where, Scully asked, does this Game Seven win rank among his pitching highlights?

"This," Sandy said smiling, "has got to be as high as any of them."

Johnson, next in line to be interviewed by Scully, yelled, "You're the greatest, Sandy! You're the greatest, baby!"

Drysdale, spotting Koufax, grabbed him after the interview and gave him a hug and kiss on the cheek.

"You beautiful, beautiful fellow!" Drysdale shouted.

When someone asked him if he had been anxious to get in the game, Drysdale remarked, "As long as we win, it didn't make any difference to me. I think I had good stuff warming up . . ."

Alston told reporters that Drysdale "must have pitched nine innings in the bullpen, but I started him early just in case Sandy developed any early trouble."

After finishing with Scully, Koufax returned to his locker. The members of the print media were slow in arriving; many of them, like Bob Broeg of the *St. Louis Post-Dispatch*, had been stuck in a crowded elevator.

"We were submerged beneath street level," Broeg recalled, "but he waited for us."

Koufax's patience impressed the Cardinals' beat writer. "For a shy guy," Broeg said, "he was very nice."

Once the reporters arrived, the questions came rapid-fire:

Did he have any control of his curve?

"I didn't have a curveball at all," Koufax said. "When I threw it, I couldn't get it over. And those first few innings, I really didn't know how long I was going to last. Then I seemed to get my second wind. In the last three innings, the fastball seemed to move better and I felt I got stronger."

Did he recall other games when he had been forced to depend so heavily on his fastball?

"Yes, but if I had a choice I'd rather not have it happen in a World Series, like it did to me today."

Was he worried at any time that he might be taken out?

"I was worried in the fifth and again in the sixth when I seemed to lose my rhythm. When Walt came out to talk to me, he told me not to try and get anything extra on the ball, just pitch to spots."

When Paul Zimmerman of the *L.A. Times* mentioned to Dodger catcher John Roseboro the difficulties Koufax faced winning Game Seven with his fastball alone, Roseboro agreed.

"Sandy," Roseboro said, "is the most exceptional pitcher in the game today."

Returning to the press box, Zimmerman filed the following lead for his next-day game story:

> It isn't often a man can win the World Series deciding game with only a fastball, but that's exactly what Sandy Koufax did at the expense of the power-laden Twins here Thursday.

Koufax's clutch performance in Game Seven enhanced his superstar status. For the second time in three seasons, he won a Corvette as *Sport* magazine's Most Valuable Player of the World Series and was named National League MVP. For the second time in three years he received the Cy Young Award, prompting Twins' ace Jim "Mudcat" Grant, who led the American League with 21 wins that season, to say that there should be two awards.

"One for Koufax," Grant said, "and one for the rest of us."

Despite his brilliant season—his 382 strikeouts in '65 were the most ever by a southpaw and led the league for the third time since '61—success came at a high price. His arthritic elbow caused him considerable pain, and he had spent the '65 season under doctor's orders not to throw between starts.

Aware that his career could end at any time because of arthritis, Koufax wanted to capitalize on his success financially. After winning Game Seven, he signed to write his autobiography, assisted by author Ed Linn, for $100,000. Linn traveled to Honolulu to spend time with Koufax, who was vacationing by himself in a beach house of a deserted golf course. In the time of his greatest triumph, Linn thought, Koufax had taken himself away from everybody and everything.

Koufax explained his vacation choice to Linn by saying that if he were to stay at a hotel and expect to have his privacy respected, he would have to be either a fool or a fraud. And Koufax needed his privacy at this time, he told Linn, to stop and take a personal inventory.

"I think everyone has a need at times," Koufax said, "to relax with his eyes wide open, and you know, think things out."

Koufax's eyes were wide open when it came to his baseball contract. Two years earlier, in the spring of '64, he had approached Dodger general manager Buzzie Bavasi and asked that his salary be increased to $75,000 per year. The Dodgers countered with an offer for $70,000, and when it was reported in the papers that Koufax actually asked for $90,000 per year, Koufax was angry. Baseball salaries weren't generally made public in the sixties, and when he saw the newspaper story with the inflated figure, he believed someone in the Dodger organization had fed the wrong figure to the press in an effort to make him appear greedy to fans. Wary of tarnishing his public image, Koufax signed the Dodgers' counteroffer of $70,000.

Privately, he was upset. He told friends he had been maneuvered into a corner, where he was forced to agree to the Dodgers' terms or be regarded by fans as greedy.

Koufax remembered the incident two years later when he approached management asking for a salary increase. San Francisco had reportedly signed slugger Willie Mays to baseball's richest contract ever—$105,000 per year—and Koufax, who made $85,000 in '65, was looking to become the sport's highest-paid pitcher. Bavasi asked him to be patient; but Koufax, now 29 and still feeling the pain in his pitching elbow, realized time was not on his side. Linn said that one of the reasons Koufax agreed to do his autobiography before the '66 season was because he knew he was going to hold out and didn't want to feel pressured for money.

"That's the only reason he did the book," Linn said.

Drysdale, the other half of the Dodgers' dynamic one-two pitching combination, made $80,000 and was also seeking a raise. In past years, Koufax and Drysdale believed that management had played one off the other during contract negotiations to keep salaries down. Since both were coming off big seasons—Koufax won 26 games, Drysdale 23—the two decided to present a united front. It was the first time two superstars of the same team had ever bargained together; Babe Ruth and Lou Gehrig had considered the strategy in their Yankee glory years, but Gehrig eventually decided not to.

In what baseball observers at the time considered an outrageous set of demands, Koufax and Drysdale not only sought to negotiate together, they wanted the Dodgers to negotiate with their lawyer, J. William Hayes, who also represented Hollywood actors. To sign with the Dodgers, Koufax and Drysdale wanted three-year contracts totaling $1 million—$500,000 to each.

Their demands came out to $166,000 each per year, and when Bavasi first heard about them in late October, he shook with laughter.

"Good luck, boys," he said, and made a counteroffer of $100,000 for one year to Koufax and $90,000 for one year to Drysdale.

The stance taken by Koufax and Drysdale reverberated beyond baseball and rocked the sports world. Dodger owner Walter O'Malley, who had been wary that his team's move from Brooklyn to Los Angeles might someday lead to his star players being represented by Hollywood agents, was irate at the demands of his star pitchers.

"I never have discussed a player contract with an agent," O'Malley said, "and I like to think I never will."

Bavasi drew another line in the sand when he said the Dodgers would never sign players for more than a year at a time. Bavasi's reasoning was that since athletes were selling their physical ability, how could they guarantee that ability three years in advance?

Koufax, Bavasi noted, would turn 31 at the end of the '66 season.

Who knew how many pitches he had left in his arthritic elbow? Drysdale was about to turn 30, and he was working on a sore knee.

The two pitchers remained unmoved. They liked Bavasi personally, but they knew that the balding, fast-talking general manager was virtually unbeatable in one-on-one contract negotiations. Bavasi had acknowledged Koufax's worth in '65 when he said he was worth $100,000 because he put an extra 5,000 people in the stands whenever he pitched. Yet he asked Koufax and Drysdale if they believed, as pitchers working every four days, they were worth as much as everyday stars.

"Do you really think you're worth more than Mickey Mantle?" Bavasi would ask. "Or Willie Mays?"

Presenting a united front and promising a joint holdout during the '66 season, Koufax and Drysdale felt it was the only way they would be dealt with to their satisfaction.

Media reaction was mixed. *Sports Illustrated* reported that Koufax and Drysdale, "the K-D entry" as the magazine referred to them, demanded not just three-year contracts but "full ownership of California and Nevada and the Strategic Air Command, plus options on the Mississippi River and Philadelphia . . ."

"We were getting headlines every day," Bavasi said. "You couldn't buy the space we were getting. But O'Malley did something I didn't like. He called the office and told them to have one of the boys call him. So the next day, Drysdale called, and Walter went to the papers and said, 'The boys are getting anxious. They called me today.' That wasn't fair really."

Koufax and Drysdale knew the Dodgers were making money on them; the club was drawing 2.5 million fans a year to Chavez Ravine, and the appearance of either Koufax or Drysdale on the mound increased attendance figures even more. When Koufax had his breakthrough season in '61 with 18 wins, the Dodgers set an all-time attendance record the next season by drawing 2,755,184 fans to Chavez Ravine.

Dodger management didn't argue the worth of Koufax and Drysdale to their club—they had combined to win three of L.A.'s four games against the Twins in the Series—but O'Malley thought it was a matter of principle to resist their demands. If they were successful, he argued, what would prevent the Dodger outfield or infield from demanding to negotiate together in future seasons?

Working in O'Malley's favor was baseball's reserve clause, a standard provision in each player's contract that prevented athletes from switching teams. From the Dodgers' standpoint, Koufax and Drysdale would pitch for Los Angeles or would not pitch at all.

Koufax, however, strengthened his position by accepting $100,000 to do his autobiography with Ed Linn; and he and Drysdale were photographed in November signing contracts with director Buzz Kulik to play feature roles in a Paramount picture called "Warning Shot."

When they told Bavasi they would lower their contract demands from $500,000 each over three years to $450,000, Bavasi shrugged.

"Good luck in the movies, boys," he said.

When the Dodgers opened spring training in February, Koufax and Drysdale remained absent from the world champions' camp. The two met with Bavasi again and agreed to drop their demands for three-year contracts and lower their asking price again, this time to less than $150,000 each. They did, however, insist on signing together for the same amount.

Bavasi, however, remained unmoved. He told Koufax he was going to pay him more than Drysdale, and suggested that if Sandy insisted on equal pay for Don, he should pay him out of his own pocket. But, the Dodger GM said, he would not sign them together for the same price.

"My price still stands," Bavasi said, "$100,000 for Sandy, $90,000 for Donald. What's your answer?"

Sticking together, Koufax and Drysdale told Bavasi to have a nice time at Dodger camp. They were prepared to spend the spring playing golf and preparing for their movie role.

Talk of the joint holdout dominated the sports news. When Alston talked of grooming young pitchers to replace Koufax and Drysdale, the two pitchers understood he was talking from management's side. But when some Dodger players said they felt the two pitchers had gone too far in their demands, Koufax and Drysdale were surprised. They felt that by holding out, they were strengthening future bargaining positions for other players.

In mid-March, the two reported to Paramount to begin filming of

"Warning Shot." Photographers snapped photos of them studying the script with star David Janssen.

At the end of March, Bavasi took a call from actor Chuck Connors. A former baseball player, Connors acted as an intermediary between Koufax and Drysdale and Dodger management.

"Chuck called me one day and said, 'Buzzie, these fellas are ready to sign.'"

Hearing this, Bavasi called J. William Hayes. The Dodgers, Bavasi said, were still insisting on separate contracts; but they would increase their offer to $110,00 for Koufax and $100,000 for Drysdale. Connors arranged to have Nicola's, a restaraunt near Dodger Stadium, open its doors at 9 A.M. on March 30 so it could serve as an office for the negotiations.

"We met there," Bavasi said, "and O'Malley had given me a $225,000 budget, and that was it. Sandy agreed to $125,000, which is what he wanted in the first place, and Drysdale agreed to $100,000. We went up to the office and drew up the contracts, and I said to myself, 'The hell with it. I'm going to give Drysdale $110,000.' So I gave him $110,000, figuring O'Malley would raise hell. He didn't raise hell, and we won the pennant that year. Then I got a note from O'Malley saying, 'It was nice of you to give Drysdale your bonus.'"

Koufax had received a $40,000 raise; Drysdale $30,000. Their raises were the biggest in baseball history, and Koufax was now the highest-paid player in the game.

"When I signed Sandy and Donald in the holdout," Bavasi recalled, "we paid Drysdale for winning games. But we paid Sandy for breaking records. Drysdale was a helluva pitcher, but I don't remember a lot of people saying, 'Let's go see Drysdale today.' But when Sandy pitched, it was, 'Let's go see Sandy.'

"I always thought Sandy's religious beliefs made O'Malley a million bucks. When we played Minnesota, Sandy couldn't pitch because it was Yom Kippur. So Drysdale tried it with two days' rest, but he just couldn't do it. He got tired and he lost. Now Sandy came back and he had five days' rest, which was too much, and he was wild and he lost. But we went on to win it, and I always say that if Sandy hadn't missed his turn we would have won in four straight. But it went seven games, and O'Malley made a million dollars."

Following the holdout, Drysdale spent the '66 season struggling to regain form. A 23-game winner the year before, he won 10 games less in '66 and his record fell below .500 to 13–16. As his victories dropped, his earned run average rose, to 3.42—Drysdale's poorest since 1961.

While Drysdale streaked in one direction, Koufax streaked in another. Putting together perhaps his finest season ever, he had 16 wins by July 14, a breathtaking pace that had observers predicting a 30-win season for the Dodger ace.

Koufax's 16–4 record was the best in the majors, but his success exacted a heavy price physically. He was losing the feeling in the fingers of his left hand, and he found himself dropping objects and unable to perform even simple tasks, like using a screwdriver to repair household items. The pain was such that Dodgers' team doctor Robert Kerlan was forced to inject cortisone directly into Koufax's elbow. Koufax's use of painkillers before games and ice baths to soak his arm afterwards continued to increase.

Through it all, Koufax remained not only baseball's dominant pitcher, but the game's dominant performer as well. Along with Cleveland Browns fullback Jim Brown and heavyweight champion Muhammad Ali, Koufax in '65 and '66 ranked as one of the sports world's premier athletes and gate attractions.

Opposing players knew of Koufax's debilitating physical condition, yet they found it almost impossible to believe that he could be in such pain and still dominate his sport.

"I'm gonna sit up all night and cry for him," Mets third baseman Ken Boyer said with dripping sarcasm after Koufax defeated New York for his 16th win. "He threw one pitch that was impossible. No ball can get up to the plate that quick. Not even his. Then he threw it again."

Before the game, Koufax told Mets' shortstop Ed Bressoud his rhythm had been fouled up for the past 10 days. After watching Sandy stifle New York, Bressoud told reporters, "I'd like to have my rhythm as fouled up as his."

Koufax had become such a dedicated craftsman he could dominate on days he didn't have great control of his pitches.

"I never saw him with less stuff," Reds' manager Fred Hutchinson said after being blanked by Koufax. "He had nothing, but we got skunked."

Pittsburgh Pirates' rightfielder Roberto Clemente, who battered opposing pitchers for a .317 batting average in '66, grew angry with reporters following an 0-for-4 performance against Koufax.

"Don't tell me about arthritis," the Bucs' future Hall of Famer said in broken English. "How can his arm hurt if he throws that hard?"

But it hurt so much that it began to wear on Koufax emotionally. On August 30, he was forced from the mound in just two innings against the Mets, and surprised both dugouts by arguing with the home-plate umpire over several close pitches. One Met said afterwards that he never thought he'd see the day when Sandy Koufax would argue for strikes.

Lowering his rubber-encased left arm into a tub of freezing water after the game, Koufax refused to use his pain as an excuse for defeat. "I was just lousy," he said.

Others, however, brought the extent of Koufax's pain to the public. *Times* columnist Jim Murray advised his readers in a September 24 article to "come out to the ball park every fourth night and see nine innings of industrial accidents."

The pain, Murray wrote, was self-inflicted. Koufax, he said, was being paid $125,000 to go to the rack every four days. "It takes the other three for the swelling to go down," Murray wrote. "Pulling your nails out with pliers is the nearest thing to it."

The toughest part, Murray said, was Koufax's unwillingness to complain. When reporters asked him about his arthritis, Koufax told them, "There's nothing wrong with my arm." Then he took his arm out of the frozen water and waited for the next injection of cortisone and dosage of painkillers.

Murray wrote that Koufax's situation was complicated by the fact that he was tired of talking about his arthritis and was eager to dispel the image of himself as a reluctant pitcher. Yet Murray believed it was inevitable that sooner rather than later, Koufax was going to snap off one of his ballerina-like curves and his inner arm would go up in flames.

Bavasi knew Koufax was pitching in pain, but he says he didn't realize how much pain Koufax was in until he had to deal with arthritis himself in his later years.

"I don't see how he did it," Bavasi said. "Every pitch he threw, he must have had tears in his eyes."

The Dodgers spent the summer locked in a pennant race with San Francisco, Pittsburgh, and Philadelphia. With Drysdale struggling, Koufax stood as the lone go-to guy in a big game. He teamed with reliever Bob Miller to beat Houston on September 11, giving the Dodgers first place in the National League.

With two weeks left in the regular season, each contending club sent its best pitcher to the mound to face Koufax. Like a sheriff facing down gunslingers in the Old West, he responded to each challenge.

He beat Pirates' 16-game winner Bob Veale, 5–1, and Phillies' 20-game winner Chris Short, 11–1. On September 25, Koufax and the Dodgers were dealt a 2–1 loss by Cubs' southpaw ace Ken Holtzman in Chicago, but Koufax came back four days later to beat Cardinals' ace lefty Al Jackson 2–1 in St. Louis.

The final weekend of the regular season matched the Dodgers and Phillies in Philadelphia. On the final Sunday of what had been a grueling campaign, the Dodgers stood one win away from clinching a second straight trip to the World Series. L.A. was one game ahead of the Giants in the pennant chase, but a loss to the Phillies in this final game and a Giants' victory over the Reds would force a tie and one-game playoff to decide the National League championship.

With title hopes on the line, Alston handed the ball to Koufax. The strain of pitching in pain showed in Sandy's face; photographer David Sutton snapped a picture of Koufax looking tired and drawn as he headed off the mound in a game at Dodger Stadium. Other photos taken that season show Koufax grimacing as he pitched.

His left arm was bent in pain, and his sports coats were altered to fit the curved shape of his arm. The pain forced him to rely more and more on cortisone shots and painkilling pills, and the medication left him feeling high on days he pitched and with a constant upset stomach on days off.

Still, he pushed on.

Rematched against Short, the Phils' ace, for the second time in September, Koufax was staked to an early 6–0 lead. He cruised through the first four innings, then felt a tremendous pain in his back after delivering a pitch in the fifth. He willed himself through the inning, then walked hurriedly off the mound and into the clubhouse.

Approaching team trainers Wayne Anderson and Bill Buhler, Koufax seized up in pain. "My back!" he said. The trainers quickly removed his shirt and had him lie on a training table.

They applied Capsolin to his back to loosen the muscles, then probed with their fingers to find the cause of the pain. A piece of his spine had slipped out of place, and the two trainers hurried to get him fixed up and back on the field. Easing him to the floor, they stretched and pulled until the disc popped into place.

Koufax quickly pulled his jersey back on and hurried to the field. Still experiencing some back pain and too tired to throw anything but fastballs, Koufax fought his way through the sixth, seventh, and eighth innings. In the ninth, an error and three consecutive hits allowed the Phillies to score three runs.

With no outs and the pennant riding on every pitch, Koufax reached back and challenged the Phils with fastballs.

Bob Uecker struck out.

Bobby Wine grounded out.

Jackie Brandt struck out.

Koufax's 6–3 win was his 27th victory of the season, capping an emotional and exhausting campaign. He led the league in games started with 41 and innings pitched with 323. Despite the tremendous workload, he also led the league in ERA at 1.73, his best ever, and in strikeouts with 317.

For the second straight season and third time in four years, Koufax had carried the Dodgers on his left wing to a pennant. In the jubilant visitors' locker room, where Koufax an hour earlier had lain on the floor while his back was manipulated, Dodger players praised his performance.

"He's beautiful," Lou Johnson said, and Maury Wills told reporters he shuddered to think where the Dodgers would be if not for Koufax. "He saved us," Wills said.

It would be the last time Koufax would save the Dodgers.

On October 6, he started Game Two of the World Series in Los Angeles against the Baltimore Orioles. The O's had won the American

League pennant that season with 97 victories, two more than the Dodgers had earned in capturing the National League flag, but L.A.'s vast post-season experience—this was their fourth World Series since 1959, and the team had engaged in playoffs in both '59 and '62—made them favorites over the young Orioles to gain a second straight world championship.

The Orioles caused a minimal stir in Game One when they beat Drysdale, 5–2, but observers shrugged. Hadn't L.A. dropped Game One against Minnesota last year and come back to win? And didn't the Dodgers have Koufax waiting to start Game Two?

Jim Palmer, a Series starter in spite of being a few days shy of his 21st birthday, took the mound with some trepidation about dueling Koufax.

"I just didn't want to embarrass myself," Palmer recalled with a laugh. "He was the best pitcher around, and you had the attitude you didn't expect to win. I was just trying to go out there and pitch the best I could."

The mound matchup between Koufax and Palmer not only pitted a 30-year-old Series veteran against a 20-year-old kid, it also involved two future Hall of Famers: Koufax, the three-time Cy Young winner, and Palmer, who had three Cy Youngs in his future.

Standing in the on-deck circle before facing Koufax for the first time, Palmer watched in fascination as Koufax whipped three fastballs to catcher Andy Etchebarren.

"Radio fastballs," Palmer said, still shaking his head at the memory some 33 years later. "You could hear them, but you couldn't see them. Everybody says the ball doesn't jump, that you can't get it to rise. Well, his ball jumped about six to eight inches."

The two matched scoreless innings through four, but Koufax ran into trouble in the fifth. Boog Powell, the Birds' big first baseman, rapped a single to left. It was just the second Oriole hit off Koufax, and the Birds, playing for one run, had Dave Johnson sacrifice Powell to second. Paul Blair followed by lofting a high fly to his opposite in center field, Willie Davis. Losing the ball in the bright California sunshine, Davis dropped it for an error, putting runners on second and third.

Etchebarren followed, and Alston flaunted baseball's traditional strategy when he ordered Koufax to pitch to Baltimore's rookie catcher and number-eight hitter rather than face Palmer, who had fanned in his previous at-bat. Alston believed Koufax would get Etchebarren, a .221 hitter in '66, and Palmer to retire the side.

Koufax did get Etchebarren to fly to center for what looked like the second out. Except that Davis lost the ball in the sun again, then compounded his mistake by throwing wildly past third. Davis's three errors in one inning was a Series record and allowed Baltimore to take a 2–0 lead. One out later, Luis Aparacio pulled a double past third to score Etchebarren and give Baltimore its third unearned run of the inning.

Koufax got out of the jam by retiring Curt Blefary, then headed toward Davis in the dugout. Some Dodgers were startled to see Sandy striding toward the despondent center fielder, who sat alone in the far corner of the dugout. Wills jumped from his seat on the bench to block his path, but Koufax nudged the small shortstop aside.

Sitting down next to Davis, Koufax draped his arm around the outfielder's slumped shoulders.

"I'm sorry, Sandy," Davis said. "I couldn't see the ball."

"Forget it, Willie," Koufax said. "Forget it. Don't let it get you down."

To some, it was a scene similar to one involving another famous fireballer decades earlier. When Washington Senators' Hall of Famer Walter Johnson lost a game on a dropped flyball by outfielder Clyde Milan, the sensitive Johnson refrained from criticizing his teammate. Asked about the error, the Big Train said gently, "Clyde doesn't do that very often."

In the sixth, Koufax gave up a long fly to Frank Robinson. Sandy turned and watched as Davis took after it, then seemingly backed off from the ball at the last instant to avoid a collision with rightfielder Ron Fairly. The ball dropped untouched for a triple, and Powell's RBI single made it 4–0 Baltimore.

Koufax retired the side without further incident, then was replaced by Alston for a pinch-hitter in the bottom of the sixth. The Orioles went on to score two more runs off Koufax's successors, and Palmer walked off with a 6–0 win.

Koufax retired to the clubhouse to soak his arm and await a Game Five start in Baltimore. It never came; the Orioles swept the Series in four games.

No one knew it at the time, but Sandy Koufax, the most famous and dominant player in baseball, had pitched his final game.

TWELVE

A t 1:08 P.M. on November 18, 1966, Sandy Koufax walked into an expensively furnished suite in the Beverly-Wilshire Hotel in Beverly Hills, California. Elegantly dressed in a royal blue sports jacket, black slacks, black slip-on shoes, a black tie, and a crisp, white button-down shirt, he moved with an athlete's grace as he took a seat at the head table next to his agent, William Hayes.

The huge room was filled with more than a hundred reporters, photographers, and cameramen. A battery of 15 microphones was positioned before the Los Angeles Dodgers' ace, and with his wavy black hair and handsome features, he could have passed for a young movie star who had come to talk about his latest picture.

Instead, the media throng knew why they had been summoned to the plush surroundings of this hastily called press conference. They knew, but still couldn't—or wouldn't—believe it. Looking at the young athlete at the head of the room, a man whom Phil Pepe of the *New York Daily News* thought was the very picture of affluence, the image of health and youthful vigor, reporters couldn't believe what Koufax was about to say.

"I have just a short statement to make," he began.

Because the Dodgers were overseas for a series of exhibitions against professional Japanese teams, L.A. general manager Buzzie Bavasi had asked Koufax to postpone his blockbuster announcement. Koufax had told Bavasi the big news the night before, and Bavasi agreed that Koufax's concern about continuing to pitch with an arthritic elbow was justified. He knew that Koufax was unable to completely straighten his left arm, that the long fingers on his left hand sometimes tingled and caused him to drop items as light as a screwdriver, and that the pitcher's sports coats had to be altered to accommodate his injured arm.

"You've got money in the bank," Bavasi told him, "you're a young man, and you've got a chance to make some money. There's no sense staying in baseball and jeopardizing your future."

Bavasi recalled that people within the Dodger organization felt that Koufax had spent the '66 season on borrowed time, and that his retirement was not a complete surprise.

"I think people close to the club had a feeling he might do this," Bavasi said. "He did the right thing and I'm glad he did. Although look at the impact he had on the club. In '66 they won. In '67, they finished what, fifth?"

Bavasi requested at the time that since team owner Walter O'Malley was in Japan, couldn't Koufax postpone his decision until the Dodgers returned stateside? Bavasi didn't want his boss picking up a Japanese newspaper the next day and reading that the greatest pitcher in team history had just quit the game.

"You've got to give Walter a chance to take part in something as important as this, Sandy," Bavasi said. "I think we both owe it to him."

Koufax, however, remained adamant. He had been suggesting to management late in the season that he was seriously considering retiring. He avoided accompanying the club overseas because he knew Japanese fans would expect him to pitch. They wouldn't understand why he couldn't, and it wouldn't be fair, Koufax thought, to Japanese fans or the Dodgers if he went to the games and didn't participate.

Since the final out of the World Series loss to Baltimore, Koufax felt he had been living a lie. He knew he was retiring, but he had been forced to mislead reporters inquiring whether he would pitch the 1967 season. His phone rang constantly, and even when he sought refuge out of the house, he was asked about his plans for the next season. Whether he was on the golf course at the Crystallaire Country Club outside L.A. or in restaurants, the questions were always the same: "How's the arm, Sandy? Have you reached any decisions whether you're going to play next year?"

Koufax always wondered if he deflected the questions politely enough. For his own peace of mind, he felt a pressing need to tell the public the truth, that the pain in his pitching arm and the consequences of continuing to snap off flaring fastballs and twisting curves concerned him deeply.

Bavasi understood, but he told Koufax that because O'Malley and the team were overseas, the Dodger organization wasn't going to be represented at his momentous press conference.

"Well," Koufax replied, "I'm going to do it anyway."

"He had his mind made up," Bavasi remembered. "You know, Dr. Kerlan was my closest friend in the world, and he told me, 'There's no way this young man can go another year. He could, but it would be detrimental to his future.' He had every right to do what he did. Maybe O'Malley was a little annoyed, because he saw the dollar signs. Every time Sandy pitched, we had five, ten thousand extra people."

In the Beverly-Wilshire the next day, Koufax watched quietly as a crush of media gathered in the hotel suite. The room was so crowded that reporters and cameramen had to push and shove their way inside.

Koufax was flanked on his right by his agent, but no member of the Dodgers' organization was there in an official capacity. As the clock moved towards 1:15 P.M., Koufax took a breath and leaned into the battery of microphones on the table before him.

"A few minutes ago," he said, "I sent a letter to the Dodgers asking them to put me on the voluntarily disabled list."

His voice was smooth and steady, reflecting few of the emotions that usually accompany such a moment. As he spoke, flashbulbs popped through the room, reminiscent of the sparkling lights that accompany the first pitch of a World Series game.

"I feel I am doing the right thing," he continued. "I've got a lot of years to live after baseball, and I would like to live them with the complete use of my body.

"I have taken too many pills and too many shots. I am just afraid that something might happen that would cost me the use of my arm the rest of my life.

"I don't regret one minute of the last twelve years," he said. "The only thing I regret is leaving baseball."

Except for the clicking of camera shutters and the low hum of television cameras, the room was silent. Finally, a reporter asked the obvious.

"The question," he said, "is 'Why?'"

Koufax issued a faint smile. "The question is 'Why?'," he said, repeating the reporter's query. "I don't know if cortisone is good for you or not. But to take a shot every other ballgame is more than I wanted to do, and to walk around with a constant upset stomach because of the pills and to be high half the time during a ballgame because you're taking painkillers, I don't want to have to do that."

"What is your thought," someone asked, "about the loss of income?"

"Well, the loss of income," Koufax said. "Alright, let's put it this way. If there was a man who did not have the use of one of his arms and you told him it would cost a lot of money if he could buy back that use, he'd give every dime he had, I believe.

"That's my feeling, and in a sense, maybe this is what I'm doing. I don't know. I don't regret one minute of the last twelve years, but I think I would regret one year that was too many."

In the long history of professional baseball, which dates back to 19th-century America, Koufax's retirement stood as an unprecedented event. No other star in the sport's history had ever stepped down at the peak of his career, and only a handful of other professional athletes—heavyweight champions Gene Tunney and Rocky Marciano, and Cleveland Browns fullback Jim Brown—had retired while still dominating their sport.

In 1966, Koufax led the major leagues with 27 victories, 323 innings pitched, 317 strikeouts, and a 1.73 earned run average. His win total and ERA were the best of his career, and in an era when the Cy Young Award was given to just one pitcher from both leagues, he won for the second straight year and third time in four years.

"I don't know of any other athlete," Bavasi said, looking back, "who retired after his greatest season."

Koufax was still a month away from his 31st birthday, and he was retiring as the game's greatest pitcher. He was walking away from a guaranteed quarter of a million dollars over the next two seasons, but as he told a reporter, "What good is money if I ruin my arm?"

Indeed. Doctors had warned him that his left arm, already bent unnaturally, might become deformed if he continued to pitch. Former teammate Ed Roebuck looked back at Koufax's retirement and saw perhaps another reason why he left the game when he did.

"I think he wanted to get out when he was on top," Roebuck opined. "He was a very proud guy, and I think he decided it was time. You know, Al Campanis asked me about Sandy once and what I remembered most about him, and I said, 'Sandy couldn't cope with mediocrity.'

"And Al said, 'That's it! That's exactly right.' And that's the way Sandy is. He gets into something, like baseball, and he really wants to be the best. I think he was really thinking about getting out of it if he wasn't going to be the best."

Asked upon retirement what his plans were for the future, Koufax laughed. "Right now, I guess you'd have to say I'm unemployed."

He didn't stay unemployed for long. On December 30, the date of his 31st birthday, NBC hired him at $100,000 for 10 years to become a color analyst on its Saturday afternoon "Game of the Week" broadcast. He joined former Dodger teammate Pee Wee Reese and play-by-play man Curt Gowdy.

The job excited Koufax, who loved baseball and wanted to stay in the game. He had wanted to get into a business he could learn, and working as an announcer seemed the perfect opportunity.

"I want to give this everything I've got," he said, "because this is my future."

Apart from postgame interviews through the years, Koufax had little experience before the television cameras. In 1962, he had made a guest appearance on the "Dennis the Menace Show," starring alongside young Jay North in an episode called "Dennis and the Dodger." Koufax also joined Drysdale in a comedic song-and-dance routine with top-coat and tails on Milton Berle's variety show.

The latter appeared after Koufax and Drysdale ended their joint holdout in '66, and Bavasi said it cost the Dodgers thousands of dollars.

"The night after we signed them, they went on with Berle and did a tap-dance routine in white tie and tails," Bavasi remembered. "A newspaper man asked me about it the next day and I said, 'I could have saved a lot of money if I had seen this show the night before we signed them' instead of the night after.' They were terrible."

As an employee of NBC, Koufax was given a complimentary seat in the press box for Super Bowl I, the historic first meeting between the NFL and AFL. Played on January 15, 1967, in the Los Angeles Coliseum, the game matched Vince Lombardi's Green Bay Packers against Hank Stram's Kansas City Chiefs. *Green Bay Press-Gazette* sportswriters Art Daley and Lee Remmel approached Koufax before the game for his prediction, but he graciously declined to venture a guess.

"I wouldn't have any idea who is going to win," he smiled. "I'm just here to watch."

Koufax spent the spring of 1967 in various major league camps, talking to players and managers to pick up background information. When Atlanta Braves' manager Bill Hitchcock saw Koufax wearing casual clothes rather than a uniform, he told reporters, "The Dodgers start 27 games back." It was a reference to Koufax's victory total the season before.

Koufax's first broadcast was Saturday, April 15, 1967, a game matching the Dodgers against the Cardinals in St. Louis. He was scheduled to interview first Don Drysdale, his former Dodger teammate, then Cardinals' slugger Roger Maris.

"I'm a little scared," he acknowledged beforehand. "This is opening day for me."

As the interview began, Koufax drew a blank on what questions he was supposed to ask Drysdale. A few seconds of dead air followed before Koufax nervously asked, "How are you feeling?"

He and Drysdale both smiled at the question, and the tension was eased. The interviews with Drysdale and Maris continued, but Koufax acknowledged later that he was more nervous facing Maris with a microphone than he had been facing him at the plate in the 1963 World Series.

"I used to think it was tough answering questions," Koufax said later. "Now I'm not sure. During my last five, six years, I was never as nervous as I was today."

Koufax drew mixed reviews. Chet Simmons, NBC's Director of Sports, acknowledged it takes time to get comfortable being in front of a camera. Producer Dick Auerbach agreed and felt Koufax had to project his voice better. But, Auerbach said, Koufax already had the basic requirements to become a successful broadcaster, and that was charm and warmth.

Some newspaper columnists weren't so sure. Barney Kremenko of the *New York World-Journal Tribune* thought Koufax came across as a rookie relief man.

Because he was shy and introverted, Koufax never seemed completely at ease behind the microphone.

"Sandy was in the training room with me in '67 before I pitched that game against Boston where I blew my arm out," recalled Jim Kaat, the Twins' pitcher at the time and later a baseball analyst for the Yankees. "I remember him coming in to do the weekend games, and he was not comfortable coming in to do that. He didn't want to talk about himself and he didn't want to be critical toward other players. I think that was the shyness and the sensitivity about him."

Working with broadcast partner Jim Simpson on NBC's backup "Game of the Week," Koufax did color commentary through the 1972 season. Research of his broadcast tapes from 1969 to 1972 reveal his style as insightful, if understated. His voice was deep and smooth as satin, and he spoke in measured, modulated tones. His analysis of players was sharp and detailed.

Bob Broeg of the *St. Louis Post-Dispatch* recalled listening to Koufax analyze Game One of the 1968 World Series between St. Louis and Detroit. The opening game pitching matchup between the Cardinals' Bob Gibson, who fashioned a record-low 1.12 earned run average, and Tigers' 31-game winner Denny McLain was one of the most anticipated in Series history.

Broeg said Koufax talked about how McLain had received more recognition that season than Gibson, and how Gibson was such a fierce competitor.

"Koufax said, 'Gibson will eat him for lunch,'" Broeg said. "And he was right. The next day, Gibson went out and struck out 17 to break Koufax's (World Series) record."

A year later, Koufax and Simpson worked a September game be-

K
O
U
F
A
X

tween the Cardinals and Astros in Houston. Steve Carlton started for St. Louis, and Koufax analyzed Carlton's new pitch, the slider.

"He's always had good stuff," Koufax said. "He didn't get the curveball over well enough or often enough. The slider is that pitch for him."

Koufax's analysis proved prophetic. Carlton developed arguably the greatest slider in baseball history, and rode that pitch to a Hall of Fame career.

In October, Koufax joined with Simpson and Mickey Mantle in doing the NBC pregame show for the World Series between the Baltimore Orioles and New York Mets. Meticulously groomed, Koufax wore a white shirt and light-gray tie, a red NBC blazer, creased gray slacks, black socks, and shiny black shoes.

Prior to Game Five, Simpson asked Koufax about Baltimore starter Dave McNally's chances of pitching the Orioles to victory over the Miracle Mets.

"I said I thought McNally's going to pitch a great ball game," Koufax said. "I'll be honest. I don't think it's going to be enough. I think a great ball game probably won't do it. I think Baltimore is believing in the Mets now and they're waiting for something to happen. They're not going out and trying to win. They're wondering what's going to happen to them now."

Koufax was right. McNally pitched shutout ball for five innings, but the Mets continued their miraculous run by scoring two runs in the bottom of the ninth to win, 5–3, and clinch the Series.

The following season, Koufax and Simpson worked the 1970 All-Star Game in Cincinnati's new Riverfront Stadium. After Pete Rose ran over catcher Ray Fosse to give the National League a 5–4 win in 12 innings, Koufax explained Rose's historic play.

"'Charlie Hustle' as you call him, Pete Rose, it looked like he was going to slide headfirst and looked up and saw the catcher had the plate blocked," Koufax said. "And you just can't slide headfirst into those shinguards, so at the last moment he just sort of hit Fosse with a body-block and broke up the play."

In the 1971 All-Star Game, Koufax and Simpson called Reggie Jackson's famous home run against Dock Ellis that bounced off the light tower high atop Tiger Stadium.

"It looked like Dock got the breaking ball up just a little bit to Reggie Jackson, and I mean, he hit it hard," Koufax explained. "I don't know when I've seen a ball hit as hard as that one. That would have gone out at the airport."

Two years later, Koufax was ready to leave the business. He had grown tired of the travel, and his sensitivity to others made him uncomfortable when he had to offer even mild criticism of a player. He had fulfilled six years of his 10-year contract with NBC when he retired at the end of February 1973. He was replaced by his former Dodger teammate, Maury Wills, who was hired on March 7.

"It was a good job," Koufax said. "But if you go to the ballpark every day hoping it's going to rain, it's obvious you're in the wrong work."

That he left TV work surprised no one. That he had even gone into the business still strikes some observers as odd.

"When you look back at it, it seems a little nuts that a guy who didn't talk much would become an analyst," said Larry Merchant. "He was not a striking personality on the air, but the thing that helped him was his knowledge of baseball."

When Koufax married Anne Widmark, the couple stepped away from public life. They lived a quiet life, splitting time between homes in Maine and California. Because he had invested wisely during his playing career, Koufax was comfortable financially. He and Anne lived quietly, and when the couple moved to Maine, neighbor MaJo Keleshian remembered them as generous, giving people.

"They cared for each other so much," said Keleshian, who was a classmate of Anne's at Sarah Lawrence College in New York. "I was primarily close to Anne. I didn't know Sandy until they moved to Maine.

"When I first met him, he was still working for NBC. I know he hated to leave every week (to do a game). They were both giving and considerate people. He used to golf a lot, and he worked around the farm, keeping it up. He did most of the work, if not all of it, himself."

Sandy and Anne maintained a home that was an extension of themselves—well kept but comfortable, unpretentious and easy to be around. Koufax loved to entertain. He was an excellent cook, and his grandmother's stuffed cabbage was a favorite recipe.

"They were fun to be around," Keleshian said.

Sandy and Anne later divorced, a breakup that Keleshian recalled as "very congenial." As the years passed, Koufax's desire for privacy built a DiMaggio-like mystique around him.

Never rude or controversial, he kept reporters and strangers at arm's length, focusing instead on a close-knit circle of friends and ex-teammates.

Following his divorce he has lived in various parts of the country, never seeming to stay in any one place too long, until planting roots in Vero Beach in 1988. In 1979, he contacted Dodgers President Peter O'Malley, whom he had known for years, to discuss the possibilities of working with the pitchers, and was hired as a part-time coach.

On March 27, 1979, Koufax was in Vero Beach for spring training and once again slipped on his famous No. 32 Dodgers jersey. "It's hard to say why this year instead of last year or next year," he said. "I had to give it a try. I guess it was time."

The 44-year-old Koufax fit in well at the Dodgers' camp. Better, he said, than even he anticipated.

"It's fun to be in a group with a single purpose," he said. "I don't mean single-mindedness but a single purpose. It's like being part of an orchestra. The violin player does his thing but he is part of a whole. I can be an individual here, but all the individuals come together with one purpose in mind."

When someone suggested that he had been hired as a public relations gimmick, Koufax bristled.

"If I wanted to do PR work," he said, "I would have been here for a week and then gone. I'm here to teach pitching."

Asked about his 13-year absence from the game, Koufax said it was time for him to find a new purpose.

"I wasn't looking for anything, just looking for time," he said. "It was a mindless period to do what I wanted to do and go where I wanted to go. I decided to take a few years to myself. I wanted to see how long I could stretch it."

And why return now, he was asked.

"I need the money," he said. "I'm like a lot of older people living on fixed incomes. I need a regular supplemental income just to keep up with inflation."

Of his time spent away from the game, Koufax said, "Sooner or later, you say, 'That's enough of that.' You need to find something to do, another purpose. Also, it's hard to be away from possibly the only thing you ever really did well."

Part of the mystique surrounding Koufax is that he did what few superstar athletes have ever done, and that is walk away from his profession at the peak of his abilities. He won 27 games his final season, struck out 317 hitters in 323 innings, posted a 1.73 ERA, and led the league in seven different categories.

And then, seemingly overnight, he was gone.

His reliance on the curveball, his number of innings pitched—658 combined his final two seasons, with 54 complete games—and his coming back on short rest were factors that eventually took their toll on an already ailing arm.

"I'm sure a lot of it (Koufax's arm problems) was the curveball, it was the innings, it was the fact we pitched every four days, and sometimes every three days," said Kaat. "In today's game, that wouldn't happen."

In today's game, Koufax would have survived the arm problems that forced him into retirement in '66. Modern medicine would have allowed him to undergo off-season elbow surgery, and he likely would have been able to pitch longer than he did.

"With the arthroscopic procedures that they have today," Kaat said, "certainly they could have done something with his arm that would have enabled him to pitch longer."

Of course, had Koufax pitched today, he would have been confronted by the daily barrage of media that is a far greater intrusion than what he faced in the sixties. How the constant exposure would have suited such a private individual is a matter of speculation.

Kaat, who lives not far from Koufax in Vero Beach, still sees him on occasion. It's an interesting footnote that the two best southpaws of the mid-sixties, the opposing pitchers in Game Seven of the 1965 World Series, now live so close to one another and are friends.

To Kaat, Koufax is anything but the mysterious recluse some have made him out to be.

"The way I read him," Kaat said, "is that Sandy is basically a very shy, caring guy who really did not want the spotlight on him but preferred they talk about the Dodgers as a team rather than him. Plus the fact that he was single and in L.A., a big celebrity town, I think that's where he got tagged with that reputation.

"I had a real treat about five years ago. They were honoring Nolan Ryan down in Arlington, and because Koufax was a hero of his, they brought in Sandy. We ended up staying at the same hotel, and so for a 24-hour period of time there I got a chance to visit with him. He's a very delightful guy.

"I think when you see what he's done as a player and you read about him or get to know him, whether we really know the true person, I see him as a guy who is shy and doesn't like the publicity."

Like Kaat, Harmon Killebrew is another member of the '65 Twins who has become friends with Koufax.

"He's a shy, private guy," Killebrew said. "I tried to get Sandy to come to Idaho for about 10 years for a charity golf tournament. Finally, he came up there and he liked it so much he lived up there for two years. He fell in love with the place. That's the kind of guy he is."

Phil Pepe of the *New York Daily News* said Koufax's quiet lifestyle is merely an extension of his personality.

"It was amazing to me that they used him on NBC and that he accepted that job because he never wanted the spotlight," Pepe said. "He never wanted to be in the public eye. He always would flee from that. It's just his nature. His character was that way.

"He never liked to go to banquets. I remember when he won the *Sport* magazine car for being the outstanding player (in the 1963 World Series). He showed up at that, but that was like pulling teeth to get him to go and speak.

"He was a very bright guy. Maybe he had some insecurity or inferiority because he never graduated from college. But Sandy always struck me as being a pretty bright guy and very good on his feet. I don't know why he would be shy about that. I never could understand it."

Pepe, who was a couple of years behind Koufax at Lafayette High in Brooklyn, recalled Koufax's retiring nature making him a difficult interview subject during his playing career. The Dodgers of the mid-sixties were a glamorous team, and since Koufax was the star, reporters naturally sought him out.

"He was never rude, never a problem," Pepe remembered, "but he was a little shy, a little aloof. He was always a good person to be around, always accommodating, but he wasn't a very good interview."

Dave Anderson of the *New York Times* covered Koufax's initial signing with the team in 1955, and later interviewed him shortly after Koufax retired in 1966.

"I still knew him enough to call him and ask, 'Can I talk to you?'" Anderson said. "He was delightful. He even told me where to meet him. I met him at La Costa Resort. I was driving from L.A. to San Diego for a football game, and he said, 'Why don't you stop (at La Costa) on your way down?'

"I walked in and he was sitting at the bar with some people and when he saw me, he got up and came over and we talked for whatever it was, half-hour, an hour. He was delightful."

Anderson said Koufax was easy to talk to about baseball. "I can't believe he was ever rude like some of these guys are today," Anderson said. "I don't think he disappeared after the game. He's very quotable if he's willing to talk. He's not controversial, but he gives you good stuff, he makes sense. He's a smart guy, he just likes to be left alone. DiMaggio was like that too. But there's always been private guys. Some people are like that. But he wasn't a hermit or a recluse."

Following the 1966 interview, Anderson didn't see or speak with Koufax again for some 30 years. He bumped into Koufax at a golf tournament in 1997, and the two exchanged small talk for a few minutes before going their separate ways.

As a sportswriter and columnist in Philadelphia, Larry Merchant covered Koufax on numerous occasions.

"He was nice enough," Merchant said. "But he was very savvy about not wanting to say anything controversial. In those days, the print media was dominant, and he wanted to stay clear of anything personal. In the last five years of his career, he was so dominant there was almost nothing he could say that would match the brilliance of his performance."

The brilliance of Koufax's performance on the mound remains vivid to Merchant even though more than 30 years have passed since Koufax's last game.

"There was always an excitement, a buzz, when he pitched," Merchant said. "He was such a beautiful, graceful athlete. He was dominant.

When you think about it, what does a pitcher do? He makes nothing happen. When a guy is overpowering like that, there's an attraction because these are the best hitters in the world.

"And he was with a glamorous team. The Dodgers were the National League version of the Yankees. So the combination of his style, his dominance with a team always in contention made him a superstar in a time when baseball was still regarded as the dominant sport. He was up there with Jim Brown and Bill Russell. He was a tremendous force. But he tries not to live in the past. He wants to live in the present."

Because Koufax is so insistent on living in the present, he has had very little to say about his past career. Friends have said that he politely asks them not to talk about his days with the Dodgers.

Long-time Dodger executive Chip Strange agreed that Koufax remains a guarded person, but pointed out that he is one of only a few ex-Dodgers who have maintained contact with him through the years. "He always sends my wife and I a Christmas card," said Strange.

By staying out of the public eye and away from the media, Koufax has protected his reputation as one of sport's more respected athletes. He has little to do with businesses seeking him as a sponsor for commercial endorsements, and has never endorsed a trading-card company. Through 1998, Koufax had appeared at just three card shows the past two years and less than 15 over the previous six years.

Because he was born in Brooklyn and became a sports hero in Los Angeles, Koufax has a fan base spanning both the East and West coasts. Because he has steered clear of controversy in his personal life, and because he is known largely for his accomplishments on the field, he is revered by two generations of Americans: those who saw him pitch in person and on television, and their children—who have had the stories passed on to them through the years.

The stories have become legend, and so too has Koufax, shielded from public view for years by his desire for privacy.

"Here was a guy who was on top of the world," Pepe said. "Good-looking, intelligent, but once he stopped pitching he disappeared. Where was he? He was a phantom. But that was part of the mystique about him."

On January 29, 1970, Koufax was named Baseball Athlete of the

Decade in a special poll taken by the Associated Press. He had received 251 votes from the sportswriters and broadcasters, almost a full 100 ahead of Mickey Mantle, who finished second with 154½. Willie Mays and Hank Aaron were a distant third and fourth, respectively.

Frank J. Shaughnessy, the former president of the International League, had seen every great pitcher from Christy Mathewson and Walter Johnson to Grover Cleveland Alexander and Lefty Grove. Of Koufax, Shaughnessy was quoted by the Associated Press as saying, "He comes as close to being unhittable as any other pitcher I ever saw."

Koufax was working on his golf game—he was an eight-handicap—at the Riviera Country Club in Los Angeles when he learned of the poll. Wearing a white turtleneck, dark pullover sweater rolled up on his forearms, and gray slacks, he posed for AP pictures and said he was surprised by the honor.

"I think it's incredible because there were guys like Mays and Henry Aaron who were great players for 10 years or more," Koufax said. "After all, my big years were spread over a full decade. I only had four or five good years."

Two years later, Koufax was honored again. He was just 36 years old, and he hadn't thrown a pitched ball competitively in six years, yet he set one final major league record.

On January, 19, 1972, Sandy Koufax became the youngest man voted into baseball's Hall of Fame. He received 344 votes, the most in the 40-year history of balloting by members of the Baseball Writers Association of America.

"I'm a little surprised I got as many votes as I did," said Koufax, who thought his injury-shortened career might dissuade voters. "I didn't have as many good years as some others in the Hall and I thought that might count against me."

Photographers rushed to get a photo of Koufax—dressed in a dark jacket, white shirt, and patterned tie—receiving a congratulatory kiss from Mrs. Yogi Berra, whose husband joined Koufax, Lefty Gomez, Buck Leonard, and Early Wynn as inductees. Baseball legends Will Harridge, Ross Youngs, and Josh Gibson were immortalized posthumously.

Koufax had packed 20 years of greatness into a 12-year career, but the fact that he had to leave the game early still bothered him.

"There are times when I miss some parts of the game terribly," he said. "If you've played you have to miss it, especially if you've had some degree of success, because it's fun."

Still, he acknowledged there were constant reminders of the parts of the game that weren't fun.

"My elbow still hurts me all the time, in varying degrees," he said. "This is the only thing that's made having to retire early a little easier. This is the biggest honor I've ever been given, not just in baseball, but in my life."

He smiled. "I've never been to Cooperstown," he said.

On August 7, 1972, Koufax stood on the steps of baseball's hallowed Hall, a picture of grace and gratitude as he was called on to speak by Commissioner Bowie Kuhn on induction day.

"I don't really have a speech to make today," he said into the microphones, "just a lot of thanks to so many people that I can't name them all."

Of his early years with the Brooklyn Dodgers, Koufax recalled them as rather inglorious. "I thought after my first six years in baseball, it was going to be 'Go out and get another job.'"

He credited Dodgers' pitching coach Joe Becker with helping him generate one of the greatest career turnarounds in the game's history.

"He pushed me, shoved me, embarrassed me, and made me work," Koufax said. "And I really have to thank him for that."

With that, Koufax stepped away from the microphone, and away from public life as well. Seven months later, he announced his retirement from NBC-TV.

EPILOGUE

S andy Koufax's place in baseball history was secure the day he was inducted into baseball's Hall of Fame in Cooperstown.

His place among the game's immortals, however, remains an open question for historians.

Was he the greatest pitcher of the pitching-rich sixties, a decade that included Whitey Ford and Warren Spahn, Don Drysdale, Bob Gibson, and Juan Marichal?

Is he the greatest left-handed pitcher ever, better than Hall of Fame predecessors Lefty Grove, Lefty Gomez, and Carl Hubbell or successors Steve Carlton and Randy Johnson?

Is he the greatest pitcher, period, better than Christy Mathewson and Walter Johnson, Dizzy Dean and Bob Feller, Tom Seaver and Nolan Ryan, Roger Clemens and Greg Maddux?

There seems little argument that Koufax was the best southpaw of the sixties, reaching his peak in 1963 just as the Cooperstown careers of Ford and Spahn were winding down.

"I knew I was not going to get many runs, so I had to match what he did," Spahn said, recalling mound duels he had with Koufax. "He was outstanding. He had the hard fastball that was intimidating and the curve, and the one complemented the other.

"If you looked for the curve, there was a tendency to chase the hard fastball up (in the strike zone). If you looked for the fastball, there was a tendency to chase the curve. The thing about him was his control."

Was he the best pitcher overall of his decade, better than right-handers Drysdale, Marichal, and Gibson?

Phil Pepe, a veteran sportswriter for the *New York Daily News,* covered both Koufax and Gibson in their prime and drew comparisons between the two.

"I always thought Gibson was the greatest competitor I ever saw," Pepe said. "But for one game that you want to win, I'd still take Koufax. As great a competitor as Gibson was, he wasn't capable of doing the things Koufax did."

What Koufax did was dominate his sport over a four-year span unmatched in baseball history. He won three Cy Young Awards in four years, pitched no-hitters in four consecutive seasons, and also threw a perfect game. He twice struck out 18 batters in a game, and his 382 strikeouts in 1965 remained a National League record for 34 years. From 1963 to 1966, Koufax averaged 24 wins and 7 losses, a winning percentage of .774, 307 strikeouts per season, and an earned run average of 1.85.

"I know whenever they talk great pitchers I keep telling people, 'Just go back and check out the years Koufax had, '63 through '66,' " said Jim Kaat, one of the top pitchers in the sixties and a color analyst with the New York Yankees. "I don't think anyone has strung four years together (like Koufax). When you take overall power, control, winning, earned run average, pitching for a team that didn't score a lot of runs, I don't think anyone dominated the game for four years like he did as a pitcher."

Bill Mazeroski, a star second baseman for the Pittsburgh Pirates in the sixties, said Koufax was the best pitcher of his era.

"Gibson approached it," Maz said, "but there was no one better than Sandy Koufax. Some guys throw hard, but not as consistently hard as he did. And he had good stuff for nine innings. He was the best I ever saw."

Pepe agreed. "Look at some of the years he had, where he struck out 380 batters and walked a hundred," he said, a sense of wonder and awe in his voice. "It boggles your mind. And he quit after winning 27 games. . .

"I put him on a pedestal as the best I've ever seen."

Bill White, a teammate of Gibson's on the 1964 Cardinals team that won the World Series, recalled Koufax's dominance over that five-year span.

"I didn't see him," White laughed, referring to Koufax's tremendous fastball. "I didn't see him. And I don't think too many people hit him. For five years, no one hit him."

Yet it is that last point, Koufax's short span of excellence, that is a sticking point for some. In his book *Stranger to the Game*, Gibson acknowledges that Koufax's five prime years from 1962 to 1966 rank with the best in history, but it bothers him that a pitcher who worked for just seven years in the sixties should be regarded as pitcher of the decade.

Yet it was one of Koufax's toughest rivals who weighed in on the topic of the best pitcher of the sixties.

"Koufax," said Juan Marichal, "is the greatest. He's the best pitcher I ever saw."

Larry Shenk, who has worked in the Phillies' media and public relations department since 1963, agreed with Marichal that Koufax is the best pitcher of the modern era.

"I saw Sandy pitch his no-hitter at Connie Mack Stadium," Shenk said. "He was overpowering. I've seen Carlton and I've seen Gibson, but with Koufax, you couldn't hit his fastball and you couldn't hit his curve. Gibson obviously had good stuff, but Koufax was the best I've ever seen. There's not much doubt about that."

Baseball historian and long-time newspaper writer Jerome Holtzman began going to major league games as a 10-year-old in 1936. In 1957 he became the baseball writer for the *Chicago Sun-Times*. Three years later, he joined the staff of the *Chicago Tribune*. Holtzman has seen or covered every great big-league pitcher in the last half-century, and of those he said Koufax is the best.

"I saw Koufax pitch 20, 30 times," Holtzman said. "He was unhittable, especially against the Cubs. I was always amazed when anybody even made contact against Koufax. He had a devastating curve ball, the best curveball I've ever seen."

To Holtzman, Koufax ranks alongside Ted Williams as the two most impressive major leaguers he's ever seen.

Dave Anderson of the *New York Times* chose Koufax as the only modern-era pitcher on his major league baseball All-Century Team, listing him alongside Cy Young, Christy Mathewson, Walter Johnson, Grover Cleveland Alexander, and Bob Feller. Interestingly, Koufax was the only left-hander Anderson named to his list of the six greatest pitchers.

"At his best he was as good as anybody," Anderson said. "There was nobody better for those five years. He was unhittable. He wasn't around for the whole decade, but for those five years he was the best pitcher in that decade. Gibson was terrific, but this guy was incredible. He was exceptional, and there's been nobody, in my mind, since him that dominant. Randy Johnson approaches it, but a lot of these guys don't even win 20 games anymore."

Anderson said that for one season, Dwight Gooden in 1984 was as dominant as Koufax. Ron Guidry's 1978 season, in which he went 25–3 with a 1.74 ERA, was close; but what sets Koufax apart in Anderson's mind is that he put together five straight seasons in which he overpowered baseball's best hitters.

"You just couldn't hit this guy, and the hitters knew it," he said. "The other team went to the ballpark saying, 'How are we going to get a run off this guy?'"

Baseball historian Bill Mazer once wrote that if you asked a fan of the game today who the best pitcher is, you would probably get a variety of answers. But, if you asked a fan in the mid-sixties who the best pitcher was, you would get only one answer: Koufax.

If Koufax was the best pitcher of the sixties, how does he rank among the greatest pitchers of all time, Hall of Famers Christy Mathewson, Walter Johnson, and Lefty Grove, and future Hall of Famer Greg Maddux?

But for the arm injuries that cut his win totals to 14 in '62 and 19 in '64 and ended his career in '66, Koufax would have won 20 or more games at least five straight seasons. Matching his peak years of 1962–1966 against the best five years of this century's pitchers of the decade—Mathewson, Walter Johnson, Grove, and Maddux—Koufax went 111–34 with a .766 winning percentage.

Mathewson from 1904 to 1908 was 147–46 with a .724 win percentage. Johnson from 1911 to 1915 went 149–63 (.703); Grove from 1928 to 1932 was 128–33 (.795); and Maddux from 1993 to 1997 went 89–33 (.730).

Koufax won five ERA titles in his peak seasons and compiled an overall ERA of 2.02. Mathewson and Johnson each won two ERA titles in their peak span and finished with combined marks of 1.93 and 1.54, respectively. Grove won four ERA titles but owned a 2.56 mark. Maddux was tops in ERA three times and owned a mark of 2.13.

Koufax dominates the group in strikeout ratio. From '62 to '66 he struck out 1,444 hitters in 1,377 innings pitched, an average of 9.4 strikeouts per game.

Mathewson struck out 983 in 1,640 innings (5.4); Johnson 1,181 in 1,746⅔ (6.1); Grove 925 in 1,408⅓ (5.9); and Maddux 883 in 1,156⅓ (6.9).

Of the six categories listed—record, win percentage, ERA, ERA titles, strikeouts, and strikeout ratio, Koufax finished first three times.

Picking his All-Century Team, Jerome Holtzman struggled to choose between Grove, whose greatness spanned two decades, and Koufax, a sixties sensation, as the best left-handed pitcher ever.

"I didn't see Grove," he said, "but I know about him. Everybody knows about Grove. He was certainly the outstanding pitcher of his time. I saw Koufax, and there were times, many, many times, when he was absolutely unhittable."

As great as Koufax was during the regular season, he had that rare ability to raise his game in the clutch. He pitched in eight World Series games and posted a dazzling ERA of 0.95. In 57 innings pitched, he allowed 36 hits and 11 walks while striking out 61.

It was enough to impress Casey Stengel, who had seen the great pitchers of the early part of the century.

"Forget the other fellow," Stengel said once, referring to Walter Johnson, whom he had played against. "The Jewish kid is probably the best of them."

Stan Musial said Koufax was the most overpowering pitcher he had ever faced. Marichal called him the best pitcher he had ever seen. Bill Mazer saw Carl Hubbell, Dizzy Dean, and Bob Feller pitch. If he was a manager and had one game he had to win, Mazer wrote once, Koufax would get the ball.

"Koufax had the incredible ability to rise to that next level when it was a 'must' game," wrote Mazer. "He was the best at it."

Said Dave Anderson, "That's what great players do. They get better. The tougher the game the better they are. That's why they're great players."

Jack Lang agreed. A veteran baseball writer and long-time member of the Baseball Writers Association of America, Lang said that for five years, Koufax was the best left-hander he has ever seen.

"If I had one game to win," said Lang, "if I needed to win one game on the final day and I had a pitching staff of Ford, Spahn, Seaver, Gibson, and Koufax, I'd give the ball to Koufax."

Don Zimmer, who has played against or seen firsthand the game's top pitchers for the past half-century, said Koufax stands alone among the great pitchers he's watched up close.

"For five years," Zimmer said, "he was the greatest pitcher I ever saw."

Writers Larry Merchant and Roger Kahn, however, dispute the notion that Koufax is baseball's best pitcher.

"He is certainly not the greatest pitcher who ever lived," said Merchant. "For five years he was as good as anybody, but that's five years."

Merchant wondered how many general managers, if they were building a fantasy team, would choose Koufax over Spahn or Carlton or Seaver? The point being, Merchant said, that a pitcher like Spahn was still winning 20 games and throwing no-hitters at an age when Koufax had already been long retired.

In an *L.A. Times* article, Kahn disagreed with what he termed "the essentially hysterical point" that Koufax was the greatest pitcher ever. To Kahn, Christy Mathewson put up more impressive numbers than Koufax.

There is, of course, no definitive answer as to who is baseball's best pitcher. But Hall of Fame pitcher Jim Palmer called Koufax as good as anyone he has seen.

"He was a two-pitch pitcher, fastball and curve, and both of them were unhittable when he was on," Palmer remembered. "His curveball was as good as his fastball, he had great control, and that's why he was as good as he was."

A more important question, perhaps, is how much was Koufax aided by conditions in the era he pitched?

His meteoric rise in the mid-sixties was influenced by two types of expansion—expansion of the player pool and the strike zone. In 1962, the National League expanded from eight to ten teams. The addition of the Houston Colt .45s and the New York Mets diluted the talent pool by rushing marginal players to the major leagues.

A more dramatic factor influencing player performance occurred on January 26, 1963, when the Official Baseball Playing Rules Committee voted to enlarge the strike zone. From 1887 until 1950, the strike zone had been defined as extending across the width of the 17-inch plate from the hitter's shoulders to his knees. When home-run production jumped following World War II, baseball officials sought to encourage the long ball—and the accompanying rise in attendance—by framing the strike zone from the hitter's armpits to the tops of his knees.

In '63, the strike zone was enlarged even further, extending from the shoulders to the bottoms of the knees. The new ruling meant pitchers gained called strikes not only on shoulder-high fastballs but on low pitches as well.

The Baseball Rules Committee's decision to enlarge the strike zone was due in part to their belief that home runs had become too cheap. It was a backlash against the historic 1961 season, when Mickey Mantle and Roger Maris both launched an all-out summer assault on what was considered to be baseball's most precious single-season record—Babe Ruth's celebrated 60-homer season of 1927. Injuries slowed Mantle in September and he finished with 54. Maris slugged 61 to set a new record, and the Yankees as a club belted a record 240 round-trippers.

Maris's 61 homers in '61 offended many baseball people, including the commissioner. Ford Frick, a former ghost writer for Ruth, ordered an asterisk placed next to Maris's name in the record book because his homer total was reached in the new 162-game season, rather than the 154-game season Ruth played in.

Ruth's total was considered more legitimate because it eclipsed the team total of every other club in the American League that season. Maris's mark had been reached in a season in which power hitters feasted on expansion pitching. Eight players hit 40 or more homers in '61, and when a record-breaking 3,001 balls left major league ballparks in '62, Frick and the Baseball Rules Committee believed the balance between pitcher and hitter had gone awry.

The commissioner challenged writers to "Take a look at the batting, home run, and slugging records for recent seasons . . . The pitchers need help, urgently."

Frick even lobbied for the return of the spitball, and the Rules Committee considered it, but decided instead to expand the strike zone. History shows that the expansion of the strike zone slammed the brakes on the game's power hitters—home runs declined in '63 by 10 percent; batting averages and runs scored dropped by 12 percent.

History also shows, however, that the rush to help the pitcher was a knee-jerk reaction to the '61 and '62 seasons. Fueled by the "M&M Boys," Mantle and Maris, the Yankees won world titles after averaging 5.07 runs a game in '61 and 5.04 in '62. Those totals are dwarfed by 6.29 runs per game averaged by the '27 "Murderer's Row" Yankees of Ruth and Gehrig and the 6.87 averaged by the '36 Yankees of Gehrig, DiMaggio, and Dickey.

The larger strike zone gave pitchers an inviting target at a time when they were also being aided by the dilution of talent through expansion. The arrival of symmetrical new ballparks also aided in pitching mastery. Older ballparks like Ebbets Field and the Polo Grounds often had close-cropped foul lines and short outfield walls because they had been built in the confines of city neighborhoods. The result was that hitters often extended their at-bat by benefit of a pop foul falling safely into seats close to the playing field, and concluded their trip to the plate by depositing the ball into short porches down either line.

When pitcher-friendly parks like Dodger Stadium began opening in the early sixties, they offered playing fields in which hurlers benefited from spacious fields that allowed their fielders to get to foul pop-ups and drives to outfield walls that were symmetrical from left to right.

Cheap homers in Dodger Stadium or the Houston Astrodome, which opened in '65, went the way of flannel uniforms. Batting averages returned to the dead-ball era as well. The increase of night games—hitters prefer to see the ball in daylight—the enlargement of fielder's gloves, and the refined skills of the fielders were advancements in the game that all arrived at roughly the same time in the early sixties.

The confluence of these pitching aids in 1963 combined to drive batting averages steadily down. New York won the American League pennant despite not having a regular player hit higher than .287. The notoriety showered on Maris in '61 and the increasing difficulty of stringing hits together were two factors that led hitters to begin swinging from their heels. Even the Chicago White Sox, who had won the American League pennant in '59 by employing a high-octane offense that earned them the nickname the "Go-Go Sox," became power-mad. At the time the only franchise never to have boasted a home-run leader, the White Sox went with young swingers like 23-year-old Dave Nicholson, who in '63 fanned a league-high 175 times in just 449 at-bats.

Pitchers profited by the swing-for-the-fences approach, and fireballers like Koufax and "Sudden" Sam McDowell of the Cleveland Indians became the first pitchers since 1946 to whiff more than 300 batters in a season. Koufax first accomplished the feat in '63 when he fanned 306 in 311 innings pitched, and repeated his success in '65 (382 in 336), and '66 (317 in 323). In '65, both Koufax and McDowell whiffed more than 300 hitters.

While the long ball continued to be the main offensive threat, it often came with no one on base, thus helping to lower earned run averages. The new strike zone squeezed the sluggers, reduced run totals, and threatened to lull both players and fans asleep. Teams like the Dodgers and Cardinals were the first to take advantage of the changes in the game, altering their style of play to meet the modern-day challenge of scoring runs.

L.A. and St. Louis both built their lineups around speed. Dodgers' shortstop Maury Wills and Cardinals' left-fielder Lou Brock were the table-setters for their respective teams, and they scored numerous runs by reaching first on a single or a walk, stealing second and often third, and racing home on an infield grounder or sacrifice fly. The success of Wills and Brock led to the return of the stolen base as an offensive weapon, and a return to the old days of playing for one run at a time rather than relying on a three-run homer.

With pitchers aiming at a larger strike zone and hitters angling to get on base any way they could, the battle over who owned home plate in the major leagues intensified in the mid-sixties. Strike zones are often as big as home-plate umpires define them, and they often define them according to the reputation of the man in the batter's box or on the mound. Boston Red Sox Hall of Fame hitter Ted Williams is reputed to have had perhaps the greatest "batting eye" ever, due in part to his extraordinary 20–10 eyesight. Williams rarely swung at pitches outside the strike zone, and umpires respected his judgment so much they gave the "Splinter" the close calls.

Pitchers who were known to always be around home plate commanded the same respect from umpires. Former Orioles' pitcher Scott McGregor said that if a pitcher proves to the ump early in the game that he can throw strikes, he can gradually expand the strike zone as the game moves into the late innings. A control pitcher like Oakland ace Catfish Hunter, whose pitches were always around the strike zone, was said to be able to expand home plate by as much as five inches by the final innings. "He's pitching to a 22-inch plate," was how one exasperated hitter put it after the Cat had rung up another win.

Koufax benefited from both the expanded strike zone and his star reputation; by 1964 he was widely considered the best pitcher in baseball. But there is a question in the minds of some regarding how much of Koufax's dramatic career turnaround can be attributed to factors such as expansion, the enlarged strike zone, pitching in Dodger Stadium, night games, and the wild swingers of his era.

Koufax's career was certainly influenced by these changes in the game; so too were the careers of other famous pitchers of the sixties. In 1968, Don Drysdale set a major league record by throwing six straight shutouts and 58⅔ consecutive innings of scoreless ball; Bob Gibson fashioned a dazzling 1.12 earned run average, the lowest of the modern era; and Denny McLain won 31 games—the first pitcher to reach the magical 30-win mark since Dizzy Dean did it in 1934.

Koufax had vanished from the scene before '68, and it's intriguing to wonder what kind of numbers he would have posted had he still been healthy and throwing in the year of the pitcher. He had thrived in the mid-sixties, yet the question remains—how much of his success in the mid-sixties did Koufax owe to outside influences?

The first two factors, expansion and the enlarged strike zone, can be dealt with quickly. Power pitchers are measured by their strikeouts-to-innings-pitched ratio. In his 1955 rookie season in Brooklyn, Koufax struck out 30 hitters in just 42 innings. The next season, he fanned 30 in 59 innings. In 1957, his strikeouts jumped to 122 in just 103 innings. In '58, he whiffed 131 in 159 innings; in '59, 173 in 153, and in '60, 197 in 175 innings. In '61, the year before National League expansion and a season regarded as the year of the slugger, Koufax set a league record with 269 strikeouts in 256 innings pitched.

In '62, the first year of National League expansion, he struck out 216 in 184 innings despite a finger ailment. His strikeout total in '63, the first season for the expanded strike zone, was 306 in 311 innings. Koufax undoubtedly benefited from pitching in the era of the high strike, but research reveals that his strikeouts-to-innings-pitched ratio was actually higher in the years before expansion, before the enlarged strike zone, and before night games.

The high strike wasn't a great factor in Koufax's strikeout totals, because batters rarely waited on his deliveries. Koufax addressed the issue of the high strike once, saying he never really needed the call because hitters, realizing he was always around the strike zone, tried to attack his fastball. The 204 home runs allowed in his career back up the assessment; had he pitched longer, Koufax would almost certainly rank alongside Spahn, Robin Roberts, and Ferguson Jenkins as the gopher kings from 1946 to the present.

That Koufax yielded so many homers, Dave Anderson said, isn't surprising.

"When you connect with his fastball, it's going to go," Anderson said. "You're going to get an extra 20 feet out of it. So all you have to do is meet it and it's going to go somewhere. And if you get a good swing, it's really going to go."

There's also no question that Koufax benefited from pitching in Dodger Stadium, a pitcher's ballpark. In the era of the high mound, Dodger Stadium's was said to be higher than most, though probably not as high as Bob Feller's "office" in Cleveland's Municipal Stadium. Indians' owner Bill Veeck said once that the Municipal Stadium mound was so high that anyone who fell off it would probably break their leg.

There were other advantages to pitching in Chavez Ravine. The stadium was enclosed by the same kind of "dead air" that hovered under the artificial sky of the Houston Astrodome. In the summer heat and smog, fly balls died in the air over Dodger Stadium. The stadium lights in Chavez Ravine were also believed to be a shade dimmer than other parks, making it harder to pick the ball up in night games.

When lefty Claude Osteen joined the Dodgers in 1965 from the Washington Senators, he immediately lowered his earned run average from 3.33 the previous season to 2.79, then followed up with a 2.85 in '66. It should also be noted that Osteen's ERA jumped to 3.22 in '67, not far from the 3.35 he had posted two years before moving to L.A.

From 1963 to 1966, the Dodger staff led the National League in ERA. But it seemed to be due more to Koufax's excellence than that they were playing half their games in Dodger Stadium. In 1967, L.A.'s first year without Koufax, the Dodgers' 3.21 ERA ranked only fifth in the 10-team National League. They improved to second in '68 with a 2.69 ERA, then fell back to third in '69 with a 3.08.

Ballpark quirks and dimensions have helped pitchers and hitters alike for time immemorial. Baltimore's Memorial Stadium was infamous for having one of the worst hitter's backgrounds in the majors—the scoreboard made it difficult to pick up the pitch from a right-hander. Jim Palmer took advantage of the background and the deep power alleys—perfect for a high-ball pitcher like Palmer—to craft a Hall of Fame career.

The Dodgers were said to do the same thing. It was believed that whenever Koufax pitched at Dodger Stadium, the left-field bleachers would be closed so that right-handed hitters would have to pick out Koufax's blurring fastball from a sea of white shirts in right field. When Drysdale pitched, it was said the Dodgers closed the right-field bleachers to affect left-handed hitters.

Southpaws like Herb Pennock, Lefty Gomez, Whitey Ford, Ron Guidry, and David Wells loved the cavernous left-center field in Yankee Stadium. When the Yanks signed low-ball lefty Tommy John as a free agent in 1979, general manager Gabe Paul said it would take "a nine-iron" to homer off John in the big ballpark.

In his book, *Whatever Happened to the Hall of Fame?* author Bill James credited the pitcher-friendly confines of Dodger Stadium for turning Koufax's career around. Using the club's move to Chavez Ravine in '62 as the dividing line, James argues that while Koufax's road ERA did not improve dramatically throughout his career, his home ERA dips significantly from '62 on.

It wasn't until the team moved to Dodger Stadium, James wrote, that "Koufax became Koufax."

A close look at Koufax's career numbers, however, suggests otherwise. His ERA at home and on the road his early years in Brooklyn clearly reflects his control problems. Pitching in Ebbets Field from 1955 to 1957, Koufax's home ERA reads 2.25, 7.50, 3.96. His road ERA those seasons is 4.15, 3.76, and 3.81. When the Dodgers moved west in '58, they played home games at the Los Angeles Coliseum, which was death on left-handed pitchers because its odd configurations favored right-handed pull hitters.

Still, Koufax's ERA at home and on the road maintains a roller-coaster look that reflects more than anything his ongoing struggle to gain control of his pitches. In the Coliseum, he posted ERAs of 5.60, 3.14, 5.27, and 4.29. His road ERA read 3.75, 5.05, 3.00, and 2.78.

Following the move to Dodger Stadium, Koufax's home ERA dropped to 1.75, 1.38, 0.85, 1.38, and 1.52. Clearly, he liked pitching in Walter O'Malley's dream park, but apart from a 3.53 mark in '62, his road ERA improved as well—2.93, 2.72, and 1.96.

The turning point for Koufax, as the numbers suggest, came after a series of occurrences between 1960 and 1962. He took the advice of catcher Norm Sherry to relax and not overthrow, and listened when Sherry told him, "Don't pick up my mitt, pick up my body." As former catcher Tim McCarver said, Sherry's idea of giving Koufax a wider target to aim for allowed Sandy to forget about being a dart thrower, which was impossible for someone who threw as hard as Koufax did.

Koufax also spent valuable time crunching numbers with team statistician Allan Roth on the benefits of throwing first-pitch strikes and working with pitching coach Joe Becker, who taught him the rocking motion on the mound that became a Koufax trademark and helped transform him from a thrower into a pitcher.

"I think that's a case of a guy who had a tremendous arm, who was late in developing his mechanics and found that good comfort zone (in his delivery)," said Jim Kaat. "Nowadays, there's so much coaching available, but back then, while you did have coaches, for the most part, you found out things on your own. You didn't have video, you didn't break down your motion, it was sort of trial and error. So it was not surprising to see a guy like Jack Sanford, who I think got to the big leagues when he was 30 years old and became a Cy Young Award winner. It was not uncommon to see pitchers take several years to develop, and when you had an arm like Koufax, certainly you were going to give him some extra time to do that.

"I think what all of a sudden made him a dominant pitcher, and he would say the same thing, is his control and his great curveball. I used to talk to Johnny Roseboro about it from time to time. Johnny came over to our ballclub about three years later and we were teammates for a year in Minnesota. And he talked about Sandy's ability to control the fastball on both sides of the plate and then throw that curveball.

"It wasn't just his velocity . . . I mean, Nolan Ryan's got raw power. So does Randy Johnson. But Koufax had that combination of power and control. Still one of the amazing statistics to me is that year (1965) when he struck out 300 more men than he walked. Ryan might strike out 370 but he might walk 200. Koufax struck out 382 and he walked 71."

By finally learning how to harness the tremendous speed on his fastball and how to throw the sweeping curve for strikes, Koufax cut his bases on balls issued from 96 in 1961 to 57 in 1962. Despite taking something off his pitches, he maintained his high strikeout ratio, fanning 216 to lead the league with a 9.4 per game average. His strikeouts-to-walks ratios from the next four seasons are 306–58 in '63; 223–53 in '64; 382–71 in '65; and 317–77 in '66.

By '66, his final season, Koufax was so dominant that his home ERA of 1.52 was just slightly better than the 1.96 he posted in enemy ballparks. Roth said that Koufax had reached a point that when anybody got a hit off him, people would turn to one another and ask, "Gee, I wonder what he did wrong?"

Former Dodger Ed Roebuck watched Koufax pitch and wondered why he didn't throw more than four no-hitters in his career. There was a Babe-Ruth-sized talent gap, Roebuck said, between Koufax and other pitchers.

Kaat agreed. "Sandy was so much more powerful and advanced in pitching than any other pitcher of that era," Kaat said. "The sixties were a great era for pitching, and he was just so much at a higher level than the rest of us it wasn't even close."

Roth played a major role in Koufax's development from thrower to pitcher. Before baseball benefited from computers, Roth was the

Dodgers' statistical guru. The club's pitchers huddled with Roth every spring to study their numbers from the previous season. In the spring of 1960, the year before he won 18 games for the first time, Koufax learned from Roth's stats that he held opposing hitters to a collective .209 batting average. That's a sterling number for a pitcher; but what really made an impression on the young pitcher was that the league was hitting a robust .349 on his first pitch. That figure topped the .325 batting average of the National League's leading hitter in 1960, Dick Groat.

Koufax and Roth worked on getting the first pitch over for a strike, and the results, as noted by John Thorn and John Holway in their book, *The Pitcher*, tell the story.

In 1960, when Koufax allowed a first-pitch batting average of .349, he went 8–13 with a 3.91 ERA and a strikeouts-to-walks ratio of 197–100.

In '61, the year after he and Roth began emphazing the first-pitch strike, Koufax allowed a .312 batting average, went 18–13 with a 3.52 ERA, and his strikeouts-to-walks ratio jumped dramatically to 269–96.

In '62, the league batting average against Koufax's first pitch dropped even lower, to .243. He went 14–7 in an injury-shortened season, posted a 2.54 ERA, and had a strikeouts-to-walks ratio of 216–57.

From 1963 to 1966, Koufax continued to emphasize the first-pitch strike. He became so deadly once he got ahead in the count that Tim McCarver, a former catcher and later baseball analyst and author, felt that if Koufax's first pitch was strike one, a hitter might just as well have returned to the dugout. If the first pitch was a ball, then he had a chance.

Koufax's control was so perfect by the mid-sixties that he pitched the entire 1966 season—323 innings—and did not hit a batter. In so doing, he set a National League record, not bad for a pitcher considered early in his career to be uncontrollably wild.

It's interesting to note, too, that many of Koufax's milepost achievements were accomplished on grounds other than Dodger Stadium, in recognized hitter's parks.

On August 31, 1959, he tied Bob Feller's major league record by striking out 18 Giants in the L.A. Coliseum. On April 24, 1962, he struck out 18 Cubs in Chicago's Wrigley Field. On October 2, 1963, he set a World Series record by striking out 15 Yankees in Game One of the World Series in Yankee Stadium. On June 4, 1964, he no-hit the Phillies in Connie Mack Stadium. And on October 14, 1965, in what is considered by many baseball people the signature game of Koufax's career, he pitched a three-hit, 10-strikeout shutout against the Twins in Minnesota in Game Seven of the World Series.

More than 30 years later, Kaat still sounded awed by Koufax's performance that day.

"I was just so impressed," he said. "To see him dominate our lineup was pretty impressive. I just felt he belonged in a higher league after seeing him for the first time like that."

And how impressive is it for a pitcher to throw two complete-game Series shutouts in a space of three days?

"I never did it," said Jim Palmer. "But that's why Koufax is Koufax."

Three decades later, Harmon Killebrew remained impressed by Koufax's performance.

"I think that final game was probably one of the greatest pitching performances I've ever seen," he said. "Sandy pitched on two days' rest and shut us out two to nothing. I'll never forget that."

Kaat said Koufax's ability to throw consecutive complete-game shutouts in the '65 Series ranked alongside Gibson's dominating performances in '67 and '68.

"Gibby in '67 had a game like that where he dominated the Red Sox, and he also had Game One in Detroit in '68," Kaat said. "But over a (two-game) period like (Koufax in '65), I don't think anybody's done that."

And Koufax did it in a manner different from pitchers who rely on fear to intimidate hitters. Koufax, Kaat said, simply overwhelmed the opposition with his talent. "Sandy had excellent control," he said, "so it wasn't as much as being intimidated by him as you were overwhelmed by how good the guy was."

Carl Erskine said Koufax's performance against the Twins showed what an awesome talent he was.

"He had trouble with his curve, so he said, 'Forget it,' and just threw the fastball the whole game," Erskine said. "What Sandy did that day really made us raise our eyebrows and say, 'Wow.'"

Koufax's performance in Minnesota proved to critics he was just as unhittable on the road as he was at home. In *The Pitcher*, authors

Thorn and Holway examined the ballpark effects on pitchers, and noted that while Nolan Ryan was often accused of setting his record in pitcher's parks like Anaheim Stadium and the Astrodome, they believed it wasn't yet clear what effect those parks had on power pitchers. If Ryan, whose fastball was clocked at 100.1 miles per hour, is blazing the ball past hitters, park dimensions became irrelevant.

Don Zimmer applied the same logic to Koufax when asked about the dead air over Dodger Stadium.

"What difference does dead air make," Zimmer asked, "if he's striking out 14 guys a game? Listen, Koufax could have won pitching in a phone booth."

Palmer agreed. "The ball didn't carry there," he said, "but Koufax could have won anywhere."

Said Kaat, "I think in most of us mortals' case, it would be a factor. But I think in his case, he could have pitched anywhere. I don't think it would have made a big difference what park he pitched in.

"For a guy like Sandy, if he would have happened to have an off day, and they hit some long fly balls, a park like (Dodger Stadium) is a little more forgiving. Like in Wrigley Field on a windy day or in Fenway Park, fly balls end up being home runs. But I think over a period of time, as great and dominant as he was I really don't think the ballpark would have been that much of a factor."

Palmer called Koufax a power pitcher, with an emphasis on both power and pitcher.

"He had so much movement (on his pitches)," Palmer recalled, "and he was very sneaky. He had great movement on (his fastball) and his curveball is one of the best in baseball history, which is why he was as good as he was, and why he was Sandy Koufax."

And that is why the Jewish kid from Brooklyn remains such a revered figure in baseball circles. He was aesthetically pleasing to writers and artists alike, on and off the field.

To New York sportswriter Phil Pepe, Koufax was "strikingly handsome, meticulously dressed, and he moved with an athlete's grace and confidence."

To Roger Angell of *The New Yorker* magazine, Koufax was beautiful to watch on the mound because he bent his back in a way that other pitchers didn't, and there was a unique bow-and-arrow feeling about the way he used his body.

Artist Deborah Kass sought to capture Koufax's classic pitching form when she did an Andy-Warhol-like silk-screening featuring the repeating image of Koufax in motion. Kass's acrylic on canvas, titled "Sandy Koufax," is her response to Warhol's "Baseball," a photographic silk-screening that captured the repeated image of New York Yankee slugger Roger Maris batting.

In 1964, *Sports Illustrated* photographer Walter Ioos focused his lens on a darkened silhouette of Koufax delivering a pitch against the Phillies at Connie Mack Stadium. *Washington Post* sports columnist Tom Boswell saw the silhouette years later, when he and Ioos were collaborating on a 1995 baseball book called *Diamond Dreams*, and he practically gasped.

"Instantly," Boswell wrote, "you know you're gazing at the greatest pitcher of all time."

When Koufax retired in '66, Boswell was 18 years old. But inside, he said, he felt as sad as a small child. Koufax was gone, and Boswell lamented that he had never seen him pitch in person.

Others saw, and remembered.

Moss Klein, a baseball writer for the *Newark (N.J.) Star-Ledger*, saw Koufax pitch in person four times. He remembered being surprised at how broad Koufax's back and shoulders were, and at how hard he worked on the mound.

"The strain and effort in each pitch," Klein later wrote, "was apparent."

Also apparent to Klein were the reactions of the batters following their late swings at Koufax's overpowering fastball, and their frozen looks when he broke off his curve—the best curve, Klein believes, ever.

Angell used to hear hitters use the word *unfair* after facing Koufax. "It's an unfair contest," they would say, and Angell, who saw Koufax pitch on several occasions in the sixties, remembered watching hitters flail at Koufax's hopping fastball as it jumped over their bat at home plate and then shooting a glance toward the mound, as if to ask, "What was that?"

Koufax, Angell concluded, had dramatically altered the game.

Larry Shenk agreed. "It was not much of a contest," Shenk said.

"He was so overpowering, hitters were like, 'Don't give me a bat. I'm not going up there.'"

Phillies catcher Bob Oldis knew the feeling. "When Koufax is pitching," he said, "the batter should get four strikes and three balls and the runner should be credited with one-quarter of a run for every base he occupies."

From 1962 to 1966, Koufax dominated in a way that hasn't been approached since, and left a lasting impression on those who saw him on the mound.

"Anyone who saw Sandy Koufax pitch," wrote Thorn and Holway, "will never forget the sight."

Koufax today is considered by many not just baseball's greatest living pitcher, but the dean of pitching. He has worked with pitchers for the Dodgers, Angels, and Rangers, and makes annual appearances at the Mets' Florida camp in Port St. Lucie.

"Not only to see Sandy Koufax, but to hear him, he's so succinct," Mets' manager Bobby Valentine said once. Somehow, Valentine added, the world doesn't seem to spin as fast when Koufax is looking at it.

"He sees things very clearly," Valentine said.

In March of 1999, Koufax, a college basketball fan, headed to Florida for the men's Final Four. He also made an appearance at the Yankees' spring camp in Tampa, where he touched base with coach Don Zimmer, an ex-Dodgers teammate, and manager Joe Torre, a fellow Brooklyn native.

Koufax also took time to talk pitching with Yankee right-hander David Cone.

"It was great talking to him," Cone told the Associated Press. "He gave me good advice, too."

Cone said he and Koufax talked about pitching mechanics, and that Koufax touched the top of his leg and said, "This is all you have to remember."

Said Cone, "He was right. If your back leg is strong and in proper position, that's everything. Sometimes you need to be reminded to keep it simple."

Zimmer, noting that Koufax had been invited to the Mets' camp the previous year to work with Al Leiter, told reporters that Koufax's words carried weight.

"I don't know what he told (Mets pitcher Leiter)," Zimmer said, "but whatever it was it sure worked."

Silver-haired and trim at age 64, Koufax appeared at spring training camps in 1999 comfortably clad in blue jeans and casual shirts. Writer Hubert Mizell saw Koufax at the Angels' camp in St. Petersburg and thought Koufax was stylish enough to appear in a Calvin Klein ad.

Devil Rays' coach Frank Howard, a former teammate on the Dodger teams of the early sixties, believes there is no classier person in baseball than Koufax.

Bill White agreed. "Sandy Koufax is one of those people I have a tremendous amount of respect for on and off the field," said White, first baseman for the Cardinals during the St. Louis-L.A. rivalry in the sixties and former president of the National League.

"He was a helluva pitcher and he's a helluva man," White said. "He's just a good guy. There are guys you don't mind being around, and he's one of them."

Mazeroski sees Koufax infrequently, but when he does, he's always struck by his low-key style.

"He's as friendly as can be," Maz said. "He's real down-to-earth; he's never had a big head. He's just a normal guy."

Koufax may consider himself ordinary, but to others he's extraordinary. When Dodger Hall of Fame pitcher Don Sutton broke a club record, someone compared him to Koufax. Sutton quickly set the record straight.

"Comparing me to Sandy Koufax," he said, "is like comparing Earl Scheib to Michelangelo."

Koufax elicits the same respectful response from modern-day players as from those of his own era. After meeting Koufax for the first time several years ago in Arlington, Roger Clemens described him as "a perfect gentleman."

Clemens at the time went on to talk with Don Drysdale and other players from the sixties to get additional information on this living legend.

"I didn't realize how great his career was," Clemens said.

Wade Boggs did. A superstar hitter and a future Hall of Famer, Boggs asked Koufax for his autograph on a baseball in '98 when Koufax made an appearance at Tropicana Field in St. Petersburg.

Boggs had never met Koufax before, and at least one observer thought the tough, 39-year-old hitter grinned like a little boy as he handed over a new ball for Sandy to sign. Boggs was still grinning later when he studied the prized signature.

"What a thrill," Boggs said, smiling.

Quiet and humble and seemingly free of the tragic flaws that bring down so many famous athletes, Koufax appeals to America's traditional views of what a hero should be. He may not like it, but he has become a sports icon, rivaling the late Joe DiMaggio in mythic grace and style. Like DiMaggio, Koufax has appeal because his persona is nonthreatening, he never said or did anything mean, and his face and name are instantly recognizable.

In the movie *Dirty Dancing*, there's talk of Koufax in the background of the scene in which the family arrives at the hotel. In *One Flew Over the Cuckoo's Nest*, Jack Nicholson fakes a narration of a Yankee-Dodger game and mentions Koufax.

Like DiMaggio, Koufax seemed to have come down from some higher league that Tom Seaver once spoke of, joining with Earth's mortals to play nine innings before returning to his place alongside the game's immortals. And the image he left behind—a quick tug on the bill of his blue Dodger cap, a quick pinch of the rosin bag, the high leg kick and classic over-the-top delivery, the left arm slamming across his body as he released the ball, and then the little recoil of his left shoulder as he cut loose with a hopping fastball or big, breaking curve—still captures the imagination.

Jeffrey Wildfogel, a consulting professor of psychology at Stanford University, said true sports heroes are those who combine style, makeup, character, and performance into some model of the ideal. They are something we are supposed to be in our dreams.

For many, Koufax is such a model. He remains a standard of excellence, the measuring stick for greatness, outside of baseball as well as inside the game.

In the September 22, 1973, issue of *TV Guide*, "Hawaii Five-O" star Jack Lord was described as "a Sandy Koufax who thinks he can pitch without an outfield."

Rick Dudley, the general manager of the NHL's Ottawa Senators, recently recalled Koufax when talking about the dominance of Buffalo

Sabres' goalie Dominik Hasek. "With a guy like Hasek," Dudley said, "it's like having Sandy Koufax pitch every game against you."

After Michael Jordan announced his second retirement from the NBA after leading the Chicago Bulls to their sixth title of the nineties, he was compared to Koufax as an athlete walking away while still at the peak of his considerable powers.

But it is inside baseball that Koufax is most revered. When Jaret Wright burst upon the majors in 1997 as a flame-throwing 21-year-old rookie, Hall of Fame pitcher Bob Feller was asked to assess the kid's 95-mile-per-hour heater.

"His fastball's pretty live," Feller said. "It's not as live as Koufax, but it's pretty live."

Rigoberto Herrera Bentcourt, a left-handed pitcher who gained fame in the Caribbean leagues, has been referred to as "the Cuban Sandy Koufax."

When Jim Leyland was managing the Florida Marlins in the 1997 NLCS, he was second-guessed by writers for starting Livan Hernandez in Game Five against Atlanta.

"I can't pull a rabbit out of my hat and put Sandy Koufax in a Marlins' uniform," Leyland said, "so we have to improvise."

Said Buzzie Bavasi, "When you talk to me about Sandy Koufax, you're talking about the best. On and off the field. He's every mother's son, and there's so many things when you go over Sandy's record . . . particularly pitching with arthritis."

When Moss Klein talks to ex-players from the sixties, he occasionally swings the conversation around to Koufax. Klein does it deliberately, just to see the reaction of the person he's talking to. Inevitably, he said, they will sit back, shake their head, and say something filled with superlatives.

Klein recalls once holding his two-year-old nephew up in front of the television screen when Koufax was pitching against the Mets.

"Years from now," Klein told his toddling nephew, "you'll be able to tell your friends you saw Koufax."

Years later, Klein heard his nephew, then 24, proudly telling friends he had seen the great Koufax pitch.

Astros' manager Larry Dierker remembers seeing Koufax pitch, remembers Game Seven against the Twins. It is, Dierker said, his fondest World Series memory. That game impressed him above all others, he said, because Koufax shut the Twins out on just one pitch.

"He hardly threw any curves after the third inning," Dierker said in disbelief. "Mostly fastballs."

That fact amazed Palmer as well. "And that," Palmer said, "is why Koufax was Koufax."

And that's why no one will ever be like him, even among current major leaguers. In the aftermath of Pedro Martinez's 17-strikeout performance against the Yankees on September 10, 1999, *Boston Globe* columnist Dan Shaughnessy called the Red Sox star "the Man Who Would Be Koufax." Bob Feller, using Koufax again as a measuring stick for greatness, said Martinez had a great season in '99, but added, "He's not Sandy Koufax yet."

Nor is anyone else likely to be.

When San Francisco Giants third baseman Charlie Hayes charged the mound after a heated exchange with Arizona pitcher Todd Stottlemyre in an April 1999 game, he angrily accused Stottlemyre of talking too brash for a .500 pitcher.

"Who does he think he is," Hayes asked, "Sandy Koufax?"

APPENDIX

CAREER STATISTICS

Season	Games	Games Started	Games Completed	Innings Pitched	Hits Allowed	Walks	Strikeouts	Wins	Losses	Saves	Shutouts	ERA
1955	12	5	2	41.2	33	28	30	2	2	0	2	3.02
1956	16	10	0	58.2	66	29	30	2	4	0	0	4.91
1957	34	13	2	104.1	83	51	122	5	4	0	0	3.88
1958	40	26	5	158.2	132	105	131	11	11	1	0	4.48
1959	35	23	6	153.1	136	92	173	8	6	2	1	4.05
1960	37	26	7	175	133	100	197	8	13	1	2	3.91
1961	42	35	15	255.2	212	96	**269**	18	13	1	2	3.52
1962	28	26	11	184.1	134	57	216	14	7	1	2	**2.54**
1963	40	40	20	311	214	58	**306**	**25**	5	0	**11**	**1.88**
1964	29	28	15	223	154	53	223	19	5	1	7	**1.74**
1965	43	41	27	335.2	216	71	**382**	**26**	8	2	8	**2.04**
1966	41	41	27	323	241	77	**317**	**27**	9	0	**5**	**1.73**
TOTALS	397	314	137	2,324.1	1,754	817	2,396	165	87	9	40	2.76

NOTE: Boldface indicates statistical leader.

HONORS AND AWARDS

1961–66	National League All-Star Team
1963, 1965–66	National League Cy Young Award
1963	National League Most Valuable Player
1963, 1965	*The Sporting News* Major League Player of the Year
1963, 1965	World Series Most Valuable Player
1963, 1965	Associated Press Male Athlete of the Year
1963, 1965	Hickok Belt
1965	*Sports Illustrated* Sportsman of the Year
1972	National Baseball Hall of Fame
1972	Uniform number 32 retired by the Los Angeles Dodgers

BOX SCORE
WORLD SERIES GAME 7
OCTOBER 14, 1965

```
L.A.  0  0  0    2  0  0    0  0  0  –  2  7  0
Min.  0  0  0    0  0  0    0  0  0  –  0  3  1
```

Los Angeles	AB	R	H	RBI	PO	A	E
Wills, ss	4	0	0	0	2	4	0
Gilliam, 3b	5	0	2	0	2	1	0
Kennedy, 3b	0	0	0	0	0	1	0
Davis, cf	2	0	0	0	1	0	0
Johnson, lf	4	1	1	1	3	0	0
Fairly, rf	4	1	1	0	0	0	0
Parker, 1b	4	0	2	1	6	0	0
Tracewski, 2b	4	0	0	0	1	0	0
Roseboro, c	2	0	1	0	12	0	0
Koufax, p	3	0	0	0	0	1	0
Totals	32	2	7	2	27	7	0

Minnesota	AB	R	H	RBI	PO	A	E
Versalles, ss	4	0	1	0	0	2	0
Nossek, cf	4	0	0	0	0	0	0
Oliva, rf	3	0	0	0	4	0	1
Killebrew, 3b	3	0	1	0	2	2	0
Battey, c	4	0	0	0	8	1	0
Allison, lf	4	0	0	0	1	0	0
Mincher, 1b	3	0	0	0	10	0	0
Quilici, 2b	3	0	1	0	1	3	0
Kaat, p	1	0	0	0	0	1	0
Worthington, p	0	0	0	0	1	1	0
a Rollins	0	0	0	0	0	0	0
Klippstein, p	0	0	0	0	0	0	0
Merritt, p	0	0	0	0	0	0	0

b Valdespino	1	0	0	0	0	0	0
Perry, p	0	0	0	0	0	0	0
Totals	30	0	3	0	27	10	1

a-Walked for Worthington in fifth.
b-Fouled out for Merritt in eighth.

Doubles: Fairly, Quilici, Roseboro.
Triple: Parker. Home Run: Johnson.
Sacrifice Hit: Davis.
Hit by Pitcher: Davis (by Klippstein).
Left on Bases: Los Angeles 9, Minnesota 6.
Umpires: Hurley, Venzon, Flaherty, Sudol, Stewart, Vargo.
Time of Game: 2:27. Attendance: 50,596.

Pitching	IP	H	R	ER	BB	SO
Los Angeles						
Koufax (W)	9	3	0	0	3	10
Minnesota						
Kaat (L)	*3	5	2	2	1	2
Worthington	2	0	0	0	1	0
Klippstein	1⅔	2	0	0	1	1
Merritt	1⅓	0	0	0	0	1
Perry	1	0	0	0	1	1

*Pitched to 3 batters in 4th.

1st Inning

LOS ANGELES

1 Wills took a called third strike.
Gilliam singled to left-center.
2 Davis sacrificed Gilliam to second, Kaat to Mincher.
3 Johnson popped to Oliva in short right who made a diving catch.

MINNESOTA

1 Versalles struck out.
2 Nossek grounded to short.
Oliva walked.
Killebrew walked.
3 Battey struck out.

2nd Inning

LOS ANGELES

1 Fairly popped to Battey in front of the plate.
2 Parker fouled to Mincher.
3 Tracewski took a called third strike.

MINNESOTA

1 Allison struck out.
2 Mincher took a called third strike.
3 Quilici popped to short.

3rd Inning

LOS ANGELES

Roseboro doubled into the right-field corner.
Koufax walked.
1 Wills grounded to second, both runners advancing.
2 Gilliam lined to right.
3 Davis fouled to Battey.

MINNESOTA

1 Kaat struck out.
Versalles singled to center.
2 Nossek was ruled out for interfering with Roseboro's throw to second as Versalles tried to steal but on the out had to return to first.
3 Oliva struck out.

4th Inning

LOS ANGELES

Johnson hit a line drive home run which hit the left-field foul pole.
Fairly doubled down the right-field line.
Parker singled over Mincher's head, scoring Fairly. Parker took second when Oliva fumbled the ball.
For Minnesota—Worthington replaced Kaat on the mound.

1 Tracewski popped to
   Worthington on an
   attempted sacrifice.
   Roseboro walked.
2 Koufax grounded back to
   the pitcher, both runners
   advancing.
3 Wills fouled to Killebrew.

MINNESOTA

1 Killebrew grounded to the
   pitcher.
2 Battey flied to center.
3 Allison grounded to third.

5th Inning

LOS ANGELES

1 Gilliam grounded to second.
2 Davis fouled to Killebrew.
3 Johnson flied to Oliva in
   deep right-center.

MINNESOTA

1 Mincher fouled to Gilliam.
   Quilici doubled off the left-
   center-field screen.
   Rollins, batting for Worthington, walked.
2 Versalles forced Quilici at
   third, Gilliam unassisted
   after a good diving stop.
3 Nossek forced Versalles at
   second, Wills to
   Tracewski.

6th Inning

LOS ANGELES

For Minesota—Klippstein
   pitching.
1 Fairly flied to left.
   Parker tripled off the center-
   field screen.
2 Tracewski struck out,
   bunting foul on the third
   strike.
   Roseboro intentionally
   passed.
3 Koufax lined to short.

MINNESOTA

1 Oliva struck out.
2 Killebrew fouled to Johnson.
3 Battey lined to short.

7th Inning

LOS ANGELES

1 Wills grounded to short.
   Gilliam singled to right.
   Davis was hit by a pitch.
2 Johnson grounded to
   third, advancing both
   runners.
   For Minnesota—Merritt
   came in to pitch.
3 Fairly flied to right.

MINNESOTA

1 Allison grounded to short.

2 Mincher fouled to Roseboro.
3 Quilici struck out.

8th Inning

LOS ANGELES

1 Parker grounded to second.
2 Tracewski grounded to third.
3 Roseboro struck out.

MINNESOTA

1 Valdespino, batting for
   Merritt, fouled to Johnson.
2 Versalles flied to deep left.
3 Nossek grounded to short.

9th Inning

LOS ANGELES

For Minnesota—Perry
   pitching.
1 Koufax struck out.
   Wills walked.
2 Wills caught trying to steal
   second, Battey to
   Quilici.
3 Gilliam grounded to short.

MINNESOTA

For Los Angeles—Kennedy
   playing third.
1 Oliva grounded to third.
   Killebrew singled to left.
2 Battey took a called third
   strike.
3 Allison struck out.

Chicago Cubs	AB	R	H	PO	A	E
Young, cf	3	0	0	5	0	0
Beckert, 2b	3	0	0	1	1	0
Williams, rf	3	0	0	0	0	0
Santo, 3b	3	0	0	1	2	0
Banks, 1b	3	0	0	13	0	0
Browne, lf	3	0	0	1	0	0
Krug, c	3	0	0	3	0	1
Kessinger, ss	2	0	0	0	2	0
a-Amalfitano	1	0	0	0	0	0
Hendley, p	2	0	0	0	5	0
b-Kuenn	1	0	0	0	0	0
Totals	27	0	0	24	10	1

Los Angeles Dodgers						
Wills, ss	3	0	0	0	2	0
Gilliam, 3b	3	0	0	0	1	0
W. Davis, cf	3	0	0	2	0	0
Johnson, lf	2	1	1	2	0	0
Fairly, rf	2	0	0	3	0	0
Lefebvre, 2b	3	0	0	1	0	0
Tracewski, 2b	0	0	0	0	0	0
Parker, 1b	3	0	0	4	0	0
Torborg, c	3	0	0	15	0	0
Koufax, p	2	0	0	0	0	0
Totals	24	1	1	27	3	0

a-Struck out for Kessinger in ninth.
b-Struck out for Hendley in ninth.

Chicago	0	0	0	0	0	0	0	0	0	—	0
Los Angeles	0	0	0	0	1	0	0	0	0	—	1

Run batted in: none • *Double:* Johnson • *Sacrifice hit:* Fairly • *Stolen base:* Johnson • *Left on bases:* Los Angeles 1, Chicago 0 • *Bases on balls:* off Hendley 1 (Johnson) • *Strikeouts:* by Koufax 14 (Young, Beckert, Williams 2, Santo, Banks 3, Browne, Krug, Amalfitano, Hendley 2, Kuenn), by Hendley 3 (Lefebvre 2, Koufax) • *Runs and earned runs:* off Hendley 1-0 • *Winning pitcher:* Koufax (22-7) • *Losing pitcher:* Hendley (2-3) • *Umpires:* Vargo, Pelekoudas, Jackowski, and Pryor • *Time of game:* 1:43 • *Attendance:* 29,139.

INDEX